DEMOCRATIZING

the

CONSTITUTION

Reforming Responsible Government

Peter Aucoin
Mark D. Jarvis
Lori Turnbull

 2011 / EMOND MONTGOMERY PUBLICATIONS / TORONTO, CANADA

The EMP Political Perspectives Series
This new series features respected authors presenting short, accessible books on key topics in politics, government, and related fields, exploring both Canada and beyond. In addition to presenting material in a clear and digestible form for students and non-expert readers, these books often incorporate authors' own proposals and perspectives. For more information, visit **emp.ca/pps**.

Emond Montgomery Publications Limited
60 Shaftesbury Avenue
Toronto ON M4T 1A3
http://www.emp.ca/highered

Printed in Canada on recycled paper.
17 16 15 14 13 12   2 3 4 5

We acknowledge the financial support of the Government of Canada through the Canada Book Fund for our publishing activities.

Acquisitions and development editor: Mike Thompson
Marketing manager: Christine Davidson
Director, sales and marketing, higher education: Kevin Smulan
Supervising editor: Jim Lyons
Production editor: Andrew Gordon
Copy editor: Gillian Scobie
Typesetter: Debbie Gervais
Indexer: Paula Pike
Text designer: Tara Wells
Cover designer: Stephen Cribbin & Simon Evers

Library and Archives Canada Cataloguing in Publication
Aucoin, Peter, 1943-
    Democratizing the constitution : reforming responsible government / Peter Aucoin, Mark D. Jarvis, and Lori Turnbull.

Includes index.
ISBN 978-1-55239-463-2

    1. Federal government—Canada.   2. Constitutional law—Canada.   I. Jarvis, Mark D., 1975-   II. Turnbull, Lori B. (Lori Beth), 1978-   III. Title.

JL27.A93 2011   321.020971   C2011-902608-2

Brief Contents

Detailed Contents

CHAPTER ONE

Introduction: A Fundamental Democratic Problem

CHAPTER TWO

Responsible Government: Theory and Practice

CHAPTER THREE

When Conventions Fail: Constitutional Governance Without Clear Rules

CHAPTER SIX

Conclusion: Reforming Responsible Government

Preface

Rusted wire and tilted posts more a symbol of restraint than a fence per se.
—David Foster Wallace, *The Pale King*

[Stephen Harper should] reinstate a culture of openness, transparency and account-ability on Parliament Hill. Now that the Conservatives have a majority, there is no excuse (not that there ever was) for the paranoia, secrecy, rule-bending, shirking of due process and committee bullying that rightly has become the subject of opposition ire in recent years.
—From an editorial in the *National Post*, May 4, 2011,
following Stephen Harper's federal election victory

By the late 1990s and early 2000s, many Canadians had come to lament how the prime ministers of single-party majority governments seemed able to undermine parliamentary democracy. By the middle of the last decade, as a prolonged period of minority government set in, many expected that this change would serve as an effective antidote for the perceived authoritarian rule that had come to be associated with majorities.

Over the course of seven years (2004 to 2011) that saw the minority governments of prime ministers Paul Martin and then Stephen Harper, it became crystal clear that this expectation was far too optimistic. Most, if not all, would agree that minority government has failed to constrain the power of prime ministers over Parliament. If anything, minority government only intensified the degree to which prime ministers were able to, and did, abuse power to undermine Canadian parliamentary democracy. In large measure, this was possible because of the erosion of the conventions meant to guide the practice of responsible government. These conventions have become the rusted wire and tilted fence posts of Canadian democracy.

There are many reasons for this erosion, including a lack of care and attention from academic experts, the media, pundits, and politicians in the preservation of a common understanding of the meaning and requirements of the unwritten Canadian constitution. What is clear is that something must be done to address this situation. While the problems did not start in December 2008, the prorogation that occurred then made it clear that Canada has a crisis of parliamentary democracy afoot, even if the effects of that crisis are not always plainly evident. Unfortunately, there is little reason for optimism, given that we have seemed content to allow the confusion and disagreement over the King–Byng affair to fester for more than 85 years.

This book is a modest response to this state of affairs. It is an attempt to document the resulting abuses and failings of differing parts of the system, and to address them, as well as to place the practice of Canadian parliamentary democracy in historical and comparative context. But perhaps the most important purpose of this book is to argue for the need for formal reforms that might address the eroding Canadian constitution.

The response by some to the most recent episodes of this deterioration has been to vilify Prime Minister Harper, suggesting that if we had a more accommodating leader or could enact some sort of cultural change, the problems would simply vanish. We reject this outright. While it's notable that the *National Post* has also acknowledged that there is a problem, as seen in the quotation above, in this book we demonstrate that Harper is far from the only leader to abuse power in this regard. Concrete change is required. Rather than attempt to remake the Canadian system as a republic, we propose reforms aimed at reinvigorating responsible government and democratizing the Canadian constitution.

Acknowledgments

The authors would like to thank the following individuals who assisted us with their insightful comments, undertook helpful discussions that helped refine our thinking, and/or provided invaluable pieces of information when needed: Jennifer Smith, Andrew Heard, David E. Smith, Paul Thomas, Ralph Heintzman, Bruce Hicks, John Nethercote, Jonathan Boston, Anne Twomey, Herman Bakvis, Philippe Lagassé, Dennis Baker, Andrew Coyne, Aaron Wherry, Dan Gardner, Susan Delacourt, Kady O'Malley, Lawrence Martin, Alison Loat and Samara, Lawrence Buhagiar, Wes Yocom, and Phil Prins.

The authors and publisher wish to acknowledge the following people for their insights and suggestions during the early stages of this project: Thomas Bateman, James Kelly, Rainer Knopff, Heather MacIvor, Peter McCormick, Andrew Potter, and Peter Russell.

Notwithstanding the great assistance of those who provided comments or other guidance, the authors alone are responsible for the analysis, opinions, and any errors found herein.

The authors would also like to thank Frank Graves and EKOS Research Associates for their generosity in providing access to public opinion data that were ultimately not used in the book.

We are especially grateful to Mike Thompson, Gillian Scobie, Paul Emond, Jim Lyons, and the rest of the staff at Emond Montgomery who adeptly guided us, and this book, through what could have been a far more difficult publication process under complex circumstances.

Finally, the authors would like to thank Margot, Malcolm, and Joanna for their enduring patience and support.

Dedication

This book is dedicated to the memory of our friend David Alexander Joseph Mac Donald. Those who knew him remember David as a scholar, teacher, comedian, fan of *The Simpsons*, and exceptional raconteur. He was all those things, but most of all David was an exemplary public servant dedicated to strengthening his profession and its role in the governance of this country. David was taken from the world far too soon. We miss him greatly.

About the Authors

Peter Aucoin (1943–2011) was a professor emeritus of political science and public administration at Dalhousie University and a senior academic fellow at the Canada School of Public Service, Government of Canada. Among his many honours and distinctions, he was also a Fellow of the Royal Society of Canada and a Member of the Order of Canada. He authored or edited 16 books, wrote over 80 articles and book chapters, and is cited extensively in Canadian and international publications. Peter passed away shortly after the completion of this book.

Mark D. Jarvis is a doctoral candidate at the University of Victoria. He is the author of "The Adoption of the Accounting Officer System in Canada: Changing Relationships?" in *Canadian Public Administration*, and co-author with Peter Aucoin of *Modernizing Government Accountability: A Framework for Reform*.

Lori Turnbull is an associate professor and undergraduate adviser in the Department of Political Science at Dalhousie University. She is the author of *Regulations on Post-Public Employment: A Comparative Analysis* for the Oliphant Commission, and co-author with Peter Aucoin of "Removing the Virtual Right of First Ministers to Demand Dissolution" in *Canadian Parliamentary Review*.

Website

For additional information on this book, please visit the website: **www.emp.ca/dtc**.

CHAPTER ONE

Introduction: A Fundamental Democratic Problem

A Uniquely Canadian Problem

The Canadian system of parliamentary government faces a fundamental problem that has been allowed to undermine Canadian democracy. The prime minister wields too much power over the operations of the House of Commons. The House of Commons is the parliamentary assembly of the people's elected representatives, the pre-eminent democratic institution of representative government (Franks 1987; Smith 2007). Too much power in the hands of a prime minister over the House of Commons in a parliamentary democracy is always a problem. Unconstrained power in any form of government invariably leads to the abuse of power. When power is abused, democracy is diminished.

The potential for unconstrained prime ministerial power has always been a risk inherent in parliamentary democracies, like Canada's, that are based on the British, or Westminster (after the name of the Gothic-

STRUCTURE OF THE FEDERAL GOVERNMENT

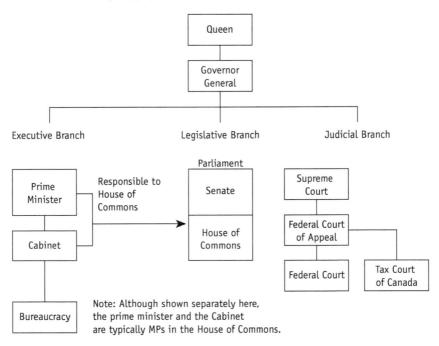

Note: Although shown separately here, the prime minister and the Cabinet are typically MPs in the House of Commons.

style building in which the British Parliament meets in London) model. The prime minister occupies a crucial position in this structure. The prime minister is both the political head of the executive government *and* the leader of the governing party in the House of Commons. As the political head of the government, the prime minister advises the governor general to summon Parliament after an election, to prorogue Parliament for a period of time, and to dissolve Parliament in advance of an election. These decisions are not subject to the approval or consent of the House of Commons. They are separate executive powers. At the same time, the prime minister and his or her government, in order to retain office, must maintain the confidence of a majority of the members of Parliament—the people's elected representatives in the House of Commons. The tenure of the prime minister, as well as the life of the government, is thus subject to the control of the House of Commons. In this way, the constitutional system of parliamentary government is democratic.

In this book, we focus specifically on the capacity of the Canadian prime minister to control the operations of the House of Commons, including using the powers legally assigned to the governor general. Prime ministerial control of the operations of the House of Commons weakens the House's responsibilities and capacities:

- to review and approve or reject the government's legislative proposals;
- to scrutinize the government's administration of public affairs;
- to hold the prime minister and other ministers to account for their performance (collectively and individually);
- to withdraw its confidence in the prime minister and government when a majority wishes to do so; and
- to replace the prime minister and government with an alternative prime minister and government that has the confidence of a majority.

Prime ministerial control of the operations of the House risks an abuse of the basic premise of responsible government, namely, that the House be *in session* in order to carry out these responsibilities. The House cannot do so when it has not been summoned, has been prorogued, or has been dissolved.

The Canadian problem has two dimensions. One dimension is constitutional; the other is a matter of parliamentary government. The constitutional dimension concerns the capacity of the prime minister to abuse the constitutional powers to summon, prorogue, and dissolve the House of Commons to advance the partisan interests of the governing party. For example, there are no firm rules for the governor general to refer to when the prime minister has lost the confidence of the House of Commons and then wants to dissolve it. This was demonstrated following the March 25, 2011 defeat on confidence of the

Harper government. As far as we are aware, Governor General David Johnston did not consult with the leaders of the opposition to see whether a new government could be formed from the opposition with the confidence of a majority. This would be standard procedure in Australia, Great Britain, and New Zealand, where it is fully accepted that the House decides who forms the government.

The parliamentary government dimension concerns the capacity of the prime minister to abuse the rules and procedures of the House of Commons that are meant to allow the government to manage the business of the House in an orderly and efficient manner. It also concerns the prime minister's powers as party leader to run roughshod over parliamentary practices meant to advance parliamentary democracy; for example, by imposing excessive party discipline on the governing party's own members of Parliament who are not ministers—the backbench MPs who sit behind the ministers in the House.

In both of these ways the prime minister governs in bad faith, allowing the government's partisan interests to subvert the opportunities for backbench government MPs and opposition MPs to perform their basic parliamentary responsibilities properly. Public opinion, at least in theory, especially the threat of electoral defeat, should induce the prime minister and MPs to act in good faith when they are inclined to act otherwise. But there is little evidence from the practices of several prime ministers in recent decades to support an assumption that public opinion and elections are sufficient constraints.

The Constitutional Dimension

When the prime minister abuses these powers—to summon, prorogue, and dissolve the House—in order to shut down the House of Commons, the House is either not in session (not yet summoned or has been prorogued) or it no longer exists (it has been dissolved). Shutting down the House to protect the governing party strikes at the very foundation of responsible government as parliamentary democracy. The House is the democratic foundation because it is composed of the people's directly elected representatives. The people directly elect only their MPs; they do not directly elect the prime minister and government. Who becomes prime minister is determined by the decisions of the political parties in the House according to the numbers of MPs each party elects. When one party elects a majority, the decision is simple. When no one party has a majority of MPs, the matter is necessarily more complicated, but it is still the House that decides by a majority.

Parliament needs to be summoned so that the people's representatives, their MPs in the House of Commons, can perform their critical functions. MPs have no power when the House is not in session. Parliament is prorogued so that the government can efficiently organize sessions, allowing it to conclude one session when its legislative program has come to an end and it wishes to introduce a new legislative program. (Each session begins with the Speech from the Throne, when the governor general reads the government's new legislative program.) Parliament is dissolved for the election of a new House when the government has concluded its agenda or when a new election is required after the government has lost the confidence of the House. The life of a parliament cannot exceed five years. The norm for elections in Canada has been about four years.

The prime minister can abuse these constitutional powers, however, by using them for mere partisan advantage. When this occurs, Canadian academic experts, pundits, and politicians disagree over whether these abuses are constitutional. The most glaring abuse of the power to summon Parliament after an election occurred when Prime Minister Joe Clark's government did not summon Parliament for 142 days, after the 1979 election that brought his Progressive Conservatives to power. As a new minority government, the Conservatives went for more than four months fully exercising the powers of government without having had the confidence of the House in this new government confirmed by a vote in the House. This would not have been acceptable in Australia, Great Britain, or New Zealand, where Parliament is summoned very quickly after an election. In 2010 in Great Britain, for example, Parliament was summoned two weeks after the election, an election that brought a new government to power, and a coalition government of two parties at that. Two weeks was also the time it took to summon the Australian Parliament after the 2010 election, even though it was uncertain for a number of days which party would form the government. The Australian constitution requires that Parliament be summoned no later than 30 days after the election day. The New Zealand constitution sets the limit at six weeks.

Abuse of power also occurs when the prime minister prorogues Parliament in order to postpone a vote of non-confidence against the government or to escape being questioned, scrutinized, and held to account for the maladministration of public services or public moneys. Again, Prime Minister Jean Chrétien abused this power in November 2003, forestalling the release of the auditor general's report to the House on the sponsorship scandal—a major scandal that occurred during Chrétien's tenure as prime minister. Prime Minister Harper went one step further in December 2008 when he prorogued Parliament in order to postpone the publicly declared intention of the three opposition parties to defeat his government on a vote of non-confidence. The following December he again prorogued Parliament, this time for several weeks, to postpone being questioned and held accountable for allegations the government had misled the House on matters relating to the handling of detainees in the war in Afghanistan.

Further abuse occurs when prime ministers call early or snap elections (so-called because they are called at the snap of the prime ministerial fingers) at a time that favours their governing party, usually in the first two or three years after the previous election. Liberal Prime Minister Lester Pearson called an early election in 1965 and Liberal Prime Minister Jean Chrétien called early elections in 1997 and 2000, in all three cases to take advantage of the political situation then favouring their party. In 2008, Conservative Prime Minister Stephen Harper called an early election, two years after the 2006 election, also for partisan reasons. He did so even after Parliament passed his government's own law to eliminate the power of the prime minister to call elections at will, fulfilling a 2006 election campaign promise. The reform fixed election dates to a specified date every four years but, as is discussed in Chapter 3, the legislation contained an important loophole that limited its effectiveness.

The previously mentioned 2008 prorogation was significant for a second reason. Because it merely postponed the vote of non-confidence in Stephen Harper's government, the question arose about what would happen if the Conservatives, who did not have a majority in the House, lost the vote when Parliament was back in session. The opposition parties, with a majority of the MPs, had already publicly proposed, in an open letter to the governor general, that a new Liberal–New Democratic coalition government, led by the Liberals, be installed, with the support of the Bloc Québécois, instead of holding another election. This government would have had the confidence of a majority of the House. Prime Minister Harper attacked this proposal as undemocratic, claiming that only the people through an election should determine who forms the government. His claim sparked a major public debate about the constitution of Canadian parliamentary democracy, a debate that has reached no conclusion because the constitutional conventions in Canada, as interpreted by academic experts, politicians, and pundits, provide no firm rules on this matter.

The three key players in the King–Byng affair (left to right): Prime Minister Mackenzie King, Governor General Lord Byng, and Conservative leader Arthur Meighen.

Unwritten Rules

Canada has not developed clear rules, guidelines, or expectations on the use of these powers when the prime minister has lost the confidence of the House. New Zealand, for instance, has adopted guidelines to establish that if a government loses the confidence of the House, the governor general is to ascertain whether an alternative government can be chosen from the same House. A prime minister who is defeated in the House has no right to demand that the House be dissolved. This reflects what should be a basic reality of responsible government: that, absent the confidence of the House, the prime minister is just an ordinary member of Parliament. A defeated prime minister must respect the authority of the House to form a new government as long as the House commands the confidence of a majority of MPs. In Canada, the absence of clear rules in this situation has given even defeated prime ministers tremendous power.

The uncertainty about the exercise of the governor general's reserve powers began in 1925, when the governor general, Lord Byng, denied dissolution to the prime minister of a minority government, a Liberal, Mackenzie King, who had not been defeated in the House on a confidence vote. King was facing imminent defeat and was trying to pre-empt it with an election. When Byng rejected his advice for dissolution, King was forced to resign[1] and Arthur Meighen was appointed by Byng to form a Conservative minority government with the support of a majority in the Opposition, without an election. It was soon defeated in the House, however, and Byng accepted Meighen's request for dissolution without consulting the opposition parties. In the subsequent election in 1926, King challenged the governor general's 1925 decision not to grant him dissolution. King won the 1926 election by campaigning, not against his opponent, Conservative leader Meighen, but the governor

---

1. Although agreement is not unanimous on this assertion, it is suggested that constitutional convention requires that a prime minister whose advice is refused by the governor general must resign.

general, by implying that Meighen had governed illegally with Byng's help, thus unleashing a rising Canadian nationalism, and winning enough seats to form a minority government.

Since that time, the debate has been polarized between opposing views on whether Byng or King was correct. The debate has never been resolved. However, since then, no governor general has ever denied dissolution to a prime minister or refused any other advice, even in cases where the government has been defeated on a vote of confidence and the prime minister's government thus no longer commands the confidence of the House—the prerequisite to being the government.

Accordingly, at present, constitutional scholars still disagree about the appropriate use of the prime minister's prerogative powers to summon, prorogue, and dissolve. Some argue that there are qualifications on, and exceptions to, the prime minister's use of prerogative powers and that the governor general can use his or her personal discretion to decide whether to refuse the prime minister's recommendation, at least under certain circumstances. The prime minister must go to the governor general to request the use of the powers to prorogue and dissolve Parliament. But there is an absence of clarity—not to mention outright disagreement and political dispute—as to what these qualifications or exceptions are, and when (if ever!) they might be applied by a governor general in refusing such a request.

This means that there are no firm rules to govern the use of the governor general's powers in summoning, proroguing, or dissolving Parliament. All experts claim that there are some guiding principles. Some even assert that matters are clear. But others challenge them. Without the clarity of firm rules, however few in number, politicians will inevitably put their own partisan political spin on their interpretation of the constitution to advance their own interests.

For example, in 2009, the University of Toronto Press published an edited volume called *Parliamentary Democracy in Crisis* in response to the controversial prorogation of the House of Commons in December 2008. The authors who wrote the chapters were among the most respected constitutional scholars in the country. Among them there was significant disagreement about the following issues: whether the prime minister actually held the confidence of the House of Commons when he requested prorogation in 2008; whether the governor general made the right choice in granting his request; whether the governor general ought to have considered political factors, such as the viability of the proposed coalition, when reaching her decision; and whether the event constituted a true constitutional crisis. Further disagreements exist about the functioning of the other elements of the Canadian constitution.

Since then, the situation has gotten no better. A 2011 workshop led by Professor Peter Russell that included a number of Canada's leading constitutional experts, as well as individuals connected to the major party leaders, sought to address the lack of consensus on many of the fundamental aspects of the constitution. The group failed to come to consensus on a number of the fundamental aspects of how our democratic system is supposed to work, including: what factors a governor general should consider in responding to a request for dissolution in the early months of a new Parliament; whether a change of government between elections is democratically or even constitutionally legitimate; how a governor general should ascertain who is likely to have the ability to command the confidence of the House following an election when no party has a clear majority; and whether, and if so how, to suitably constrain confidence votes to reduce brinkmanship and increase the stability of minority governments. We no longer have a touchstone reference that grounds the Canadian constitution in practice or in principle.

By not addressing the disagreement engendered by the King–Byng debate, even with the election in the interim of several minority governments, Canada has allowed the disagreements that have broken out since the 2008 prorogation to spread confusion and uncertainty about the basic principles and rules of Canadian parliamentary democracy, effectively undermining our system.

By contrast, as noted, New Zealand took steps nearly two decades ago to prevent this from occurring, when everyone realized that the adoption of a new voting system for its House of Representatives (the equivalent of the Canadian House of Commons) was likely to produce party standings in the House where no single party would have a majority. As part of its *Cabinet Manual*, New Zealand has set out in writing the procedures that the prime minister, the governor general, and the party leaders are expected to follow if a government loses the confidence of the House before the next scheduled election. Great Britain started the process to do the same when the outcome of the 2010 election appeared likely to produce what the British call a "hung parliament," a House where the election has not provided a single party with a majority of seats. In Australia, governors general have exercised discretion in a few cases, most notably in a 1975 case somewhat akin to the Canadian King–Byng case. But even there, the behaviour of the political party leaders following the election of 2010, when no one party won a majority in the House, also confirmed the same constitutional understanding of parliamentary democracy articulated in New Zealand and Great Britain. This shared understanding has three basic rules:

1. The Queen in Great Britain and the governor general in both Australia and New Zealand do not intervene politically in the exercise of the powers of summoning, proroguing, and dissolving Parliament.
2. The House of Commons (House of Representatives in Australia and New Zealand), through its party leaders, is consulted on which party leader is prime minister and forms the government.
3. The Queen or governor general is not to be dragged into partisan politics by the party leaders, including the prime minister who has lost the confidence of the House, in any fashion (New Zealand 2008; Hazell and Yong 2010, 5; Twomey 2011).

The experience in these three parliamentary democracies does not appear to have had had much, if any, significance for the Canadian practice. There is scant evidence that more than a precious few among the Canadian media, politicians, and the experts even knew about the New Zealand development when the 2008 debate erupted. By 2011, the British development—the transfer of power from the Labour Party to the Conservative–Liberal Democrat coalition government—was known by many more. That did not inhibit Prime Minister Harper, standing alongside the new prime minister, David Cameron, after the British election, from putting his own political spin on what had happened, including describing the Liberal Democrats—one part of the coalition government—as "losers," Harper's definition of every party that does not elect the most MPs. Harper also claimed that only a coalition formed by the party that won the most seats was legitimate. That was definitely not the understanding of the British constitution articulated before the 2010 election, which stated clearly: "It is for the Monarch to invite the person who appears is most likely to be able to command the confidence of the House of Commons to serve as Prime Minister and to form a government" (United Kingdom 2010).

The Parliamentary Governance Dimension

The second dimension of the democratic problem concerns the Canadian prime minister's capacity to exercise excessive power over the day-to-day operations of the House—powers easily abused purely for partisan purposes. There are several ways a prime minister is able to abuse power with respect to the operations of the House. These include:

- The prime minister can declare all government legislative proposals (bills) to be matters of confidence for the government's MPs, thus forcing government MPs to vote with their party and thereby diminishing the prospects for serious review and examination by House committees of ways to improve such bills.
- The prime minister can decide to have all government bills go to committee only after passing "second reading" in the House,

which means that no amendments can be considered in committee that would go against the basic principles of a bill as accepted by the House at second reading. This too reduces the effectiveness of House committees.

- The prime minister can select the chairs of all the committees chaired by a government MP. This includes all but a few committees chaired by an opposition MP because those committees, such as the public accounts committee, examine the government's administration of program and financial resources. This power invariably means that these chairs do the prime minister's bidding in chairing committees, especially when they operate under strict directions from the prime minister's political staff.
- The prime minister can undermine the work of committees by constantly changing the government MPs on committees as a way of keeping them under tight control.
- The prime minister determines, through the government's expenditure budget, the level of budgetary resources for expert staff and operating costs provided to House committees. All recent governments have been reluctant to provide committees with the resources they need to perform their responsibilities at an effective level.
- The prime minister, as party leader, is able to use his or her power to approve all party candidates to arbitrarily interfere in local nomination contests, including "parachuting in" preferred candidates. Combined with the inability of party caucuses to appoint or dismiss party leaders, this power reduces the likelihood that governing party backbench MPs will play any kind of serious role in scrutinizing and holding the government to account or constraining the prime minister, especially in committees.
- The prime minister has a major say in the scheduling of the business of the House and can use this power to postpone so-called opposition days, when the opposition is able to put

forward non-confidence motions and to raise issues that the government does not want examined in the House.

• The prime minister is able to determine in some instances what actually constitutes a vote of non-confidence and to decide when the government has been defeated on confidence.

House committees are now the primary forum for MPs to do their legislative review and administrative scrutiny and accountability work. Prime ministerial abuse of any or all of these powers means that MPs cannot help but fall short in fulfilling their responsibilities to citizens of effective democratic representation (Samara 2011). The need to bring the parliamentary process into the 21st century requires many new approaches, but none will have their intended effect if parliamentary reform does not diminish the powers of the prime minister over the people's elected representatives in the House of Commons.

The past 50 years is littered with failed efforts at reform precisely because this prerequisite of reduced prime ministerial power over the House was not met. There were some achievements: the strengthening of the mandate and independence of the auditor general in 1977 under the Trudeau Liberal government; the introduction of the *Access to Information Act* with its information commissioner in 1985 under the Mulroney Progressive Conservative government; and the creation of the parliamentary budget officer in 2007 under the Harper Conservative government. The last two have not fared as well as expected, because governments have failed to implement these reforms in ways that allow them to be fully effective.

The Prime Minister and Responsible Government

Prime ministers have always been more than first-among-equals in their Cabinet of ministers and have had the power to impose party discipline on their MPs. Canadian prime ministers have had greater control over their ministers and MPs than in Australia, Great Britain, and New Zealand ever since the Liberal, and then the Conservative parties, removed the power of their party caucus to select and dismiss their party leader. Instead, the parties, beginning with the Liberals in 1919, adopted the practice of national party conventions, with delegates from across the country, ex officio party officials, and the party's MPs, to select the party leader, including when the party leader would become prime minister after the party was in government.

Since at least the 1960s, prime ministers in all Westminster systems have become more powerful in relation to their elected parliaments and, with few exceptions, the constraints or checks on their power have weakened. Several developments have enhanced the power of the prime minister in relation to the House of Commons. Among them, two stand out.

First, the federal government has expanded its roles into almost every aspect of society and the economy. This has required an enhanced capacity for coordinating government policy-making and thus managing the government's legislative agenda in the House of Commons. This enhanced capacity is located at the centre of government under the direction of the prime minister.

Second, television had a significant effect on personalizing party leadership, with election campaigns becoming even more leader-centred and focused (Savoie 2010). In addition, the Canadian prime minister, as the government's "chief executive officer," has greater control over non-partisan public service executives and has the largest partisan political staff among the Westminster democracies. It is not surprising that Canadian prime ministers have not been inclined to reduce their powers. Why would they if the main objective is to be in power and stay there? The two most recent prime ministers, Martin and Harper, both expressed interest in reform before they gained office. As discussed in Chapter 4, neither succeeded after he became prime minister.

In 1997, between periods in his career as an elected politician, Stephen Harper co-authored an article with his one-time adviser, Professor Tom Flanagan, entitled "Our Benign Dictatorship." They argued: "We persist in structuring the governing team like a military regiment under a single commander [the prime minister] with almost total power to appoint, discipline and expel subordinates [Cabinet ministers and members of Parliament]" (Harper and Flanagan 1997). In 1999, Professor Donald Savoie wrote a widely cited book, *Governing from the Centre: The Concentration of Power in Canadian Politics*, in which he portrayed the concentration of power under the prime minister as a governance structure resembling a powerful monarchy, with the prime minister surrounded by a cabal of courtiers, all dependent for their influence in "the king's court" on the personal whims of the prime minister (Savoie 1999). In 2001, Jeffrey Simpson, *Globe and Mail* columnist, penned a book about Liberal prime minister Jean Chrétien, whom he described as a "friendly dictator" (Simpson 2001). And, in 2010, Simpson's colleague at the *Globe and Mail*, Lawrence Martin, published a bestseller called *Harperland: The Politics of Control*, in which he describes how Stephen Harper, now prime minister, has taken prime ministerial power to even greater heights (Martin 2010).

We will argue that the abuse of these and other constitutional powers by the prime minister is more damaging to parliamentary democracy than the much publicized practice of recent prime ministers centralizing government decision making in their own office. The consequent bypassing of the structures of Cabinet government and individual ministerial responsibility has received far greater attention to date. Even Prime Minister Stephen Harper's two controversial prorogations are seen as simply part and parcel of highly centralized and tightly controlled prime ministerial government, rather than abuses of power.

We acknowledge that centralization under the prime minister and his or her political staff in the Prime Minister's Office is indirectly related to the prime minister's capacities to control the House of Commons. This centralization diminishes the likelihood that the prime minister's Cabinet colleagues, let alone his or her party's MPs, will be able to constrain the prime minister from abusing the governor general's powers or running roughshod over the parliamentary process. But centralization within the executive branch of government does not by itself lead to the abuse of the governor general's powers. Something more is required: the willingness of the prime minister to exercise these powers simply and merely to promote and protect the political interests of the governing party. In other words, the willingness to act in bad faith.

A Note on the Effect of Partisanship and the Malaise of Modern Politics

Partisanship, in and of itself, is not damaging to parliamentary democracy. Indeed, it is an integral and positive part of our system of parliamentary government. Our system is one of "party government" in several important respects. Competing political parties are freely organized by citizens. These parties structure the choices for voters at elections by nominating party candidates, offering a party platform, and identifying their party leader. After the election, they organize Parliament into two sides: the government and the opposition. The members of Parliament on the government side support the prime minister and Cabinet ministers as the political executive. By democratic convention, the prime minister and almost all other ministers are also MPs, rather than members of the Senate, the unelected house of Parliament. Since 1867, the Canadian experience has seen the government side always composed of just one party, as is the case at the time of writing, with the Conservative Party in office.[2] Since the 1920s, the opposition has comprised two or more parties. Today, it is made up of four parties—the New Democrats, the Liberals, the Bloc Québécois, and the Green Party. In all these ways, partisanship serves important democratic purposes.

However, partisans can sometimes be excessive in their partisanship. They can demonize their opponents. They can fail to listen to the arguments of the other side. They can deliberately misrepresent what their

---

2. A possible exception was the Union government put together by the Conservative prime minister during the First World War that included some Liberal MPs in the Cabinet. But it was not a coalition because the Liberal Party, with the rest of the Liberal MPs, remained in opposition.

opponents have said or stand for. They can portray robust democratic competition as a war between enemies. And partisanship can go beyond simple excess. Partisanship leads to the abuse of the prime minister's conventional powers to summon, prorogue, and dissolve the House of Commons whenever they are exercised solely to protect or advance the interests of the governing party. The prime minister is constrained in the use of these powers only by public opinion and the prospects of voter disapproval in a subsequent election.

The malaise of modern politics encompasses a number of developments, some of which are easily observed but not well understood. These include a general decline of citizen engagement and interest, especially among youth, in the traditional and still basic forms of voting, associating with a political party in some manner (even if only as loosely considering oneself a partisan for one party), and generally being attentive to politics and government. When citizens become disengaged in large numbers, the likelihood of their being concerned about the state of Canadian democracy is diminished. The influence of the mass media, to which the great bulk of the population paid some attention for most of the latter half of the 20th century, has also diminished, in part because the various new electronic media have captured so many of the specialized or niche markets that these other developments themselves helped to fracture.

Citizens, pundits, scholars, and politicians themselves have singled out partisanship and political parties for special criticism. Many would like to see MPs voting more freely, based either on what their constituents want (assuming MPs could know) or the MP's personal conscience. They oppose the excessive party discipline imposed by party leaders that occurs when leaders silence the voices of their MPs and turn them into robots who merely echo the party line. All party leaders have been responsible at times for succumbing to both these temptations, although it is ironic that the Conservative Party has probably been the party most characterized by this practice, despite the fact that the core of the new party is the defunct Reform Party of Preston Manning, a party formed precisely to advance the ideals of reduced partisanship and party discipline in parliamentary government (Smith 1999).

Many—though not all—of those who support reforming how Parliament works on a day-to-day basis have set their sights on reducing, if not eliminating, partisanship. However, the entire parliamentary process is predicated on partisan politics, which sees institutionalized adversarialism as the best means of securing democracy. Partisanship is thus an essential dynamic of public accountability in our democratic system and any efforts to improve democracy by reducing partisanship are doomed to failure. Efforts to improve democracy should instead be focused on reducing excessive party discipline.

The Need for Reform

As we have indicated and will argue more fully in later chapters, unconstrained prime ministerial power undermines the democratic spirit of the Canadian constitution of parliamentary government as institutionalized by the conventions of responsible government. "Prime Ministers who violate the spirit of the constitution may not understand its requirements or are prepared to violate the norms of behavior it prescribes because of their obsession with winning and holding power. There is a critical issue of character with leaders who are prepared to ignore or violate the rules of the game" (Thomas 2011). These conventions are meant to govern how the democratic elements of the constitution should operate. The logic here is that MPs in the House of Commons are the people's directly elected representatives. This makes the system democratic: the people have the ultimate control. But they have this control only insofar as MPs are able to constrain the prime minister and government.

This was the democratic spirit that motivated British political reformers in the third decade of the 19th century in Great Britain. The prime minister became responsible to the House of Commons and not the Queen. It was the same democratic spirit that emerged shortly thereafter in the British North American colonies (as well as in the British colonies in Australia and New Zealand). These colonial reformers also won out, and their structures of parliamentary government adopted the British practices.

One must acknowledge that while citizen, pundit, academic, and political reformers are now active on several fronts and are advancing reform proposals, the effort is scattered and lacks coherence at this time. Although most reformers have the fortitude to keep going, there is a level of frustration that characterizes the reform movement(s) generally. None of the major parties has endorsed a comprehensive and coherent program of democratic reform, although all speak to the issue. Leadership failure on this front cannot but discourage reformers and breed cynicism on the part of citizens who are not active in reform circles yet nevertheless have a low opinion of the state of parliamentary democracy.

The problems that are undermining Canadian democracy demand reform. The problem is not the result of any one governing party. Nor is it the consequence of minority government; majority government, in many ways, enhances the democracy problem even if it gives it a façade of stability or, worse, gives it the veneer of legitimacy (the false god of autocrats) (Russell 2008). The reforms we propose in this book seek to establish firm, clear rules for the practices governing confidence and the summoning, prorogation, and dissolution of Parliament, around which a consensus could build among politicians, analysts, and the public. These rules would constrain the power of prime ministers to silence the House in order to protect their partisan interests. We also seek to advance proposals that would reduce the power of the prime minister and government to dominate parliamentary structures and processes merely to serve their partisan interests.

While it is neither possible nor desirable to prescribe rules for every situation, a complete absence of rules leaves the integrity of the system vulnerable to abuse. It should also be noted that having a few firm rules does not forgo flexibility within, or preclude future evolution of, our parliamentary system.

Outline of This Book

Before we present our case for reform and our proposals for addressing the problem of the abuse of prime ministerial power and the shortcomings of our existing system in Chapter 6, we need to examine the reasons why we face this major problem in our system of democratic government. We need to consider how the system of responsible government emerged and then evolved. We also need to consider the problem from a comparative perspective, especially against the experiences of Australia, Great Britain, and New Zealand. And, of course, we need to consider the recent debates about the current state of responsible government in Canada.

In Chapter 2, we provide a brief comparative account of the principles and structures of responsible government, its origins, and the evolution of its practices to this point in Canada, Great Britain, Australia, and New Zealand. We introduce what we see as the Canadian problem of unconstrained prime ministerial power, when adherence to the spirit of responsible government is diminished or disappears.

In Chapter 3, we examine the critical role of unwritten constitutional conventions in the practice of responsible government. We discuss what happens when conventions become unclear or subject to dispute, and thus ultimately fail to be effective constraints. Whenever this is the case, what may or may not happen when the rules come into play turns out to be uncertain.

In Chapter 4, we describe how the prime minister has come to be able to exercise the governor general's powers at his or her discretion and to use them to give the governing political party a political advantage over the opposition parties that not only serves no public purpose, but actually diminishes the quality of parliamentary democracy. In several critical respects, responsible government has been turned on its head: the prime minister controls the House of Commons, not the other way around. He or she does so as the leader of the governing party *in* the House. In this capacity, the prime minister has the legitimate authority to dictate to his or her party's MPs, including ministers, how they will vote in the House of Commons. This capacity to impose what is called "party discipline" gives the prime minister enormous leverage against the opposition parties when the MPs who belong to the prime minister's governing party constitute a majority of all MPs. But even when this is not the case—when the prime minister's party has only a minority of the MPs on its side (known as a minority government)—the prime minister can be just as dominant. This has been fully evident most recently in the case of Prime Minister Stephen Harper, who governed between 2006 and 2011 with only a minority of Conservative MPs in the House of Commons. Maintaining power by political tactics that keep the three opposition parties disunited, as Prime Minister Harper did so successfully, is simply good political leadership. Abusing the prime minister's powers of prorogation and dissolution is something else altogether.

In Chapter 5, we examine why periodic elections are a necessary, but not a sufficient, condition of a robust democracy. Neither elections nor the constant pressures of public opinion have been sufficient to constrain prime ministers from abusing their powers. The chapter reviews the indirect role of elections in the formation of government in a parliamentary system. While this parliamentary system of selecting governments functions with relatively little complaint when voters elect a majority of members of Parliament from a single party, the system faces greater complexity when no single party wins a majority of seats. Perhaps the most controversial and contested aspect of Canadian democracy, even among constitutional scholars, is the legitimacy of changing governments between elections.

Some argue that elections should be the only way to change a government from one party to another. This was the argument advanced by Prime Minister Harper and his supporters following the December 4, 2008 prorogation of Parliament (see, for example, Flanagan 2009), facing defeat and the proposed Liberal–New Democrat coalition government. We examine the competing claims of the democratic legitimacy of changing governments between elections. One does not have to dispute that elections are the cornerstone of our democracy to be able to reject the argument advanced by the Conservatives that only elections can decide who is to be prime minister, and thus which party will be the governing party. In a parliamentary democracy, it is the House of Commons that must decide who constitutes the government after the people have elected their MPs.

Because, at times, Canadian voters do not elect a majority of the MPs belonging to one party, requiring an election to be held every time the prime minister and government loses the support of a majority in the House of Commons is simply not respectful of what voters have decided in the election. The only way to respect the democratic wishes of the people when no one party has a majority of MPs is to abide by the founding principle and original logic of responsible government: that a majority of MPs decides who should be the prime minister, even if that means that a majority of MPs replaces one prime minister with another between elections. In a democracy with three or more competitive political parties electing MPs to the House of Commons, this logic is even more compelling now than it was nearly two centuries ago!

Chapter 5 concludes by considering the practical implications of relying exclusively on elections to form government for the conduct of parliamentary democracy, including the requirement to entrench rigid party discipline on all MPs in order to respect the party preferences of voters, as well as the capacity of Parliament to hold government to account between and during elections.

In Chapter 6, we outline our proposals for reforming responsible government in order to democratize the constitution. We argue that the prime minister should not be able to dissolve or prorogue Parliament or to put off summoning Parliament at his or her discretion or to decide when the government has lost the support of the House of Commons. That kind of power held by a single person does not, in our view, belong in a robust democracy.

At the same time, we think that a robust democracy should not rely on the personal discretion of an appointed governor general to constrain a prime minister from abusing those powers. But that is exactly what some expect our governor general to do. And they persist in this view even though the conventions of responsible government that guide what the governor general should or should not decide, and under what conditions, are now highly contested. When a consensus on the conventions themselves does not exist, the constitution's unwritten rules are next to useless, allowing the prime minister to drag the governor general into the partisan political arena, as was most dramatically experienced in December 2008. It is also practically unrealistic and democratically inappropriate to rely exclusively on a new election every time a government loses the confidence of the House of Commons. Something else is obviously required.

We offer a four-part reform to address the constitutional dimensions of our democracy problem:

First, to constrain the prime minister from abusing the power to summon Parliament after an election, we propose a requirement that Parliament be summoned within 30 days after the date of an election.

Second, to reduce the capacity of the prime minister to destabilize parliamentary operations and undermine the effectiveness of the House and its committees in performing their critical functions in a parliamentary democracy, we propose that the dates of elections be fixed at four years. Elections would occur every four years on a specific date unless a two-thirds majority of MPs approves a motion to dissolve Parliament for an early election. This would remove what has become the virtual right of the Canadian prime minister to call an election whenever he or she wants, even after losing the confidence of a majority of MPs. It would also eliminate a partisan advantage that can be used against the opposition.

Third, to remove any disagreement about what constitutes a vote of non-confidence and to eliminate the power of the prime minister to dismiss some votes as not actually withdrawing confidence, we propose the adoption of a "constructive non-confidence" procedure. Under this procedure, the opposition can only bring down the government via an explicit motion of non-confidence. This motion would also identify the member who would become the prime minister and form a new government with the support of a majority of MPs in the House. The motion would have to be supported by a simple majority of MPs. It would require opposition leaders and their MPs to vote non-confidence in the government only when they are prepared to form and/or support a new government from the opposition side of the House. It would also make clear that the House could change governments between elections. This reform would also dramatically reduce the ability of both the prime minister and the opposition to use confidence measures (and elections) as a form of brinkmanship.

Fourth, to constrain the prime minister from abusing the power to escape scrutiny on a vote of non-confidence, we propose that the consent of the House of Commons be required before proroguing Parliament. To be an effective constraint on the prime minister of a majority government, the consent of a two-thirds majority of the House of Commons should be required.

In addition to these first four reforms, we also propose measures that will further reform parliamentary governance. These would constrain the prime minister's power over the House of Commons and strengthen the effectiveness of the House and its committees. In proposing these reforms, we use a simple four-part test that should be applied to all potential reforms.

As we will discuss, the most effective means of enacting the four proposed reforms that encompass the powers of the governor general would be formal constitutional amendments that establish these new processes. These democratic reforms should be packaged for constitutional change separate from any other measures—especially electoral system reform and Senate reform—that bring important and controversial issues of federalism into play. Electoral system reform, from the current first-past-the-post (or single-member-plurality) voting system to any proportional-based voting system, would not adversely affect our proposed changes in any way and could well help to bring about the desired objectives. The effects of a reformed Senate, on the other hand, can only be considered with reference to fully formed proposals for a reformed Senate. The proposals put forward by the Conservatives since 2006 do not meet these criteria.

Although the changes we propose require the consent of the provinces, they do not affect the legislative powers or rights of the provinces in any way. At the same time, we recognize Canadians' assumed collective phobia of "opening the constitution." This phobia has become an impediment to democratic reform. We thus discuss what reforms might be accomplished, short of formal constitutional change, by looking at what has been done in New Zealand and Great Britain.

References

Flanagan, Tom. 2009. Only voters have the right to decide on the coalition. *The Globe and Mail*, January 9, A13.

Franks, C.E.S. 1997. *The Parliament of Canada*. Toronto: University of Toronto Press.

Harper, Stephen, and Tom Flanagan. 1997. Our benign dictatorship. *Next City* 2 (2) [Winter 1996–97].

Hazell, Robert, and Ben Yong. 2010. Submission to the Political and Constitutional Reform Committee: Lessons from the process of government formation after the 2010 election. House of Commons. http://www.publications.parliament.uk/pa/cm201011/cmselect/cmpolcon/734/734we01.htm.

Martin, Lawrence. 2010. *Harperland: The politics of control*. Toronto: Viking Canada.

New Zealand. 2008. *Cabinet manual*. http://www.cabinetmanual.cabinetoffice.govt.nz/node/68.

Russell, Peter H. 2008. *Two cheers for minority government: The evolution of Canadian parliamentary democracy*. Toronto: Emond Montgomery.

Russell, Peter H., and Lorne Sossin, eds. 2009. *Parliamentary democracy in crisis*. Toronto: University of Toronto Press.

Samara. 2011. *"It's my party": Parliamentary dysfunction reconsidered.* http://www.samaracanada.com/downloads/ItsMyParty.pdf.

Savoie, Donald. 1999. *Governing from the centre: The concentration of power in Canadian politics*. Toronto: University of Toronto Press.

Savoie, Donald. 2010. *Power: Where is it?* Montreal and Kingston, ON: McGill-Queen's University Press.

Simpson, Jeffrey. 2001. *The friendly dictatorship.* Toronto: McClelland & Stewart.

Smith, David. 2007. *The people's House of Commons: Theories of democracy in contention.* Toronto: University of Toronto Press.

Smith, Jennifer. 1999. Democracy and the Canadian House of Commons at the millennium. *Canadian Public Administration* 42 (4): 398–421.

Thomas, Paul. 2011. Personal correspondence with authors, February 26. Used with permission.

Twomey, Anne. 2011. The governor general's role in the formation of government in a hung Parliament. *Public Law Review* 22 (1): 52–74.

CHAPTER TWO

Responsible Government: Theory and Practice

Introduction

In this chapter, we briefly elaborate on the basic features of responsible government as it emerged in Britain and then in Britain's North American colonies, in what is now Canada. The adoption of responsible government as the foundation of parliamentary democracy built upon and retained the existing structures of government already in place. What changed were the unwritten rules or conventions as to how the democratic process should work. The evolution of this new approach was continued when the written constitution of the new Dominion of Canada—the *British North America Act*—was enacted by the British Parliament in 1867. Understanding Canada's democratic development requires perceiving the distinction between the formal or legal provisions of this *written* part of the constitution, and the *unwritten* conventions of responsible government. The complete constitution can only be understood by knowing how the unwritten conventions are meant to govern the conduct of the governor general (as the representative of the Queen), the prime minister, and MPs in the House of Commons. In this context, we need to describe how political parties make the logic of responsible government a practical form of democratic governance. As we have done in Chapter 1, we reference Westminster experiences from Australia, Great Britain, and New Zealand to better understand the Canadian experience.

Responsible Government in Great Britain

The emergence of responsible government as the constitutional foundation of parliamentary democracy in Great Britain was part of an evolution that occurred over several centuries, with various twists, turns, and even reversals of progress along the way. Bruce Hicks (2010, 19) notes the beginning of this evolution: "The decision to convene an assembly of barons, prelates and ministers, which in the 13th century was dubbed 'parliament,' was nothing more than a political mechanism to mollify challengers to the Crown's authority." Over the next three centuries, the powers of the Crown to summon, prorogue, and dissolve Parliament were established by the Crown to control Parliament, "to restrain the legislative and governing impulses of competing political interests" (ibid.).

Over the next several centuries, the struggle was between the Crown (the monarch, now the King or Queen, as the case may be), who possessed the executive powers of government, and Parliament, which controlled law-making and raising taxes. In the process, Parliament became separate from the monarch and divided into two houses: the House of Lords and the House of Commons. The former was restricted to the higher nobility, and membership became based on inheritance or being a member of the senior clergy of the church. The latter was for the second tier of English society, the growing new class of knights and burgesses, and was eventually organized geographically, with representatives from districts called boroughs. The consent of both houses was required for new laws and taxes proposed by the monarch and the ministers who assisted him or her in governance.

By the turn of the 19th century, the structure of government had evolved, with the monarch now having executive power to administer government and its operations; the power to summon, prorogue, and dissolve Parliament (subject to various restrictions imposed by successive parliaments over time); and the right to propose new laws and taxes for the operations of government (including, of course, military operations). The monarch no longer exercised the power to refuse royal ascent to laws that had been proposed and then passed by members of the two houses. Ministers appointed by the monarch to the Privy Council (or Cabinet) and drawn from the two houses of Parliament assisted in the monarch's exercise of power. One of these ministers was now designated the prime minister, as well as the First Lord of the Treasury. The monarch needed the support of the prime minister to convince Parliament to supply the funds for the operations of government as well as to coordinate the work of other ministers who headed the various departments of government to determine how those funds were spent.

By then, what were to become what we now know as political parties had developed to the point where the supporters of the monarch and his government sat on one side of the House of Commons and all other members of Parliament, as the members of the House of Commons were now known, sat on what became the opposition side of the House. The House of Commons was now composed of the elected representatives of the monarch's subjects, although the franchise (the right to vote for MPs in an election) was still restricted to a small proportion of these subjects. Increasingly, the monarch was obliged to make efforts to ensure that his or her ministers, led by the prime minister, were able to command the support of a majority in Parliament, but especially in the House of Commons, on a continuing basis. This meant that the MPs on the government side of the House should, ideally, constitute a majority. With most MPs forming themselves into two competing political parties sitting on opposite sides of the House, it became increasingly obvious that the monarch needed a prime minister who could command the confidence of a majority in the House. Support for the monarch's preferred policies by the majority of the House of Lords was rarely an issue, of course.

The result was that from 1835 on the monarch has appointed as prime minister only someone who could command the confidence of the majority in the House of Commons. A widespread public demand for democratic reform led to the *Reform Act of 1832*, which extended the franchise to a greater number of subjects (although still less than one-fifth of the male population), and gave increased representation to major population centres (and removed representation from many "rotten boroughs," where few people actually lived or were able to vote). This demand for reform fitted well with the idea that it should be the House of Commons, rather than the monarch, that decides who should form the government, and that this decision is made after a general election and after a government is defeated on confidence (as occurred with some frequency between 1832 and 1867). The prime minister and government, even though they are the monarch's government, thus became "responsible" to the House of Commons. It was this model that interested democratic reformers in the British North American colonies, hence the call for "responsible government" on this side of the Atlantic.

Before Responsible Government

In the British North American colonies of Nova Scotia, Canada (formerly Upper and Lower Canada), New Brunswick, Prince Edward Island, and Newfoundland, the structures of parliamentary government in the early 1840s were hardly democratic at all. As in Britain at the time, the franchise (the right to vote) was severely restricted. The right to vote was only gradually expanded to all adult citizens: universal suffrage took over 200 years to accomplish.

However, in each of the colonies, starting in Nova Scotia in 1758, the British government had implemented the principle of "representative

TIMELINE: THE EVOLUTION OF RESPONSIBLE GOVERNMENT IN CANADA

1758	The British government establishes, first in Nova Scotia and ultimately in all of the colonies, a system of *representative government*, whereby each colony has a legislative assembly directly elected by the people; the franchise is severely restricted.
1758–1840s	The British government appoints and controls the colonial governors, but the consent of legislative assemblies is required for the passage of laws, including laws that raise money.
Early 1800s	Support for responsible government grows in each colony as people demand an end to British control over colonial governors.
1820s–1840s	Rival political groups develop. Conservatives support the status quo, while Liberals/Reformers want change (in the form of responsible government); these groups eventually develop into disciplined parties in the assemblies.
1837	Upper and Lower Canadian rebellions, which precipitate Lord Durham's report (1839) and his recommendation for responsible government in the colonies.
1848	Nova Scotia becomes the first colony to achieve responsible government. The first executive chosen by a majority in the legislature is formed after a vote of no confidence in the previous executive.
1849–1854	The Province of Canada, Prince Edward Island, New Brunswick, and Newfoundland achieve responsible government.
1867	The British government creates the Dominion of Canada; the *British North America Act*, an act of the British Parliament, is Canada's first written constitution.
1918	The Civil Service Commission is created, with authority to hire public servants on non-partisan, merit-based grounds.
1920	The position of an independent chief electoral officer is created, to oversee the administration of elections and ensure that they are fair and impartial.
1982	The Canadian constitution is patriated with the adoption of the *Constitution Act, 1982*, which includes the *Charter of Rights and Freedoms* and amending formulas.

government." Each colony thus had a *legislative assembly* of representatives directly elected by the people. These legislative bodies were modelled on the British House of Commons, although the term "legislative assembly" was used in all provinces except Quebec, where the term "National Assembly" was, and still is, used. As was the case in Britain by the 1840s, the consent of the elected legislative assembly was required for the passage of all laws, including the laws that enabled the executive government to raise public money through various forms of taxation. However, in each of the colonies, and unlike in Britain, the people's elected representatives in the legislative assembly did not otherwise have control over the executive branch of government.

The executive branch of government, or simply "the government," was under the control and authority of the colonial *governor*. Governors were British officials appointed by the King or Queen on the advice of the British government, sent from Britain to exercise executive powers under instructions from the British government. The colonies were, after all, colonies of the British Empire.

For his part, the governor appointed a select number of local political leaders to advise and assist him in the administration of government. They became the ministers of the governor's *executive council* (or Cabinet). Under the governor's authority, these ministers headed the departments of the government. The governor selected these political leaders from both the elected legislative assembly and from the *legislative council*, a second legislative assembly whose members were not elected but were also appointed by the governor. (The House of Lords in Britain was the obvious model here.) In this structure, the governor was clearly in charge. His ministers were his subordinates; they were not his colleagues, let alone his equals.

In every colony, some more than others, there were demands to end the British governor's control over the colony. Each colony had its supporters of the status quo, however. These included the governor's ministers, other administrative officials in his government's employ, the members of the appointed legislative council, and a varying number of members of the elected legislative assembly. They opposed the establishment of responsible government, in part for obvious self-interested reasons and in part because they did not believe in political equality. Responsible government would mean that their tenure as members of the governor's "court party," along with the political influence and perks that accompanied these appointed positions, would come to an end. In these colonies, the Conservatives (also referred to as the "Tories," a nickname imported from British politics for those who wanted the British Crown to remain an important part of government) were the chief supporters of the British governors. The Conservatives wished to maintain the status quo, insofar as the structure of government was concerned. As long as the British-appointed system, with the governor in charge, stayed in place, they had political power, without needing to compete against their opponents in the legislative assembly—the Liberals (also called Reformers) in the Maritimes and the Reformers in the Province of Canada.

Responsible Government as Party Government

The struggle for responsible government in the 20 or so years leading up to the 1840s, including the 1837 rebellions in the colonies of Lower Canada and Upper Canada, was accompanied by the development of these two rival political groups—the Conservatives, who favoured the system as it was, versus the Liberals, or Reformers, who favoured change. Each group was made up of leading citizens who shared roughly similar views on public governance and/or shared vested interests in public policy. However, these groups were not tightly disciplined voting blocs in the legislative assembly; they were not political parties as we know them today. Many elected politicians preferred to take stands on an issue-by-issue basis or simply wished to have the independence to see which way the winds of public opinion were blowing.

It did not take long for those who advocated responsible government to realize that such a system would require more disciplined action in the legislature. Nevertheless, political reformers, such as Joseph Howe

The 1837 rebellions in Upper and Lower Canada arose from the frustrated demands of reformers.

SOURCE: *Back view of the church of St. Eustache and dispersion of the insurgents* by Lord Charles Beauclerk, 1840. Copyright McCord Museum (M4777.6). Reprinted by permission.

in Nova Scotia, were reluctant converts to the idea of disciplined political parties. Howe worried that government based on political parties would be divisive. Citizens would be split into at least two camps: the party that formed the government side and the party that constituted the opposition side. Nonetheless, Howe and other reformers eventually accepted that responsible government—government that was controlled by the people's elected representatives in the legislative assembly and not by the governor—required an organizational mechanism to perform at least two critical functions:

1. to determine which member of the legislative assembly would be chosen to head the government and to select the other ministers of the government; and
2. to secure a majority of members of the legislative assembly to provide continuing *confidence* in the government and to support its legislative program.

Joseph Howe left his career as a noted journalist and publisher to become a political reformer, and in 1848 he played a central role in helping Nova Scotia become the first British colony to achieve responsible government.

SOURCE: Library and Archives Canada/PA-025486.

That mechanism was political parties.

With the adoption of responsible government, parliamentary democracy thus became a form of "party government." The legislative assemblies of the colonies were organized formally so that the government members sat on one side of the assembly and the official Opposition members sat on the other. In the first years, the contending parties, the Conservatives and the Liberals, were prone to losing members as some occasionally switched sides or voted independently of the party. The democratic expectation, nonetheless, was that the two parties would periodically change sides—between government and opposition—as their support from voters waxed and waned. And, it should be noted, once responsible government was established in the colonies as the colonial policy of the British government, the Conservatives, who had originally opposed the adoption of responsible government, accepted this new constitutional regime. As a result, that particular difference of opinion between the Conservatives and the Liberals/Reformers disappeared.

The Constitution of 1867: The Written Law and Unwritten Conventions

When the struggle for responsible government resulted in democratic reform in the late 1840s and early 1850s, the power structure in the colonies was transformed. In each colony, the governor was replaced as the *de facto* executive head of government by the party leader able to form a government with the confidence of a majority in the elected representative assembly. The people's representatives in the assembly now controlled who constituted the government, not the governor. Even those who had opposed this new regime accepted the reform and its enhancement of democracy. In addition to Nova Scotia, responsible government was implemented in the Province of Canada in 1849, in Prince Edward Island in 1851, in New Brunswick in 1854, and in Newfoundland in 1855.

It is important to note that no new written constitution reflecting this transformation in power accompanied the reform, aside from the British government's written instructions to the colonial governors. Instead, the British tradition and preference for unwritten constitutional conventions was maintained. The result: the term "responsible government" appears nowhere in Canada's 1867 constitution. Written constitutions were for the French or the Americans. This meant retaining, as much as possible, the traditional formal structures of government each time a reform was adopted. At the same time, of course, it was assumed that everyone understood that the actual practice was to be governed by new unwritten rules. In adhering to this British tradition of evolutionary reform, political leaders were expected not only to know the conventions of the constitution but also to respect their spirit by acting in good faith.

The Written Constitution

When the British Parliament created the Dominion of Canada in 1867, Canada actually did obtain a written constitution of sorts, the *British North America Act* (BNA Act). This statute was a British law that applied to Canada. As a result, the newly created dominion now had both this written law as a constitution and the unwritten constitutional conventions of responsible government established two decades before Confederation. A written constitution was necessary in order to create the federal system of government that had been negotiated by the colonial political leaders, commonly referred to as the Fathers of Confederation. Thus, the BNA Act established the division of subject matters of legislation between the new federal Parliament and the provincial legislatures of Nova Scotia, New Brunswick, Ontario, and Quebec.

The written constitution also contained provisions dealing with the executive and legislative branches of government. These provisions are still found in the written part of the Canadian constitution—since 1982 entitled the *Constitution Act, 1867*. Except for the rule that a parliament not last longer than five years, the provisions describe the formal structures in ways that do not reflect the democratic distribution of powers in practice as governed by the unwritten conventions of responsible government.[1] The most important provisions of the *Constitution Act, 1867* that do *not* reflect the conventions are those dealing with the Queen and the governor general as her representative in Canada. The written constitution, for instance, states that:

- the executive powers are vested in the Queen;
- the members of the Queen's Privy Council (or Cabinet of ministers) who assist and advise the governor general are chosen by and may be dismissed by the governor general.

The written constitution reflects the legal reality that the Queen of Canada and the governor general are part of a constitutional monarchy. In Canada, as in Britain, Australia, and New Zealand, the Queen reigns but is not meant to rule.

---

1. The *Canadian Charter of Rights and Freedoms*, adopted in 1982 and part of the *Constitution Act, 1982*, also requires that there be at least one sitting of Parliament every 12 months.

The Unwritten Conventions

The positions and powers of the prime minister and Cabinet are not even mentioned in the *Constitution Act, 1867*, except for the oblique references to the Queen's Privy Council.[2] In fact, of course, the evolution of the unwritten constitutional conventions of responsible government prescribes that the prime minister and other ministers of the Cabinet exercise the powers of the executive government, with the prime minister as the head of the government.[3] This means that:

- the prime minister, and not the governor general, forms the government and decides who will be ministers (and thus formally made members of the Privy Council);[4]
- the prime minister alone, or the prime minister with other ministers, advises the governor general on the exercise of the executive powers of the Queen/governor general, including to summon,

2. The prime minister and all other ministers are formally appointed as members of the Queen's Privy Council. The operative part of the Privy Council is the governor general together with the ministers of the government of the day, called the governor in council. When the government acts in a legal manner, such as making appointments or declaring legal regulations, it acts as the "governor in council." The governor general, of course, merely rubber-stamps what the government of the day has decided. The Privy Council should not be confused with the Privy Council Office, the public service department that serves the prime minister and Cabinet.

3. At the provincial level of government in Canada, the prime minister is called premier. The two terms mean the same thing, namely, the "first minister" of the government. Historically, the two terms were often used interchangeably. In Québec, the premier is known as *le premier ministre*.

4. Senators may be appointed ministers of the government and today at least one will be so appointed and function as the government leader in the Senate. Legally, one can be a minister, even prime minister, without being an MP. John Turner was not an MP when he was Liberal prime minister for several months in 1984 after succeeding Pierre Trudeau as Liberal Party leader and prime minister. But he was expected to call an election shortly after becoming prime minister and did so. The Australian and New Zealand constitutions require that the prime minister be an MP.

prorogue, and dissolve Parliament, to make appointments to public offices that require the governor general's approval, and to approve regulations that require the governor general's approval; and

- the Queen's representative, the governor general, always gives royal assent to legislation that has been passed by the House of Commons and Senate.

The powers of the prime minister are substantial. By exercising the governor general's powers, the prime minister decides when to summon Parliament into session, when it will be prorogued, and when it will be dissolved and an election held. Except for positions in the non-partisan professional public service and a handful of other exceptions,[5] the prime minister approves all appointments to public offices, including the very top professional public service positions, which are made by the governor general with the Privy Council (referred to as "governor in council" appointments). The power to make or approve these many hundreds of appointments to dozens of government boards and commissions is considered the prerogative of the prime minister.

The *Constitution Act, 1867* further stipulates that all legislative measures that propose either to raise public money through taxes or fees or to spend public money for any purpose must be recommended by the governor general (and they must be introduced first in the House of Commons, not in the Senate). This means that these measures can only be introduced by ministers after the prime minister approves them.[6]

---

5. The members of the public service of Canada, up to the level of assistant deputy ministers, are appointed on the basis of merit under the authority of the Public Service Commission, an independent executive agency that reports to Parliament and is not under the direction of a minister. The handful of other exceptions include the president of the Public Service Commission and the auditor general of Canada, each of whom is considered a parliamentary agent and not part of the executive government under the prime minister and Cabinet.

6. A "bill" is the term used for a legislative proposal that has not yet become legislation or law (that is, a "statute" or "act").

These constitutional provisions give the prime minister and the government the lead role in moving their public policy agenda through the parliamentary processes of the House of Commons. MPs who are not also ministers of the government, which by definition includes all opposition MPs as well as the governing party's own MPs who are not ministers, cannot introduce these financial measures. The House, of course, can vote down the government's proposals. On the plus side, this allows opposition MPs to clearly place the accountability for all government tax and spending policies on the prime minister and the government.

While the prime minister assumes great power by virtue of the conventions of responsible government, which are discussed in further detail later in this chapter, it is important to note that these same conventions also require that:

- the prime minister and the government remain in office only as long as they have the confidence of a majority of the MPs in the House of Commons; and
- when the prime minister's government loses the confidence of the House of Commons, he or she must either:
  - resign along with the rest of the government so that a new prime minister may be formally asked by the governor general to form a new government to govern with the confidence of a majority of the MPs in the House of Commons; or
  - formally ask the governor general to dissolve Parliament so that a new election for the House of Commons may be held.

The application of these rules, referred to as the "confidence conventions," requires that the prime minister and government be "responsible" to the House of Commons. In this formulation, "responsible" means two things:

1. that the prime minister and the ministers must continuously provide an account to the House of their administration of

the laws, public finances, and public services as approved by Parliament; and

2. that the House of Commons has the power and obligation to hold the prime minister and ministers of the government to account, to question them, and to pass judgment on their policies and performance, including the power of a majority of MPs in the House of Commons to withdraw their confidence in the prime minister and government.

By these means, the prime minister and the ministers of the government are thereby also, but only *indirectly*, responsible to the people who have *directly* elected the House of Commons. Accordingly, when an election is held, the decision about who should form the government is turned back to the people. But even then, the decision of the people can only be made indirectly through the decisions of their elected representatives.

The Canadian Practice of Responsible Government

With Confederation in 1867, elections for the House of Commons became primarily contests between the recognized candidates of two political parties, although the Liberals took some time to develop as an organized competitive national party. To this day, only two parties, the Liberals and the Conservatives, have ever formed the government in Ottawa.[7] Whenever one party has a majority of the MPs elected to the House, it forms what is referred to as a "majority government" or, more accurately, a single-party majority government. The most recent was Harper's majority government, elected in 2011.

Due to the emergence of parties other than the Liberals and Conservatives that have gained parliamentary representation since the end of

---

7. The Union government during the First World War was essentially a Conservative government. Also, the current Conservative Party is the result of a merger between the former Progressive Conservative Party and the former Canadian Alliance Party. Both of these are discussed in more detail in later parts of this book.

the First World War, Canada has experienced single-party "minority governments" with some frequency in the 20th and 21st centuries, in each case a Liberal or Conservative single-party minority government. On 13 occasions, these other parties have denied either the Liberal or the Conservative governing party a clear majority in the House of Commons (Russell 2008). For instance, following the 2008 election, four parties were represented in the House of Commons and the governing Conservative Party did not have a majority of the MPs on its side. It was thus a minority government, having elected only 143 of the total 308 MPs in the House of Commons. For the Conservatives to stay in power, a sufficient number of MPs from the ranks of the three opposition parties—the Liberals, New Democrats, and Bloc Québécois—had to support the Harper government or at least not vote against it on matters of confidence. That lasted until 2011, when the Harper government was defeated on a vote of confidence and then won a majority of seats in the election that followed.

The practice in Canada has been to have single-party governments, whether they are single-party majority governments or single-party minority governments. In both cases, one party forms the government. The prime minister and all ministers of the government or Cabinet are from that one party. The MPs of the government party who are not appointed as ministers are therefore not members of "the government" when this term is used to refer to the political executive as government, Cabinet, or ministry.[8] The MPs who are not ministers are commonly referred to as "backbenchers," a term that comes from Britain, where all MPs, including ministers, sit on benches in the House of Commons. Ministers occupy the front benches; those who are not ministers occupy the backbenches. The ministers and backbench MPs of the governing party

---

8. The terms government, Cabinet, and ministry can be used interchangeably for most purposes. All ministers are part of the government. But, in some governments, the ministry includes ministers who are not in the Cabinet. Each of these ministers is usually the subordinate or junior minister to a Cabinet minister.

constitute the party's "caucus," a forum where the prime minister and Cabinet ministers meet with the party's backbenchers to maintain party solidarity and, depending on the leadership style of the prime minister, to allow the backbenchers some opportunity to comment on or to complain about the government's policies. Each opposition party has its own caucus as well.

A single-party majority government, of course, could only be defeated if a sufficient number of its MPs revolted against the prime minister and Cabinet and then either voted against their own government or failed to vote and thereby enabled the opposition MPs to outnumber the governing party's MPs. All of this is academic, at least so far, because no majority government has ever been defeated on a vote of confidence in the House.[9] A single-party minority government, on the other hand, does not have a majority in the House on its side. To survive, as noted above, it must count on the support of the MPs from one or more opposition parties. But the parties that support the minority government whenever there is a vote of confidence or non-confidence are not part of the government. Even when they support the government on a fairly continuous basis, as the New Democrat MPs supported the 1972–1974 minority government of Liberal Prime Minister Trudeau or the Liberals, Bloc Québécois, and New Democrats did at various times for the Harper Conservative government, they remain on the opposition side of the House.

When two or more parties are part of the government, they have formed what is called a "coalition" government. In that case, the prime minister will invariably be the leader of the party with the most MPs. But leading MPs from the one or more other parties in the coalition will

---

9. There is at least one example of a majority government falling as a result of a backbench party member voting against the government at the provincial level, however. In 1988, the NDP government of Howard Pawley in Manitoba was defeated on the budget vote and forced into holding an election when one NDP MLA, Jim Walding, voted for an opposition amendment to the budget.

also become ministers in the government. The two or more parties that form the coalition government sit on the government side of the House.

While there has never been a coalition government at the federal level in Canada,[10] there have been a few cases of coalition governments at the provincial level. The most recent was formed in Saskatchewan, when the New Democratic Party and the Liberal Party joined forces in a coalition government under Premier Roy Romanow, the NDP leader. The coalition government was formed after the 1999 election, when the NDP won 29 seats, the Liberals 4 seats,[11] and the Saskatchewan Party 25 seats, and was in office from 1999 to 2003. To have a majority government, the NDP needed the Liberals to join them in a coalition government and they did so. In this case, the coalition government was a majority coalition government. Coalition governments, however, need not be majority governments, although public discussions in Canada often assume this. In New Zealand, for instance, there have been a number of coalition governments in recent years that have been minority coalition governments. The several possibilities of different forms of government, all meeting the confidence test of responsible government, are discussed in Chapter 5.

Independent MPs

Notwithstanding the emergence of party government, neither the constitution nor the election law prohibited a person standing as a candi-

---

10. There was a Union Government created during the First World War by Conservative Prime Minister Robert Borden in 1917. It comprised both the Conservative Party and some Liberals. Borden had wanted a Conservative–Liberal coalition but the Liberal leader, Wilfrid Laurier, rejected the idea, based on his opposition to conscription. The Union Government was thus not a coalition government of two or more parties. The Liberal Party continued as a separate party in Parliament, in this instance as the official Opposition party, while a number of its former members sat under the Union banner.

11. The Liberals initially won four seats, but were reduced to three when one member defected.

date for election as an "independent," rather than as the candidate of a political party. But even in the 19th century, one could count on one hand the number of individuals who were elected as independents in any given election.[12] With parliamentary government organized along party lines, there was little room for MPs who did not belong to a political party. The structures and processes of parliamentary government give independent MPs very little say in the operations of Parliament or government. Since independents, by definition, do not belong to a party, even when there is more than one independent MP, each has only one voice and one vote. However, there can be circumstances under minority governments when the governing party needs every possible vote in the House to escape defeat. The votes of independent MPs who are not already aligned with opposition parties that intend to vote against the government can be crucial for the survival of a government. Even one independent MP can hold the balance of power. For example, the Liberal minority government of Paul Martin only survived a dramatic May 2005 non-confidence vote by securing the votes of two independent MPs.

Floor-Crossers

Although MPs are now identified on the ballot as the official candidates of a registered political party (unless running as an independent), MPs are still elected as individuals. They are free to act and vote as they see fit. This means that an MP may "cross the floor" from one side of the House to sit on the other side with another party: from government to opposition or vice versa. If they wish to leave an opposition party and join the government side, the prime minister must accept them into the

---

12. MPs can also become independents by leaving their party either by their own choosing or by being kicked out of their party by the leader. Bill Casey, a Nova Scotia MP first elected in 1988, was kicked out of the Conservative Party caucus by Prime Minister Harper for voting against the government's 2007 budget and sat as an independent MP. In the 2008 election, the popular MP was re-elected as an independent.

governing party caucus. If they wish to go from the government party to an opposition party, the leader of that party would have to accept them. They could also sit as an independent or move from one opposition party to another, again with the approval of the leader of the party to which the MP seeks to belong.

Three of the most notable floor-crossers in recent years were Scott Brison, Belinda Stronach, and David Emerson. The first two were prominent Conservatives who, at different times, had been candidates for, respectively, the leadership of the old Progressive Conservative Party and the new Conservative Party. Brison crossed the floor to the governing Liberals in 2003, and immediately became a parliamentary secretary and then later a minister. He won re-election as a Liberal in the 2004, 2006, 2008, and 2011 elections and remains a leading Liberal MP. Stronach also crossed the floor to the governing Liberals in 2005, immediately became a minister, and helped the minority Liberal government of Paul Martin survive. She also won re-election as a Liberal in 2006 but did not seek re-election in the 2008 election. Both Brison and Stronach claimed that the Conservative Party was too socially conservative for them, although both were accused of political opportunism. Even more controversial as a case of political opportunism was the decision of Emerson, a senior minister in the Liberal government and a harsh critic of Stephen Harper, to switch to the Conservatives. Emerson became a senior minister in the new Harper Conservative government just days after winning his seat in the 2006 election as a Liberal. Emerson claimed his position as a senior Conservative minister was better for his constituents. Facing an organized backlash of Liberal voter outrage in his constituency to his floor-crossing, he did not seek re-election as a Conservative two years later in the 2008 election.

The Senate and Responsible Government
We need to note here that the government is not responsible to the Senate under the conventions of responsible government described above. The reason is that only the members of the House of Commons

are elected by the people in accordance with the principle of "representation by population." The principle of representation by population
demands that MPs should be elected to the House of Commons from
geographically demarcated electoral districts (commonly referred to as
constituencies or ridings) of roughly similar size in population.

The number of constituencies (and thus MPs with seats in the House)
is currently set at 308. Each constituency is represented by a single MP.
The number of seats has grown from the 180 members in the first
House of Commons in 1867, a development that reflects both population
growth and the increased number of provinces and territories. The constitution requires that the number of seats in the House first be allocated
by province on the basis of the proportionate populations of the ten
provinces.[13] This means that no districts can cut across any provincial
boundary. In addition, the smallest provinces and the three territories are
given some preferential treatment, with the result that the principle of
presentation by population is achieved only in a very rough approximation to voter equality. As it now stands, all provinces and territories
except Ontario, British Columbia, and Alberta are overrepresented and
these three exceptions are underrepresented. The Harper Conservative
government has proposed changes to redress these imbalances, although
it is not certain that the changes will be made by Parliament. The politics
of provincial representation are intense to say the least.

The task of drawing and, as necessary, redrawing the boundaries of
electoral districts within each province in order to achieve representation by population is no longer conducted by Parliament, even though
the resulting changes are formally approved by Parliament. Rather, it is
assigned to independent federal electoral boundaries commissions for
each province. Each commission is chaired by a justice of the province's
senior court. The work of these commissions is undertaken every ten
years following the decennial census and includes public hearings in

---

13. Each of the three territories is assigned one seat, because their populations
would not otherwise provide them with more than one.

each province on draft changes proposed by the provincial commission. The objective of these structures and procedures is to remove MPs from decisions in which they have both personal and partisan interests.

In contrast to the House, the Senate's composition is based on a different principle, a modified form of regional representation. This principle seeks to ensure that the people of all the constituent units of the federation—the ten provinces and the three territories—are represented either equally, as in the Senates of Australia and the United States, or at least in an equitable fashion that gives the units with the smaller populations greater representation than their populations size alone would otherwise warrant. The current formula for the Canadian Senate reflects both historical deals made at different times and the failure of a succession of proposals to change how Senate seats are allocated to the provinces and territories. What this works out to at present is Ontario and Quebec each with 24 senators; the three Maritime provinces with 24 in total (10 each for Nova Scotia and New Brunswick and 4 for Prince Edward Island); the western provinces with 24 in total (6 each for Manitoba, Saskatchewan, Alberta, and British Columbia); Newfoundland and Labrador with 6; and 1 senator for each of Nunavut, Northwest Territories, and Yukon. In the American Senate, by contrast, each of the 50 states has two senators. And in the Australian Senate, there are 12 senators for each of the six states of the Australian federation plus 2 senators each for the Northern Territory and the Australian Capital Territory.

The Canadian Senate is also not elected. Its members are appointed, formally by the governor general and in practice by the prime minister. Once appointed, senators may remain in office until they are 75 years old. But even if the Senate were to become an elected house, the prime minister and government would remain responsible only to the House of Commons in the sense that they require the confidence of the MPs in the House. This is the case in Australia, where the Australian Senate is elected, for example, but the Australian prime minister and government are responsible solely to the House of Representatives (the equivalent of our House of Commons).[14] An elected Senate for Canada would possess greater democratic legitimacy than the current appointed Senate, and could act as a powerful constraint and check on the prime minister and government, as the Australian Senate does in Australian parliamentary government. Still, an elected Senate would not necessarily possess the constitutional power to defeat the government on a non-confidence vote. That power would likely remain with the House of Commons, the membership of which is composed on the principle of representation by population.

The Governor General's Reserve Powers: Protecting Responsible Government?

As discussed above, the written constitution does not describe, let alone prescribe, the conventions of responsible government. They are conventions, not laws. At the same time, the spirit and logic of the constitutional conventions of responsible government remove the governor general from the political operation of parliamentary democracy. This leaves the practice of responsible government to politicians, who are the people's elected representatives in the House of Commons, including the prime minister and other ministers of the executive government.

Paradoxically, in the written constitutional law, the governor general continues to be vested with the powers to summon, prorogue, and dissolve Parliament for a new election. According to the conventions of responsible government, on the other hand, the governor general is expected to exercise these powers on the advice of the prime minister. At the same time, the governor general is usually said to have the discretion to refuse to accept advice from a prime minister in certain circumstances. What these circumstances might be, however, is nowhere set

---

14. In 1975, the Australian Senate played a major role in bringing the government to an end, but it was the governor general who dismissed the prime minister and government when they failed to get crucial money bills approved by the Senate. The governor general's actions have been the subject of debate ever since.

down in any formal document and has, over time, become the subject of considerable debate.

The most that can be said is that whenever the governor general is called to exercise these so-called reserve powers—powers that are said to remain with the governor general even under the conventions of responsible government—the decision of whether or not to reject the advice of the prime minister is one that the governor general would make at his or her discretion. The governor general's decision would be final. The governor general would have no obligation to justify the decision or give an account of the reasons for the decision to anyone.

The governor general's discretion was affirmed in two very recent decisions, first by the Federal Court of Canada and then, on appeal, by the Federal Court of Appeal.[15] The decisions of these two courts constitute the final judgment on the matter because the Supreme Court of Canada decided not to hear an appeal from them. The case concerned Prime Minister Harper's election call in 2008. From a *legal* perspective, the courts concluded that there is no check on the governor general's power of dissolution (the specific issue that was before the courts). The Federal Court acknowledged that there was a *"political* limitation in the form of a constitutional convention whereby the Governor General will only exercise power to dissolve Parliament when advised to do so by the Prime Minister." But, it continued: "The Prime Minister has traditionally had unlimited discretion in regard to this advisory power" (*Conacher* 2009, para. 10). The court decided, in effect, that the prime minister's right to advise the governor general to dissolve Parliament could not be constrained because, without an amendment to the written constitution, the governor general's discretion could not be constrained.

---

15. The case in question resulted from the constitutional challenge to Prime Minister Harper dissolving Parliament for an election in 2008. The prime minister did so notwithstanding the law that Parliament had passed in 2007 as part of his own government's democratic reform agenda, fixing the date of the next election in 2009. See *Conacher v. Canada (Prime Minister)*, 2009 FC 920, aff'd. 2010 FCA 131, appeal denied 2011 CanLII 2101 (SCC).

Because these circumstances circumscribing the exercise of discretion are not set down in any formal document, there is no official document for the Canadian governor general to consult on this matter, unlike the case in New Zealand, where the governor general can consult the New Zealand *Cabinet Manual*. Nor, as discussed at greater length in Chapters 3 and 5, is there a consensus among constitutional experts on the issue. Politicians in Canada are equally divided on the subject, as clearly evidenced by political disagreements during recent controversies.

At a minimum, there would likely be agreement that if the prime minister's government had clearly lost the confidence of the House of Commons but the prime minister refused either to resign or to advise dissolution for a new election, the governor general would have to act on his or her own cognizance. In that case, the prime minister would be acting completely contrary to the most basic rule of responsible government: the confidence convention. In this extreme circumstance, the only legitimate recourse available to protect the conventions of responsible government would require the governor general to dismiss the prime minister and his ministers. The governor general would then appoint a new prime minister from the opposition side of the House to form a new government. An election might or might not have to follow very soon thereafter, depending on whether the majority of MPs supported the new prime minister and government.

Beyond this extreme circumstance, consensus among experts is more difficult to find. And what consensus may have existed just a generation ago is eroding, as we discuss in greater detail in subsequent chapters. Here we briefly note one example. Until recently, most experts would probably have agreed that the governor general could properly refuse the prime minister's advice for a dissolution following the government's defeat on a confidence vote in the House of Commons if the loss of confidence came shortly after an election. And, they would have said, this would be especially justified if the same prime minister had called that election *and* if the leader of the official Opposition was willing and able to form a new government with the confidence of the House.

While a number of experts still support this view, there are now contrary opinions, led by Prime Minister Harper. This disagreement is taken up in detail in Chapter 5.

As we shall discuss later, these very conditions might well have become the circumstance in December 2008. Less than two months after the October 14, 2008 election that he had called, Prime Minister Harper faced a united opposition with a public written declaration of non-confidence and a proposed new government. The non-confidence vote did not take place, however. Instead, on December 8, Harper requested that the governor general prorogue the House—which she agreed to do—to avoid the immediate vote of non-confidence and loss of office to a new government. The prorogation was in effect until January 26, 2009. As events unfolded after December 8, the non-confidence motion was not put forward after the House of Commons returned. The several weeks' delay saw the unity among the three opposition parties crumble and support for a non-confidence motion erode.

As is evident from the account just sketched, Governor General Michaëlle Jean did not have to choose between: (a) a defeated Prime Minister Harper asking her for dissolution and a new election, less than two months after the October 14 election that he had called; and (b) the request to her from the Liberals and New Democrats that she ask Liberal leader Stéphane Dion to form a new coalition government without an election. (The proposed new coalition government would have been a minority government. However, the Bloc Québécois, the third opposition party but not a part of the coalition government, had promised to support the new government for at least 18 months.) The prime minister's strategic request for prorogation pre-empted that choice. Nonetheless, speculation around the possibility that Governor General Jean might have had to make such a choice quickly revealed that there was no consensus among academic experts, pundits, and politicians and their partisan supporters on what she should do. Instead, the prime minister effectively reframed the public question, making it about the democratic legitimacy, rather than the constitutionality, of a new government coming to office without an election.

The lack of consensus on the exercise of the governor general's so-called reserve powers in this situation is conditioned in large part by the fact that only one Canadian governor general has ever rejected the advice of the prime minister on dissolution. That case occurred in 1926 and it has been the subject of disagreement among experts ever since. This was the controversial King–Byng affair.

In that instance, the governor general, Lord Byng of Vimy, refused the advice of Prime Minister Mackenzie King to dissolve Parliament and hold an election. King wanted an election to avoid having his minority government face almost certain defeat in the House of Commons on a motion of censure, amounting to a vote of non-confidence. The motion followed the exposure of a major scandal in the government. As noted above, King's Liberal minority government was unusual in that the Liberals did not win the most seats at the 1925 election but had been able to secure sufficient support from the Progressive MPs and others to stay in power following the election.

Byng rejected King's advice of dissolution and election on the grounds that the Conservatives had the most seats and thus deserved a chance to govern following the Liberal loss of confidence. Byng also thought it relevant that the previous election, called by King, had taken place less than nine months before, and that the leader of the official Opposition, Conservative Party leader Arthur Meighen, was willing to form a government. Rather than face defeat in the House, King resigned when Byng rejected his advice for an election. Byng then asked Meighen to form a new government without an election and he did so. Meighen's minority government itself was soon defeated and Byng granted Meighen a dissolution and election. He did not ask King, then the leader of the official Opposition, if he was willing to attempt to form a new Liberal government.

Byng's decision to reject the prime minister's advice has been debated by experts ever since. At the time, it generated great political controversy. King and his supporters refused to accept that the governor general had made the proper constitutional decision. It helped King's argument immensely that the governor general at the time was still an appointment of the British government, rather than an appointee of the Canadian prime minister, as is now the case. King and his confrères thus painted Byng as a British imperialist who did not accept the self-governing of Canada by Canadians. It is generally assumed that King won the political argument—he won the 1926 election and was able to form a strong majority government with the support of the Progressive Party. (Ironically, King had actually asked Byng to get direction from the British government when Byng first rejected King's request for dissolution. To his credit, Byng refused to do so on the grounds that that would be imperialist interference!)

This case is significant for several reasons, the most important of which, in our view, is that it makes it patently evident that there was no consensus then nor is there one now on the constitutional responsibilities and discretion of the governor general when the prime minister is about to lose or has lost the confidence of the House. One reason for the lack of agreement is political—partisans will make the argument that best serves their cause. Another is that the governor general, by convention, does not provide any explanation of substance for a decision.

Not surprisingly, then, there is also no agreement on whether the governor general could, and, if so, should, refuse to accept the prime minister's advice of prorogation if the government is about to be defeated on a non-confidence vote in the House. This was the case in December 2008 when Governor General Jean gave Harper his prorogation. Since the decision, both experts and pundits have disagreed on the constitutional correctness of her decision (see Russell and Sossin 2009).

A Constitution Without Effective Constraints

A robust democracy requires elections so that citizens can elect those who govern them. However, elections, even free and fair elections, are not sufficient. A robust democracy also requires a vigilant and informed public, supported by a free press and competent media, if public opinion is to function as a constraint on ministers and MPs between elections. However, as the Canadian experience amply demonstrates, institutional constraints are also required to ensure that no one branch of government, especially not the executive, is able to exercise unconstrained power. Elected dictatorships—where a prime minister or president is able to exercise unconstrained power—are sham democracies. In the absence of effective constraints, political executives are able to misuse and abuse power at their discretion and to their political advantage.

In our view, the Canadian conventions of responsible government are inadequate and have become more so over time. Neither the governor general nor the House of Commons can effectively constrain the prime minister from abusing power. The House of Commons is unable to constrain the prime minister from abusing power, beyond attempting to mobilize public opinion, because the powers to summon, prorogue, and dissolve Parliament are assigned to the governor general and not to the House. Moreover, the fact that the House of Commons does have the power to withdraw its confidence in the prime minister's government with a simple majority of 50 percent plus one of the MPs voting is rendered academic when the prime minister's party has a majority of the MPs, especially if the prime minister has excessive control over Cabinet and caucus, as has been the case in Canada for some time (Samara 2011).[16] Even when the government is a minority government, however, the House's power to withdraw its confidence can be contained when, as happened in 2008, the prime minister imposes prorogation and shuts down the House.

Furthermore, as discussed in more detail in Chapter 3, what counts as a vote of non-confidence is subject to disagreement and uncertainty. In some cases, there is clarity and agreement—for instance, under a motion that says, "This House does not have confidence in the Prime Minister and government." At times, the prime minister has been able to decide

---

16. MPs are not required to show up and vote. Those who are not present for a vote are not counted in the total vote from which the simple majority is calculated. A quorum of 20 MPs is required for a valid vote.

whether a vote on an opposition motion or government bill will be acknowledged by the government as a vote of non-confidence.

In addition, even when the prime minister acknowledges that his or her government has been defeated on confidence, the practice in Canada has come to be that the prime minister still gets to decide whether to resign, so that a new government can be formed without an election, or whether to dissolve the House for an election. In the second case, the prime minister and government get to stay in office during the election campaign period because there must always be a government in power. In the Canadian tradition, these two options have come to constitute a choice for the Canadian prime minister. The latter occurred in 2005, when the minority government of Liberal Prime Minister Paul Martin lost a November 28 non-confidence vote moved by Stephen Harper, then leader of the official Opposition. Following the vote, Martin immediately dissolved Parliament for the January 23, 2006 election. The same occurred again in 2011, when Harper lost the confidence of the House and called an election. Given this virtual right to a dissolution, the opposition majority can be placed in a position where the prime minister can accuse it of causing an unnecessary and unwanted election, as Harper did in 2011. The threat to call an election further reduces the effectiveness of the confidence convention as a constraint because it removes the opportunity for a new government to be formed from the opposition without an election. This is discussed further in Chapters 5 and 6.

In contrast, in New Zealand the accepted convention is that the prime minister offers his or her resignation to the governor general when defeated on a vote of non-confidence. The governor general then asks the leader of the Opposition if he or she is willing and able to form a government with the confidence of the House. If the answer is yes, the new prime minister is appointed and the new government is formed. If the answer is no, the House is dissolved and an election held. In the latter case, the defeated prime minister and government remain in office but must operate under a clearly understood convention, with published protocols, that requires them to act merely as a "caretaker government" through the election period. This convention restricts them from doing anything other than routine government business. The caretaker government period lasts from the date of the election call until after the election and a government with the confidence of the House is in place. This procedure takes the power out of the hands of both the prime minister and the governor general and transfers it to the House to determine who has its confidence. Canada does not have a caretaker government document to guide the government, the governor general, or the public service, at least not one that is public so everyone is aware of the rules. (Evidently, there is a document of sorts but it is a secret document!) (Russell and Milne 2011.) In the absence of a public document, Mel Cappe (2011, 2–3) notes that, "Several times in our history the Caretaker Convention has been called into question. ... In each of these circumstances, whether followed or not, the Caretaker Convention arose as an issue of some import and controversy." This is yet another example of Canada failing to modernize and establish a few firm rules.

As discussed above, the Canadian governor general's reserve power to reject the advice of the prime minister in certain circumstances is the subject of dispute, with only Byng having ever rejected the prime minister's advice to dissolve the House. And, as described earlier, Byng's decision has not been universally accepted as a valid precedent. As also noted above, two recent court decisions have declared that the governor general's discretion in responding to a prime minister's request for dissolution is legally absolute. But the Federal Court, which addressed the matter in some detail, went further when it implied that even a prime minister who had lost the confidence of the House could still expect a positive response to such a request. In short, the court decisions do nothing but provide a kind of imprimatur to rubber-stamp the decision of the PM in what has been labelled the virtual right of the prime minister to do whatever he or she wants to do (Aucoin and Turnbull 2004).

Even if there was greater agreement about the reserve powers, the claim that the governor general has discretion—albeit limited by convention—hardly supports the understanding of responsible government as a structure with *democratic* constitutional constraints on the prime minister and government. A major objective of the struggle for responsible government was to remove the appointed governor from the political processes of governance. Accordingly, under responsible government, the most critical responsibility of the governor general is to ensure that the prime minister complies with the first rule of responsible government, to resign or seek dissolution if defeated on confidence. However, to be able to fulfill this responsibility in a non-political manner, the governor general must be guided by clearly articulated and accepted conventions. When such conventions do not exist and the governor general must therefore exercise discretion in what cannot be other than a controversial case, he or she is dragged into the partisan political arena and caught between a rock and a hard place. This was amply demonstrated in the dramatic case that unfolded as a result of the December 2008 request by Prime Minister Harper for a prorogation, even though he had not yet lost the confidence of the House and was not seeking dissolution.

The inability of the House of Commons or the constitutional conventions as applied by the governor general to effectively constrain a prime minister who is intent on abusing constitutional powers is not what the reformers who struggled to establish responsible government meant to happen. They thought that the basic convention of responsible government—*the prime minister and government must have the confidence of a majority of the members of the House of Commons in order to govern*—established the House of Commons as the check on both a governor and a prime minister who sought to use executive powers to undermine the democratic powers of the elected legislature.

Over time, unfortunately, these constraints, which the reformers thought would make responsible government a robust structure of democratic governance, have diminished in practice. The democratic system works only when the prime minister is willing to abide by the spirit and logic of responsible government and thus exercises executive powers in good faith. When the prime minister acts otherwise, the system becomes one of unconstrained prime ministerial power. As we seek to show in subsequent chapters, several prime ministers have abused their powers to partisan advantage. Recent episodes by prime ministers Chrétien, Martin, and Harper provide sufficient examples of the violation of the spirit of the constitution to cause concern, though such abuse certainly did not begin this recently. While the abuse of prime ministerial powers for tactical political advantage may not always produce the intended result, there is little evidence to suggest that offending prime ministers pay a serious or lasting price in the political arena. We explore the reasons for this state of affairs in Chapters 5 and 6.

When Good Faith Goes Missing

Prime Minister Stephen Harper figures prominently in this book because in a period of less than two years he made three unilateral decisions, discussed below, that illustrate clearly and dramatically how a Canadian prime minister can exercise unconstrained power to prorogue and dissolve Parliament. Further, as discussed in Chapter 3, he was willing to declare on what he would accept or not accept as a vote of confidence. At the same time, it is important to stress that Stephen Harper is not the first prime minister to abuse constitutional powers and exercise unconstrained power vis-à-vis the House of Commons, even if he has taken the practice to great new heights in several critical respects.

Harper also sought to present his own understanding of what democracy requires for the formation of a government, arguing against the democratic legitimacy of a new government being formed without an election even when the incumbent government is defeated on a confidence vote. He did so even though he took the opposite position in 2004 when he was leader of the official Opposition. In a letter written alongside the leaders of the two other opposition parties to then Governor General Adrienne Clarkson, he said:

> As leaders of the opposition parties, we are well aware that, given the
> Liberal minority government, you could be asked by the Prime Minister

to dissolve the 38th Parliament at any time should the House of Commons fail to support some part of the government's program.

We respectfully point out that the opposition parties, who together constitute a majority in the House, have been in close consultation. We believe that, should a request for dissolution arise this should give you cause, as constitutional practice has determined, to consult the opposition leaders and consider all of your options before exercising your constitutional authority. (Harper, Duceppe, and Layton, 2004)

It should be noted that the affirmation of the legitimacy of a change in government between elections is clear here, regardless of whether or not Harper or the other signatories had actually hoped to pursue this course of action or not.

The September 2008 Election Call

The first of Harper's three decisions demonstrating bad faith was taken on September 7, 2008, when he dissolved the House for an election to be held October 14. Prior to this particular dissolution, the election call, even as an abuse of power, would not have been viewed as unusual since the Canadian prime minister has come to enjoy a virtual right to call an election at a time of his or her choosing. The only effective constraint is that there must be an election once every five years, as required by the *Constitution Act, 1867*. This was, nonetheless, an early or snap election call, since the previous election had been held on January 23, 2006.

Prime ministers have been criticized for calling snap elections before the standard four years since the last election was up, when the timing was politically advantageous to their party. In these instances, the prime minister's decision is motivated solely or primarily by partisan interests. In 1965, Liberal Prime Minister Lester Pearson called an election less than three years after the 1963 election that elected his minority government. He did so in the hope and expectation that he would secure a majority. (He did not.) In calling snap elections, prime ministers ignore the good faith requirement that the prime minister abide by the spirit and logic of responsible government and not abuse constitutional powers.

Not surprisingly, prime ministers have always faced criticism when calling snap elections. For instance, when he was opposition leader, Harper was highly critical of Liberal Prime Minister Jean Chrétien for calling early elections in 1997 and 2000 for this very reason. However, in every instance of a snap election the criticism soon faded as the campaigns and the media turned their attention to the most pressing differences between the parties and leaders.

In 2006, nonetheless, Harper and the Conservatives took this issue seriously. A central plank in the Conservatives' 2006 campaign platform was the promise to enact a law to eliminate the prime minister's discretion to abuse the power of dissolution. This reform would fix the date of elections in law, a scheme that is known in Canada as "fixed election dates" and that had already been put in place in seven provinces and one territory. In every case, it was adopted as a democratic reform measure to constrain the premier who, as head of government, has the same powers as the prime minister within the provincial sphere of jurisdiction.

On May 26, 2006, Prime Minister Harper, now in power, was explicit as to why the idea of a fixed election date was required:

> Fixed election dates prevent governments from calling snap elections for short-term political advantage … from trying to manipulate the calendar simply for partisan political advantage. This is a very useful advantage that we're willing to give up. (CBC News, May 26, 2006)

With an amendment to the *Canada Elections Act* that all parties in the House of Commons supported, the new law came into force on May 3, 2007. The prime minister was now to be constrained by law from calling an election whenever he believed it to be politically advantageous to do so. Under the new law, elections are to be held every four years on the third Monday of October. The first election under this system was to have taken place on October 19, 2009.

The new law, however, provided for the possibility of an election earlier than the fixed date. The reasons for this provision were twofold.

First, there was a desire to avoid having to amend the *Constitution Act, 1867* itself so that the law would set rules for the governor general's exercise of the power of dissolution. A constitutional amendment affecting the powers of the governor general requires the approval not only of Parliament but also of all the provincial legislatures. That may not be easy to accomplish, at least not as quickly as simply getting Parliament to pass the law proposed by the government. Second, there had to be a way to allow an early election to take place if, following a government's loss of confidence of the House, the prime minister refused to resign and thus prevented the opposition from forming a new government without an election, thereby making dissolution required in order to have a new election. For both reasons, then, there had to be a provision in the amended *Canada Elections Act* that said that the powers of the governor general to dissolve Parliament for an election were not affected.

The insertion of this qualification in the amended *Canada Elections Act*, however, was not characterized by the government as, or assumed by others to constitute, a legal loophole for a prime minister to get around the law in order to call a snap election. As was the case in each of the provinces that had adopted the fixed election date law, it was assumed that the prime minister would be constrained by the explicit purpose and logic of the law and act in good faith.

As it turned out, the expectation of good faith was not sufficient to constrain Prime Minister Harper. He called an election for October 14, 2008, one full year before the scheduled October 19, 2009 election. He was legally able to ignore the new law by getting Governor General Jean to approve his decision. And, as already noted, neither the Federal Court of Canada nor the Federal Court of Appeal had any objection to the legality of his snap election call. They effectively declared the fixed election date law to be meaningless as a constitutional constraint on the prime minister (as did the Justice Canada lawyer defending the prime minister's decision before the Federal Court).

As part of his justification for calling the 2008 election, Harper argued that the fixed election date law applied only to majority governments and not to minority governments. Aside from the fact that this argument was invented after the law was passed, the logic here is perverse. The fixed election date law is even more important during minority government, because the prime minister can proceed to call an election despite the fact that a majority of MPs are on the opposition side of the House. This is what Harper did in 2008; it is what Pearson did in 1965; and what Diefenbaker did in 1958. All three were prime ministers of minority governments, calling an election for partisan reasons. In none of these cases was the majority of MPs on the opposition side of the House of the Commons able to constrain the prime minister, because the power to dissolve Parliament belongs to the governor general. And in none of these cases could opposition MPs withdraw confidence in the government, because the House was already dissolved. In short, the argument that the fixed election date law applies only to majority governments completely misses the need to constrain the abuse of power, whether the prime minister has a majority or minority government.

With this first of his three decisions to abuse the constitution, Prime Minister Harper not only did what he had previously criticized Chrétien for doing, he did it even after instituting a democratic reform to constrain himself and all future prime ministers. In calling the 2008 election, he rendered his own fixed election law devoid of meaning. He also reinforced the prime minister's virtual right to a dissolution. This precedent, in effect, shows that good faith is no constraint on a prime minister willing to put partisan advantage ahead of the spirit of responsible government in parliamentary democracy. There is no evidence that Harper paid a price for his decision to call the 2008 election in the face of the new election law. Even in a major examination of the election, his decision is not mentioned (Pammett and Dornan 2009).

The December 2008 Prorogation

Harper's second decision demonstrating bad faith came on December 4, 2008, when, to escape a vote of non-confidence by the combined opposition in the House of Commons that had been scheduled for December 8, Harper prorogued Parliament until January 26, 2009. Following the October 14, 2008 election, Harper's Conservative government was still a minority government. He had failed to win his desired majority. The Conservatives elected 143 MPs out of 308 in the House, or 46 percent. The other 54 percent of the MPs were thus on the opposition side: 77 Liberal MPs, 49 Bloc Québécois MPs, 37 New Democrat MPs, and 2 independent MPs. With the opposition united in its decision not only to vote non-confidence in the Harper government but also to replace it with a Liberal prime minister heading a Liberal–New Democrat coalition government, the Conservative government was in severe trouble.

Harper's ability to shut down the House of Commons by proroguing Parliament in order to evade a humiliating defeat highlighted the uncertainty about the conventions of the Canadian constitution. The governor general did not immediately approve the advice for a prorogation. Rather, the approval came only during a two-hour closed meeting of Prime Minister Harper and Governor General Jean at Rideau Hall, the governor general's residence, with advisers in tow for both. This made for great television, newspaper, and Internet commentary and discussion, at least for political junkies. What was said was not revealed. Nor were the reasons for the decision to approve. The governor general, by convention, is not expected to provide any reasons for her decision. From all accounts, the governor general appears to have exercised discretion, thus not abiding by the position that the governor general has no discretion on prorogation (MacDonald and Bowden 2011). In this instance, any exercise of discretion occurs without firm rules or binding conventions. In any event, the outcome was what everyone should have expected to occur in Canada: the prime minister got what he wanted. Governor General Jean did not repeat the King–Byng decision by refusing to accept the prime minister's advice, even if this was a case of prorogation, not dissolution. Most commentators have concluded that that was the right outcome, given a range of concerns with the proposed coalition's likely stability, Dion's weak and temporary leadership, and the fact that the coalition, as a minority government, would require the support of the Bloc Québécois.

What happened after prorogation was granted was even further evidence of the uncertainty about our constitutional conventions. Disagreement and confusion reigned over the constitutional and democratic legitimacy of a new government being formed from the opposition without an election, the democratic legitimacy of the Liberals and New Democrats forming a coalition without having campaigned in the 2008 election on that basis, and the legitimacy of a Canadian government being supported on confidence votes by the Bloc Québécois, given the party's primary purpose of breaking up the country. The Conservatives, of course, led the way in denying the constitutional and democratic legitimacy of the proposed Liberal–New Democrat coalition government being formed without another election. They claimed that only the electorate could decide who formed the government, thus rejecting the idea that if Harper's government were defeated on a vote of confidence it should resign and allow the governor general to call upon the Liberal Party leader, as leader of the official Opposition, to form the coalition government. If this option was not legitimate, the only option would then be another election, even though the dust had hardly settled on the election held on October 14, 2008. Further, the prospect of a diet of successive elections in a short period of time could also not then be ruled out.

As it turned out, Harper and his government survived after the prorogation ended and a new session of Parliament began. This was due in no small measure to the prorogation and its length of several weeks. The lengthy prorogation allowed the Conservatives to mount an aggressive media campaign against the constitutional and democratic legitimacy of the coalition taking power without a new election. They also questioned the legitimacy of a coalition government being formed and surviving with the support of the Bloc Québécois. The Conservative campaign was successful in turning public opinion as well as converting many media pundits to their position. The coalition's unity crumbled, particularly after Stéphane Dion stepped aside as Liberal leader and the Liberals selected Michael Ignatieff as acting party leader to replace him.

The mix of constitutional uncertainty, disagreement, and confusion, even illiteracy, over the spirit and logic of the conventions of responsible government among the electorate, as well as among experts, pundits, and politicians, further facilitated the government's survival. The outcome muddied the waters of our constitution even more than was the case prior to the prorogation. As with the election call in 2008, there is no evidence that the prime minister was much concerned about public opinion over his abuse of prorogation. If anything, it appears that having successfully employed the first prorogation as an effective partisan tool to avoid defeat in the House, Conservative strategists seized on it as a handy tool for future use.

The December 2009 Prorogation

Harper's third demonstration of bad faith came on December 30, 2009, when he again prorogued Parliament, this time for two months, until March 3, 2010. He shut down Parliament to postpone having his government subjected to scrutiny and held to account for its handling of information about how the Canadian military had managed the custody of Afghans taken prisoner by Canadian soldiers. This time the prime minister, it is reported, simply telephoned the governor general to announce that his advice was being sent to her for her approval.

On this occasion, the prime minister's decision to shut down the House of Commons produced a widespread outcry that included even sharp criticism from persons and sources who usually strongly favoured Prime Minister Harper and his government. They included a highly critical commentary on the 2009 prorogation by *The Economist*, published in London and perhaps the most prestigious newsmagazine in the English-speaking democracies.

For their part, the Liberals and the New Democrats each responded by proposing reforms to enable the House of Commons to constrain the prime minister's ability to prorogue Parliament to save his or her own skin.[17] The New Democrats proposed that the prime minister not be permitted to prorogue Parliament for more than a seven-day period without the approval of the House of Commons. The House then approved this motion, the combined opposition parties outnumbering the Conservative MPs who voted against the motion. The motion has no status as law,[18] however, and thus can only constrain a prime minister with assistance from the force of public opinion. Neither of these opposition party proposals, as we discuss in Chapter 6, adequately addresses the basic problem in the constitution.

The Harper government did take a hit in public opinion for this second prorogation decision. This was due to the fact that the criticisms of the decision resonated with a broad cross-section of Canadians, with no complicating threat from the opposition proposing an alternative coalition government backed by the Bloc Québécois. The public's conclusion was that the government was trying to escape public scrutiny, pure and simple. The government also did not want any attention brought to the issue of Afghan detainees that might detract from the free and

---

17. The Liberal proposal was more complex, including demands that: at least 10 days' written notice be given by the prime minister of his intention to seek to prorogue, as well as the specific reasons for doing so; the prime minister bring the issue of prorogation before the House of Commons for full debate; a request for prorogation within the first year after a Speech from the Throne be prevented, unless the House consents; a prorogation longer than one calendar month be prevented without the consent of the House; a request for prorogation be prevented if a matter of confidence has been scheduled in the House, unless the House consents; and that parliamentary committees be permitted to continue to function during the period when Parliament is prorogued until the start of the new session (http://www.liberal.ca/newsroom/news-release/liberals-pledge-to-prevent-abuse-of-prorogation/).

18. A motion is simply an expression of intent moved by a member of Parliament to be approved by the House. Motions are not laws, as they do not go through committee or Senate scrutiny, nor do they receive royal assent. Therefore, they are not "binding" on the government or anyone else in the way that laws are.

Protesting prorogation in Toronto, January 2010.
SOURCE: Joey Schwartz/Creative Commons.

positive publicity and boost in public opinion it assumed it would get from the Winter Olympics in British Columbia. In this case, Harper's decision backfired, in part because many Canadians saw Harper, his ministers, and MPs giving themselves a paid holiday to attend the Olympics. Nonetheless, there is no evidence to suggest that the negative public reaction had a lasting effect.

The Need for Reform

Not surprisingly, there are only two general views of Prime Minister Harper's decisions in each of these cases. One view is that each of his decisions was a crafty political manoeuvre that was constitutionally legal and ultimately produced results that served Canadians' best interests, even if it stretched the limits of our largely open-ended constitution. The opposing view is that these three decisions were an abuse of prime ministerial powers that went beyond the pale of the spirit, logic, and principles of our conventions of responsible government.

We think that both these views support our contention that the constitution has a serious democratic problem that needs to be addressed by institutional reforms. The two views, each in its own way, acknowledge that there is nothing but public opinion—especially the threat of negative electoral consequences—to constrain the prime minister from using the governor general's powers to protect or promote the partisan interests of the governing party. But there is no evidence to suggest that public opinion constrains prime ministers who are willing to act in bad faith.

As a result, the governor general was effectively sidelined by the Canadian prime minister's virtual right to use these powers even after he was defeated in the House on confidence. For its part, when the House of Commons is prorogued or dissolved, it loses the power that was intended to be the democratic achievement of responsible government: to hold the government to account and to withdraw confidence when a majority decides not to support the government. In addition, the House's power to decide who forms the government is effectively negated by the unilateral power of the prime minister to dissolve the House when it withdraws its confidence in the government. The prime minister is, in short, in charge at all times.

Some experts, pundits, and politicians maintain that the governor general retains the constitutional power to reject the advice of the prime minister *in certain undefined circumstances*. Ever since 1926 and the King–Byng incident, the actual practice has been that the governor general accepts what the prime minister advises, a practice that has been recently confirmed by all three of Harper's decisions and by Governor General Jean's acceptance of his advice. This would suggest that the only certainty is that the prime minister gets to decide what the constitution means. He or she makes the rules.

The current situation, accordingly, can be described as follows.

- The legal provisions of the constitution vest the executive powers of government with the Queen, to be exercised by the governor general.
- The conventions of responsible government provide no firm rules for the governor general's exercise of the powers to summon,

prorogue, and dissolve Parliament, except that they are to be exercised following the prime minister rendering advice to the governor general.

- With no consensus on the conventions, the governor general can be dragged into the partisan politics of parliamentary democracy whenever the prime minister's advice becomes controversial and risks being criticized for whatever decision is made—to accept or not accept the prime minister's advice.
- With no consensus on the conventions, the actual practice is that the prime minister has unrestrained power to decide when to exercise the governor general's powers. Those powers now effectively belong to the prime minister.

This is our view of the current state of affairs in Canada. This state of affairs is the reason for the problem in the constitution. It is no way to run a modern parliamentary democracy.

Before we go further with this discussion, we discuss in Chapter 3 why the conventions of responsible government that occupy such a critical place in our current constitution have succumbed to uncertainty and disagreement over time and why there is now an absence of consensus on even the basic rules of responsible government.

References

Aucoin, Peter, Jennifer Smith, and Geoff Dinsdale. 2004. *Responsible government*. Ottawa: Canadian Centre for Management Development (now Canada School for Public Service). http://www.csps-efpc.gc.ca/pbp/pub/pdfs/P120_e.pdf.

Aucoin, Peter, and Lori Turnbull. 2004. Removing the virtual right of prime ministers to demand dissolution. *Canadian Parliamentary Review* 27 (2): 16–19.

Cappe, Mel. 2011. *The caretaker convention in Canada*. http://www.aspercentre.ca/Assets/Asper+Digital+Assets/Events+and+Materials/Constitutional+Conventions+Workshop/Workshop+Papers/Cappe-caretaker-article.pdf.

Conacher v. Canada (Prime Minister). 2009 FC 920, aff'd. 2010 FCA 131, appeal denied 2011 CanLII 2101 (SCC).

Harper, Stephen, Gilles Duceppe, and Jack Layton. 2004. Letter to Governor General Adrienne Clarkson, September 9.

Hicks, Bruce M. 2010. British and Canadian experience with the royal prerogative. *Canadian Parliamentary Review* 33 (2): 18–24.

MacDonald, Nicholas A., and James W.J. Bowden. 2011. No discretion: On prorogation and the governor general. *Canadian Parliamentary Review* 34 (1): 7–16.

Pammett, Jon H., and Christopher Dornan, eds. 2009. *The Canadian federal election of 2008*. Toronto: Dundurn Press.

Russell, Peter H. 2008. *Two cheers for minority government: The evolution of Canadian parliamentary democracy*. Toronto: Emond Montgomery.

Russell, Peter H., and Cheryl Milne. 2011. *Adjusting to a new era of parliamentary government: Report of a workshop on constitutional conventions*. Toronto: David Asper Centre for Constitutional Rights.

Russell, Peter H., and Lorne Sossin, eds. 2009. *Parliamentary democracy in crisis*. Toronto: University of Toronto Press.

Samara. 2011. *"It's my party": Parliamentary dysfunction reconsidered*. http://www.samaracanada.com/downloads/ItsMyParty.pdf.

CHAPTER THREE

When Conventions Fail: Constitutional Governance Without Clear Rules

Introduction

Conventions are an essential part of our democratic constitution. As noted in Chapter 2, responsible government—the lynchpin of Canadian parliamentary democracy—is based entirely on constitutional conventions (Heard 1991). The unravelling of the consensus on these conventions threatens the integrity of our democracy.

In this chapter, we discuss the uncertainty and disagreement surrounding the components and requirements of our most fundamental constitutional conventions. These especially include the three practices at the core of the functional operation of responsible government: the procedures involved in prorogation (the end of a parliamentary session), the confidence convention, and dissolution (the termination of a parliament). Considerable uncertainty and disagreement have emerged among politicians, pundits, and constitutional experts about the rules that govern these processes and thus the related powers of the House of Commons, the prime minister, and the governor general.

We start with a brief discussion of the political and legal significance of constitutional conventions in Canada, emphasizing the need for a strong consensus so that they can function properly. We then outline the rules and principles that are usually said to govern each of the three practices mentioned above. Finally, we draw upon historical precedents and the expressed opinions of constitutional experts, pundits, and politicians to demonstrate that there is insufficient agreement in Canada about the constitutional rules that apply to these three practices. It is our contention that the absence of consensus, particularly with regard to the discretionary powers of the governor general, serves to enhance the unconstrained power of the prime minister to control the operations of the House of Commons. In so doing, it abets the decay of democratic parliamentary governance.

What Are Constitutional Conventions?

The term "convention" has more than one meaning. In some circumstances, convention is synonymous with agreement. In diplomacy, for instance, conventions are *treaties* agreed to by signatory countries, such as the Geneva Convention governing conduct in war. In other contexts, "convention" is used to describe an uncodified rule, a tradition, or a custom. For example, in some cultures it is conventional to shake hands upon first acquaintance.

Constitutional conventions can be understood to invoke both of these interpretations to some extent. Constitutional conventions are non-legal rules of conduct about which wide and general agreement is presumed. The fact that constitutional conventions are not enumerated in written law is the primary reason why a shared understanding of their meaning and significance is required. In Westminster parliamentary democracies such as Canada's, the constitution includes many unwritten rules that are of primary importance for the practice of democracy.

Disagreement about these rules is a recipe for confusion and, in some cases, a threat to democratic governance.

The Canadian constitution encompasses both the written constitution, specifically the *Constitution Act, 1867* and the *Constitution Act, 1982*, and the conventions that have developed through political agreement and experiences. Political scientist Andrew Heard echoes other noted constitutional authorities such as Eugene Forsey, Peter Hogg, Geoffrey Marshall, and Graham Moodie in defining conventions as "binding rules of behaviour" that cannot be enforced by the judiciary (1991). Because these rules are not legally enforceable by the judiciary, they are "binding" only in the political sense, including the obligation to act in good faith.

Conventions and the Courts

Constitutional experts disagree about the legal status of constitutional conventions and the extent to which conventions can and ought to be transformed into written law. For instance, J.R. Mallory (1984) believed in the courts' ability to adopt a convention as law, whereas Eugene Forsey (1984, 42) insisted that courts cannot—and ought not—"decide what the conventions of the Constitution are." If the courts did so, Forsey argued, they would overstep the boundaries of judicial power and, consequently, wade too far into political waters, legalizing something that had always been and ought to remain political. In Forsey's world, public opinion and elections should be a sufficient check on those who do not act in good faith.

In fact, there are now clear examples of judges' willingness to acknowledge the existence of conventions as part of the constitution. The Supreme Court of Canada did just that in its 1981 reference decision on the resolution to amend the constitution—the Patriation Reference—put to the court by Prime Minister Pierre Trudeau. Clearly, then, conventions are not irrelevant to judicial decisions. On the contrary, they have been cited as component parts of the constitution, equal in weight to the written parts. This means that conventions are understood not as a form of constitutional "law," but as constitutional rules with important implications for judicial decisions and opinions in constitutional cases decided by the courts as well as for politics. For instance, in the 1981 reference case noted above, Prime Minister Trudeau asked the court for its opinion on whether Parliament could unilaterally amend the written constitution to make it independent of the British Parliament without the consent of the provincial legislatures. A majority of the Supreme Court found that this course of action by the federal government would be *legal* but *unconstitutional* in the conventional sense. The majority declared that there was an established precedent that substantial provincial support was required for a constitutional amendment affecting the provinces, which this one surely did. In other words, what is "unconventional" is unconstitutional.

However, the courts are not in a position to pursue a judicial remedy when a convention is found to have been broken. In other words, the courts cannot enforce compliance with conventions even though these unwritten rules are understood to be binding. The courts cannot impose penalties of any sort for non-compliance. This means that the obligatory forces underpinning conventions are *entirely political*. A sense of political obligation should compel a prime minister to respect the spirit of a convention, even in the absence of political sanctions for ignoring it, because it is the "right" and "honourable" thing to do (Heard 1991, 10–11).

Political sanctions for a prime minister or government that offends conventions can be applied in different forms by opposition parties, media, constitutional experts, and voters. For example, Prime Minister Stephen Harper's decision to prorogue Parliament twice in roughly one year for obviously political reasons had consequences for his reputation and for the popularity of his government, at least after his second prorogation. His critics were only partly successful in framing his actions as dictatorial and disrespectful of the spirit of parliamentary democracy. For instance, a CBC poll conducted after the second prorogation in 2009 revealed that among the 67 percent of respondents who were aware of Harper's decision, 58 percent were against it. Sixty-three percent of those aware of his decision agreed with the statement that "suspending Parliament is anti-democratic" (CBC News 2010).[1] In the weeks that followed, public opinion polls showed a reduction in the Harper Conservatives' lead over the Liberals. But as made clear by the 2011 election, in which the Conservative government moved from minority to majority status, there is little evidence that either of these prorogations have had a lasting negative impact on voters' preferences. This undoubtedly reflects, in part, the reality that elections are not referenda on particular policies or decisions. We address this issue at greater length in Chapters 5 and 6.

Conventions and Consensus

Since conventions are political rather than legal in character, there must be a consensus on what a convention requires in order to nurture a sense of *political* obligation on the part of the relevant actors to follow the convention, and for the political community to demand that they do. Brun and Tremblay (1982) describe conventions as shared agreements, contracts, or "ententes" between political actors, the terms of which must be agreed to for the conventions to have meaning or effect. An agreement or consensus on the part of political actors, experts, journalists, and voters is what generates and reinforces the political obligation to respect the convention. Hence Forsey's (1984, 13) claim that conventions are the products of politics: "First and foremost, they are political: political in their birth, political in their growth and decay, and political in their applications and sanctions." In other words, it is the responsibility of the political community to use the political process to establish and re-establish conventions. This is not to say that the rules of the conventions could not be written down for greater certainty, as has been done, for instance, in New Zealand. New Zealand wanted to make certain that there were both clarity and consensus about what the

---

1. It is interesting to note that while 63 percent of the respondents aware of Harper's decision agreed that "suspending Parliament is anti-democratic," only 58 percent were against the decision.

confidence conventions of responsible government require of the prime minister and the governor general. That is one option for addressing a situation where the consensus on one or more constitutional conventions has disappeared or appears to have disappeared.

Unanimous agreement on a single understanding of a convention's particulars is neither likely nor necessary. A constitutional rule can stand up to the protestations of at least some detractors but too much disagreement brings about the convention's demise. The question is: What degree of consensus is sufficient (a) to confirm the existence and meaning of a convention in the first place, and (b) to ensure its application if a constitutional question surfaces?

The renowned British constitutional scholar Sir Ivor Jennings (1959) posited that we can be sure that a practice is not merely a pattern or an expectation but a *convention* if it satisfies the following three-part test: (1) Is there a precedent (at least one case where the rule appeared to be accepted as a convention)?; (2) Did the actors involved believe themselves to be bound by the rule?; and (3) Is there a reason for the rule?

Not everyone agrees with Jennings that a precedent is a necessary condition for a convention to exist. Heard (1991, 13) has argued that conventions can be born of "express agreement of the prime political actors" even in the absence of a single precedent (see also Heard 2010).

In our view, each of these approaches to convention making has limitations. Jennings's insistence on the need for a precedent dismisses the fact that binding rules of behaviour can indeed arise from mutual agreement among the relevant actors without having a precedent as a reference point. For instance, experience would suggest that there is agreement on the convention that a prime minister, upon losing the confidence of the House, must either (a) resign, and the leader of the Opposition be asked by the governor general to form a new government without an election, or (b) request that the governor general dissolve Parliament for an election. In fact, though, no Canadian prime minister has ever chosen the first of these two options. Despite the absence of a precedent, constitutional scholars almost always cite this option as an accepted part of constitutional convention (Desserud 2006, 7).

The "explicit agreement" approach has its limitations as well. For one thing, it is not always easy to determine who the "relevant political actors" are who must agree on what a convention does or does not require. For example, if there is a dispute about whether the governor general is obliged to grant the prime minister's request for dissolution when the prime minister's government has been defeated on a vote of non-confidence, who, if any, are the relevant actors in this case, besides the prime minister and the governor general? Given the change in the prime minister's status following a loss of confidence, is he or she still considered a relevant actor? And, regardless of who the relevant political actors are, is the "explicit agreement" confined to those in government or the House? If so, this makes the meaning of constitutional conventions all the more uncertain whenever political elites disagree with one another.

The Case of the 2008 Dissolution and Election Call

A constitutional challenge was brought before the Federal Court of Canada against Prime Minister Harper's 2008 dissolution of the House of Commons. As described in Chapter 2, Harper dissolved the House despite the fixed election date law initiated by his Conservative government in 2007, which amended the *Canada Elections Act* and scheduled the next election for October 2009. Although the challenge was unsuccessful, it serves as a useful case study to demonstrate the uncertainty that surrounds the creation and confirmation of constitutional conventions.

Duff Conacher, the director of the advocacy organization Democracy Watch, challenged the prime minister's dissolution in court on the grounds that calling the early election violated the new fixed election date law. Conacher further argued that the 2008 election violated "a constitutional convention that had been created by the provincial precedents, parliamentary debates, and enactment by Parliament of the [fixed election date] provisions" (Memorandum of Argument of the Applicant, 67). He referred to both of the tests discussed above in his submissions to the Federal Court of Canada, the Federal Court of Appeal, and the Supreme Court of Canada (which has declined to consider Conacher's appeal).

Starting with Jennings's three-part test, Conacher noted that several provincial jurisdictions in Canada have fixed election date laws and none of them had ever held an "early" election once the law had been passed. This, he argued, satisfies the first part of Jennings's test: there is an established precedent that fixed election terms must be respected unless the opposition expresses non-confidence in the government and an election is held as a result. With respect to the second and third parts of Jennings's test, Conacher cites a number of quotations from Prime Minister Harper and Minister for Democratic Reform Rob Nicholson, who was responsible for presenting the government's case in the House of Commons. These quotations make it clear that when the bill was introduced and debated in the House, the prime minister and his government believed that the law would be establishing a *binding rule* with a *clear purpose*: to provide for "greater fairness in election campaigns [and] greater transparency and predictability" (Canada, House of Commons 2006) by eliminating a prime minister's ability to call a snap election when it is politically convenient for the governing party. Nicholson was frank in his assessment of the prime minister's virtual right to demand dissolution:

> When the prime minister, under the current system, requests the dissolution of the House, the Governor General, unless there are unusual circumstances, agrees and the country finds itself in an election. What we have is a situation where the prime minister is able to choose the date of the election, not based necessarily on the best interests of the country but on the best interests of his or her political party. I believe Bill C-16 would address those concerns. (ibid., 1105)

Nicholson acknowledged that the bill would not alter the basic requirement that the government needs the confidence of the House in order to govern legitimately. Therefore, he said, "the prime minister's prerogative to advise the Governor General on the dissolution of Parliament is retained to allow him or her to advise dissolution 'in the event of a loss of confidence.' ... *Having legislation like this—that again in no way constrains the Governor General—will begin a new convention about when and how Canadian elections will take place*" (ibid., 1110, emphasis added). Nicholson's statement clearly indicates that, at the time of the debate, the government's intent, under the fixed election date regime, was that only a loss of confidence could trigger dissolution and an election.

Conacher argued that the second test for creating conventions—the expressed agreement of the relevant political actors—was also met. All four of the parliamentary party leaders, including Prime Minister Harper, supported the fixed election date law in the House of Commons. Surely, Conacher argued, these leaders are the relevant political actors in this case.

According to Conacher, the fixed election date amendment to the *Canada Elections Act* established a new convention, limiting a prime minister's discretion to advise a governor general to dissolve Parliament to the following two situations: "first, in accordance with the electoral schedule [for the fixed date of the next election] in Subsection 56.1(2), and second, in a situation of a vote of non-confidence in the House of Commons" (Applicants' Memorandum of Fact and Law 2009).

In its 2009 judgment, the Federal Court of Canada defined conventions as "non-legal rules that modify the strict legal rights of political office holders. They emerge through political usage and become political rules once the relevant officeholders view them as being obligatory" (*Conacher* 2009, para. 11). The court, in other words, seems to agree with Jennings's view that a convention must have at least one precedent, or "usage," in order to qualify as a true convention, and that the relevant actors must believe themselves to be bound by the rule. In fact, the Federal Court acknowledged both Jennings's precedent test and the "explicit agreement" test as mechanisms to determine whether a convention had been established. The court also acknowledged that because conventions are political rather than legal in nature, they "have not been enforced by the courts and no legal sanction exists for their breach" (ibid.). Therefore, any punishment for a breach of convention could only be meted out in the political realm.

The court determined that no new convention had been established by the fixed election date law. Hearing the case on appeal, the Federal Court of Appeal for its part, in a very brief judgment issued in May 2010, declined to "make a declaration that there is a new constitutional convention that limits the ability of the Prime Minister to advise the Governor General in these circumstances" (*Conacher* 2010, para. 12). The appeal court did not provide any further analysis of the tests for determining constitutional conventions. It simply concurred with the Federal Court's finding.

The Federal Court argued that Jennings's three-part test was not satisfied in this case because there was no precedent by "relevant political actors" and no consensus among these actors on the existence of a new convention. In the court's view, the relevant political actors were the prime minister and the governor general and no one else. The court rejected Conacher's contention that the relevant political actors included all of the parliamentary party leaders and not just the prime minister. It noted that "the leaders of the political parties [other than the prime minister] have no power, be it conventional or legal, to dissolve Parliament" (*Conacher* 2009, para. 46). The court concluded that the explicit agreement test was not met for the same reason: the prime minister and the governor general, according to the court, were the only relevant actors and, despite what Harper had said on the matter when proposing and explaining his reform of fixed election dates, the court concluded that there was no evidence from either the prime minister or the governor general to suggest that they agreed a new convention had been created.

The court did not elaborate on why it adopted this extremely narrow interpretation of who counts as a "relevant political actor," but its approach makes it virtually impossible for either of the tests for conventions to be satisfied whenever the prime minister disputes what others may believe, or may have believed, constitutes a convention. Indeed, the court even ignored the prime minister's own previously stated beliefs about the fixed election date reform. This view of how conventions come to be accepted is counterintuitive to the spirit and logic of constitutional conventions, which the court acknowledged as rules that "modify" strict legal interpretations of the constitution. If the conventions of responsible government can be modified only by the prime minister and the governor general acting together, it is as though the prime minister and the governor general then have a veto on changes to constitutional conventions.

Ideally, conventions make the constitution an organic set of rules that can and should evolve in response to changing political realities. However, to give the prime minister a veto over change is to stifle the political evolution of a parliamentary democracy that encompasses not only the prime minister but also the elected House of Commons. In this instance, the prime minister was even able to veto a change in the convention after he had both proposed it as a campaign promise and then endorsed it as government legislation.

Before concluding this discussion of what constitutes a convention and the murkiness that surrounds the establishment of conventions, we wish to acknowledge that there is evidence of a durable consensus on the *principle* of responsible government. Everyone agrees with the basic principle that the government must have the confidence of the House of Commons in order to govern. At the same time, we need to emphasize that conventions comprise more than just founding principles.

Even with a strong consensus on this need for confidence, there is significant disagreement about the ways in which the confidence of the House can be expressed, revoked, and ascertained. For instance, what if opposition leaders express their lack of confidence in the government outside the walls of the House of Commons? Does (or *should*) this "external" expression count when the House is not in session or when the opposition is unable to move a motion of non-confidence because the prime minister and government control the parliamentary agenda? Or, notwithstanding a public statement by the opposition leaders, is an explicit vote of non-confidence against the government in the House of Commons required? To take another area of disagreement, if an expression of non-confidence comes from the opposition in the form of a procedural motion (such as a House instruction to a House committee) rather than an explicit motion of non-confidence or a vote on a substantive matter of government policy (such as an important piece of government legislation), does this mean that the government has lost its legitimacy to govern? These examples are given fuller attention in the next section of this chapter, but they are raised here to demonstrate that, though a consensus on the principle of a convention is a necessary condition for the functional survival of the convention as part of the constitution, it is not a sufficient condition. There must be agreement on the rules of behaviour as well.

In the next section, we identify the practices and behaviours that are thought to govern confidence votes and the prorogation and dissolution of the House of Commons. In the subsequent section, we demonstrate the lack of a solid consensus to support these conventions.

Confidence, Prorogation, and Dissolution

As outlined in Chapter 2, responsible government requires that the prime minister and government be accountable to the House of Commons and command the support of a majority of MPs in order to govern legitimately. In practical terms, it means that, to survive, the government needs the majority of the MPs present to vote in favour of any of the confidence measures that are tabled in the House of Commons. At least two principles give purpose to the confidence convention. First, this convention is meant to ensure that the government is held to account, not only at election time, but all the time. Second, it is meant to empower MPs, as the people's representatives, to withdraw their confidence in the government, when they find it necessary. The balance of power between the government as the political executive and the House of Commons as the directly elected representatives of the people is meant to lie with the latter as a constraint on the former.

Confidence Votes

It is a widely accepted convention that not all government bills and motions are, or need to be, considered matters of confidence. This means that the government need not win each and every vote to maintain its legitimacy.[2] Minority governments must live constantly with this fact of parliamentary life. Even a majority government can lose the occasional vote—for example, when the Liberal majority government of Prime Minister Jean Chrétien lost a vote on a Conservative motion put forward by Opposition leader Stephen Harper to remove the power of the prime minister to appoint the chairs of House of Commons committees. This motion of the House was then respected by Prime Minister Chrétien.

Andrew Heard divides confidence votes into three categories: (1) those that are designated as such in advance by the prime minister; (2) those that would approve crucial government policy; and (3) motions by the Opposition that are worded to express a clear lack of confidence (Heard 2007).

In the first category, the prime minister might designate as a confidence vote the vote on a government bill or motion that would not otherwise be considered a confidence vote. The prime minister would do this to send a message to his or her MPs, the opposition parties, and the public that the government was staking its right to govern on the outcome. In this way, the vote is given the status of a confidence measure. In this situation, the MPs of the prime minister's party are expected to toe the line and vote with the government. The Chrétien Liberal government took this approach, for instance, with the 2002 vote on the Kyoto Protocol (CTV 2002).

A minority government prime minister might use the confidence convention in this manner as a political tactic against the opposition parties

---

2. A motion is a proposal, made by a single member of the House, that the House "do something, order something done or express an opinion with regard to some matter." A bill is a proposed piece of legislation that has not yet been passed into law. For more information, see Marleau and Montpetit (2009).

to force them either to pass the government's bills or to risk an election that either the public does not want or that one or more of the opposition parties do not want, or both. A minority government is vulnerable, of course, because it is outnumbered by the MPs on the opposition side of the House, making defeat on confidence measures a real possibility. But the government also might be more likely to lose votes on important government bills if they are not declared to be confidence measures beforehand. By declaring that a vote is a matter of confidence, the government raises the stakes. If enough opposition members do not support it, the government loses its claim to power. In Canada, this has always resulted in the dissolution of the House, then a general election. As we have noted, no prime minister has ever chosen the second conventional option: resigning, and having the governor general ask the leader of the official Opposition to form a new government without holding an election. And no defeated prime minister has ever been forced to resign or been dismissed by the governor general in order to have a new government without an election. Accordingly, if one or more opposition parties want to avoid an election, and they often do, they find themselves "holding their noses" as they vote for government motions and bills or simply do not show up to vote, a tactic thereby reducing the number of votes cast against the government.

In Heard's second category, some votes have always been considered to be questions of confidence. These include the votes on the address in reply to the Speech from the Throne, which presents the government's policy agenda for the session;[3] the budget; and the budget implementation and supply bills (Heard 2007).[4] Defeat on any of these measures would

---

3. The "address in reply" is an address of thanks to the governor general for the Speech from the Throne, read by a government member the day after the governor general reads the Speech.

4. The "business of supply" includes the procedures by which "the government asks Parliament to appropriate the funds required to meet its financial obligations and to implement programs already approved by Parliament." See Marleau and Montpetit (2009).

indicate a lack of confidence in the government's policy platform and decisions. Government defeats on these votes have occurred on a number of occasions, the last instance being the defeat in 1979 of the budget of the Progressive Conservative minority government of Prime Minister Joe Clark.

In the third category are the opposition's motions that are explicitly worded to convey a lack of confidence in the government. These are not very common, as they are likely to occur only when the opposition side of the House is able to set the agenda for the House of Commons. At present, the rules of the House provide for only 20 "opposition days" per calendar year and the government gets to choose the days on which they are held. Prime Minister Harper did this in 2008 when he rescheduled the opposition day set for December 1 back a week to December 8 to postpone a vote on an expected opposition motion of non-confidence. (On December 4, of course, he prorogued Parliament.) An example of an opposition motion to express non-confidence is the following: "That this House has lost confidence in the Government" (Canada, House of Commons 2005). This was the motion moved by Opposition leader Stephen Harper against Paul Martin's Liberal government on November 28, 2005. It passed, which resulted in Martin's request for the dissolution of Parliament and the January 23, 2006 election. Another explicitly worded motion, which also conferred the House's finding of the government in contempt of Parliament, was used to defeat the Harper Conservative government in March 2011.

Loss of Confidence

When the prime minister and government are defeated on a confidence question, the prime minister has two options: resign or ask the governor general to dissolve Parliament for an election. The first of these options, as previously noted, would give the governor general an opportunity to ask the leader of the official Opposition to form a new government from the existing House of Commons. This has never occurred in Canada, although there are precedents in other Westminster systems.

The possibility of it occurring in December 2008 drew hostile criticism from Prime Minister Harper and his Conservative supporters. Harper claimed that only an election should be able to determine who forms the government. This claim contradicted what he did as official Opposition leader in May 2005, when he demanded that the Martin Liberal government resign. Harper changed his tune in December 2008 to cast doubt on the legitimacy of the proposed Liberal–NDP coalition. His rallying cry was that the proposed coalition had not been chosen by voters in the 2008 election and that, therefore, a change of government without an election from his Conservative government to a Liberal–NDP coalition government, even if it had the confidence of a majority of the MPs in the House, was not a legitimate option. If Harper's view were to be accepted, the only option would be the second one: dissolution and an election to choose a new House after every loss on a confidence vote.

In a majority government situation, of course, the prime minister can take the confidence of the House for granted. Losing a confidence vote would require that some MPs from the government party caucus vote against the government, and thus, with the opposition, constitute a majority against the government. However, party discipline virtually eliminates the possibility that a majority government will be defeated. In fact, in the 1940s, when majority government was the norm and the expectation, constitutional scholar R.M. Dawson (1948) interpreted *all* government motions and bills as confidence matters, which makes sense given the safe assumption that majority governments would always be able to command the support of their own caucus members. However, minority governments do not have the same degree of security. This is not to say that opposition parties are always eager to defeat minority governments; on the contrary, only six minority governments in Canada's history have been defeated on confidence votes (in 1926, 1963, 1972, 1979, 2005, and 2011).

Minority government situations, particularly the two most recent examples of Liberal Prime Minister Paul Martin and Conservative Prime Minister Stephen Harper, have been characterized by excessive partisanship. Obviously, prime ministers do not prefer to govern with minorities and are thus tempted to engineer their own defeat and an election if winning a majority government seems like a reasonable possibility. This occurred in 1974 in the case of the Trudeau Liberal government.

But neither the government nor the opposition wants to be seen to be triggering an election that voters do not want. Each side will engage in a blame game in an attempt to shift responsibility to justify an election. For instance, when Prime Minister Harper called an election in September 2008, notwithstanding his new law setting the date of the next election for October 2009, he claimed that the House had become "dysfunctional." And, of course, he blamed the opposition parties. This was a contested opinion, to say the least. Opposition MPs rejected Harper's description of Parliament as dysfunctional, and cited steady and productive committee work and the passing of bills into law as reasons for allowing Parliament to continue its work (CTV 2008).

Canada's recent experience with minority government has revealed considerable confusion about the application and enforcement of the confidence convention. Before the 2004 election, when the Liberal government under Paul Martin was reduced to a minority government, Canada had had majority government for 24 years. This long period gave us a kind of false security about our knowledge of unwritten constitutional conventions. Because majority governments do not lose confidence, the conventions were not tested. Canadians might have assumed that they would know a defeat on a confidence vote if they saw one, but the matter has proven more complicated. We expand on this issue more fully in the next section of the chapter.

Prorogation and Dissolution

As we have noted but repeat here for greater clarity, the powers of prorogation and dissolution are legally the powers of the governor general as the representative of the Crown in Canada. To prorogue Parliament is simply to end a session. The prorogation order also sets the date for the start of a new session. The written constitution stipulates that there shall be a sitting of Parliament at least once every 12 months, so a prorogation cannot exceed that period. The House of Commons and the Senate do not meet during a prorogation, nor do their committees. Any government bill that is still in process when the session closes must be reintroduced in the subsequent session (although private members' bills can be picked up from where they stood once the House resumes). Prorogations are routine. At the time of writing, the House had been prorogued a total of 120 times in the 144 years since 1867. Within 14 months of the election of October 2008, however, Prime Minister Stephen Harper prorogued Parliament on two separate occasions.

In contrast, to dissolve the House of Commons is to terminate government business completely and to bring an end to the tenure of the MPs there. A general election must then be held following dissolution in order to select a new House of Commons. As Marleau and Montpetit (2000) express it, dissolution has the effect of releasing members of Parliament from their responsibilities. In short, they are no longer MPs, even if they become election candidates for the new House of Commons. The prime minister and the ministers of the government stay on as ministers, but they too are no longer MPs.

The powers to summon and dissolve Parliament are assigned to the governor general by the written constitution. The power to prorogue Parliament is thus a prerogative power of the Crown. Prerogative powers, as Dicey explains, are the "residue of discretionary or arbitrary authority which at any given time is legally left in the hands of the Crown" (Dicey 1885, 424). The scope of the Crown's prerogative has been modified and reduced over time in different parliamentary systems throughout the British Commonwealth. For instance, many of the original prerogative powers of the British Crown in Canada, including the declaration of war, the negotiation of treaties, and the appointment of ministers, are now recognized as the de facto powers of the prime minister. In other words, they are exercised at the prime minister's discretion—not the governor general's. The governor general's role in these matters is strictly symbolic.

As discussed in Chapter 2, the House of Commons cannot be prorogued or dissolved by the prime minister alone. The prime minister must formally advise that the governor general use the powers vested in the office legally to achieve these ends. At the same time, it would be unconventional and, therefore, unconstitutional for a governor general to take these measures without a request from the prime minister. Also as noted in Chapter 2, some experts argue that the Crown has some discretion on these matters in certain but unspecified circumstances, especially when the prime minister and government have lost the confidence of the House. The precedents have been for governors general to act on the advice of the prime minister.

In Canadian history, there is not a single example of a prime minister's request for prorogation being denied. Only once was a request for dissolution denied—the famous King–Byng affair of 1926, discussed in Chapter 2. Again, this is but a single example of a governor general refusing to take a prime minister's advice, but it is often cited as proof of the Crown's discretionary power. In the election campaign that followed the defeat of the Meighen Conservative government, which had replaced King's Liberal government, Mackenzie King took aim at the governor general and his use of the Crown's prerogative. King insisted that Byng's refusal to grant his request for dissolution was illegitimate because, he claimed, the governor general had no discretion to deny a request from a prime minister. No governor general has said "no" to a Canadian prime minister since, so perhaps it was King's interpretation of the constitution that set the definitive precedent.

The rules that govern the practices of confidence, prorogation, and dissolution have become the subject of considerable confusion and debate. For instance, some observers, including Edward McWhinney (2006), suggest that the King–Byng example is too out of date to be considered a guiding precedent and that, in the current climate of populist democracy and citizen empowerment, in which the voters ought to hold the balance of power, discretion on the part of an unelected and unaccountable governor general is unthinkable. Others, including Andrew Heard (2009), maintain that the governor general's discretion is a fundamental component of parliamentary government that enhances democracy by providing a check on any unconstitutional behaviour by the prime minister. In the following section of the chapter, we explore the differences of opinion about these constitutional conventions. The obvious lack of consensus drives home the need for the greater certainty that could come with written rules or protocols.

The Consequences of a Crumbled Consensus

In this final section, we demonstrate the lack of consensus on the conventions that govern the practices of confidence, prorogation, and dissolution. Constitutional scholars, judges, and politicians hold differing views, not only on tests that determine what constitutes a convention but also on the actual meaning and the practical requirements of the conventions.

Earlier in the chapter, we identified the two tests that have been used for determining whether a rule, pattern, or tendency qualifies as a constitutional "convention." Jennings had a three-part test: at least one precedent, actors who believed themselves to be bound by the rule, and a discernible purpose for the rule. The second, alternative test, as advanced by Hogg and Heard, requires that conventions be established and supported by explicit agreement of the relevant political actors.

However, neither test is able to settle the debates surrounding confidence, prorogation, and dissolution. Each leaves too much unresolved and open to interpretation. For instance, Jennings's test demands that the relevant political actors in a given situation must believe themselves to be bound by convention. But how can we know with certainty what they do or do not believe unless they say so? What if they say they do not believe themselves to be bound? Jennings also insists that there must be a precedent. But what if there are conflicting relevant precedents? And Jennings says that there must be a discernible purpose. But who decides what constitutes a discernible purpose? Conversely, Hogg and Heard's "explicit agreement" test does not specify who the "relevant political actors" are. How would we know whether this criterion has been satisfied?

In short, there is disagreement about the existence and meaning of at least some of our conventions, and none of the established tests for assessing whether a convention exists resolve these disagreements. For these reasons, we argue that written rules or protocols are now necessary in order to construct a constitution that can operate more firmly and certainly. When there is a consensus to support them, conventions can be a useful way to achieve both stability and flexibility. However, when there is no consensus to support them, conventions simply do not work. They lose their obligatory force so are unlikely to be effective. As a result, the integrity of responsible government suffers.

We focus here on the practices of confidence, prorogation, and dissolution because they are integral to the fundamental principle of responsible government in parliamentary systems. All three relate specifically to the balance of power between the prime minister, government, and the House of Commons, and especially Parliament's ability to hold the government to account. The uncertainty about the unwritten parts of the constitution gives prime ministers the opportunity to ignore the conventions at will, thereby furthering confusion over how responsible government should be practised. We have seen several examples of this phenomenon in recent decades, to which we refer in the following section.

The Confidence Convention

The requirement that the prime minister and government must have the confidence of a majority of MPs in the House of Commons in order to govern legitimately sounds fairly straightforward. Yet scholars and practitioners disagree about the ways in which confidence can be confirmed or denied. Prime Ministers Paul Martin and Stephen Harper were each faced with what some constitutional experts would character-ize as expressions of non-confidence, but each chose to ignore them and got away with it because there was no one to constrain them. We now consider these episodes, and reactions to them. In our view, these episodes expose the lack of consensus about the meaning of the con-fidence convention and the extent to which this lack of consensus contributes to the empowerment of the prime minister over the people's representatives in the House of Commons.

In May 2005, before Martin's Liberal minority government presented its budget, Conservative MP Jay Hill introduced a motion in the House of Commons that his party later insisted was meant as an expression of non-confidence. The motion came as a directive that instructed the Standing Committee on Public Accounts to amend its report to recommend that "the government resign because of its failure to address the deficiencies in the governance of the public service addressed in the report" (Canada, House of Commons 2005). The motion passed by a vote of 153 to 150, but the government did not resign nor did Prime Minister Martin seek dissolution.

Paul Martin proclaimed that the motion was procedural (instructing the committee to undertake a particular course of action) rather than substantive (a vote either on confidence itself or on government legislation or the budget) and therefore did not qualify as a confidence motion. Further, he contended that, in any case, the motion's intent remained unsatisfied unless and until the committee voted to accept the recommendation and then returned its amended report to the House for a vote. Both Conservative leader Stephen Harper and Bloc Québécois leader Gilles Duceppe heartily disagreed. Both inside and outside Parliament, they claimed that their party MPs meant to vote non-confidence in the government by supporting Hill's motion. The NDP voted against the measure after having agreed, during the Easter break in April, to support the government on upcoming confidence measures, suggesting that the NDP also saw the May 10 vote as a matter of confidence (Heard 2007).

Historical precedent does not support Martin's interpretation of the constitution in this case. Four previous Canadian governments have been defeated on non-confidence motions by the opposition, three of which were "procedural" in nature, just like the one introduced by Hill.[5] Andrew Heard concludes that in this instance Paul Martin wilfully ignored a clear expression of non-confidence and, therefore, was in breach of one of the confidence conventions.

---

5. For a thorough analysis of these events, see Andrew Heard (2007).

Fellow political scientist Don Desserud sees things differently. After the dust settled on Hill's motion, the Liberals went on to pass their budget and a number of other bills. They did not lose another confidence vote until November, following which Prime Minister Martin requested dissolution. Desserud's logic is simple: if the government had truly lost the confidence of the House in May, surely it would not have been able to continue to govern and pass its budget. Desserud (2006, 16) posits that confidence is not won or lost on a single vote, "but must be seen instead as an ongoing process of discovery, a discovery furthermore that the executive has the sole prerogative to make." For Desserud (ibid.), confidence is a "political rather than a legal event" and it is for the prime minister to determine whether the government has or has not lost confidence, and thus the legitimacy to govern. Desserud concedes that if he is correct in his assessment, this reality can only contribute to the unconstrained concentration of power in the hands of the prime minister over the House of Commons (ibid.). While this argument may be unusual, it is not dissimilar to the arguments advanced by some to justify the governor general's approval of Harper's 2008 prorogation, although these arguments were developed after the fact with the 20/20 vision of hindsight.

After the May 2005 vote that Martin dismissed, Harper had this to say on the floor of the House of Commons:

> Mr. Speaker, we have just voted on a motion that was agreed to on a clear majority, a motion which calls upon the government to resign. By all of the established conventions of our democratic system, when the government faces a clear vote on such a question, it is required to do at least one of three things: it is required to fulfill the terms of the motion and resign; to seek a dissolution; or at the earliest moment, to ensure that it indeed has the confidence of this chamber, which is the only democratic mandate this government has to spend our public money. (Canada, House of Commons 2005)

Harper's comments are relevant to our discussion in three ways. First, he confirms his belief that the May 10 vote constituted a confidence vote. Second, he grants the prime minister the prerogative to choose how to respond to a loss of confidence. Third, his interpretation illustrates the confusion about and disagreement on the confidence convention.

Harper lists three options for a government to pursue in the immediate aftermath of a non-confidence vote: to resign, to request dissolution, or to seek a clear expression of confidence from the House. As previously noted, the first two of these are almost always cited as rules of the confidence convention, at least until Harper's own recent rejection of the first option of resignation, when he stated that an election is the only legitimate method of changing the hands of government. But the third is not commonly cited, if at all.

Why Harper added this third possibility is not clear. Nor is its logic. Why, if the government lost a vote of confidence on a clear and explicit question, as Harper says the Liberal government did in this instance, should it have the right to ask for another confidence vote? Why not an immediate resignation or dissolution?

As described in Chapter 2, almost exactly two years after the defeat of the Martin government the Harper government faced a crisis of confidence of its own, just weeks after the general election of October 14, 2008. The government's Speech from the Throne passed with the support of the Liberals under Stéphane Dion's leadership. But then, a few weeks later, on November 27, Finance Minister Jim Flaherty gave Canadians a "fiscal update," which included a package of controversial proposals that proved unacceptable to the opposition parties. The government proposed the following: that federal public servants' right to strike be suspended until 2011; that federal employees' right to seek pay equity remedies be suspended; and that the public subsidy for federal political parties ($1.95 per vote) be eliminated (Valpy 2009). These proposals were not part of the Conservatives' fall campaign or the Speech from the Throne, so they came as a surprise to the other three parties. The third proposal to the party financing regime was especially controversial because it threatened the financial stability of the three opposition parties.

The three opposition leaders were united in their desire to defeat the government, and because the proposed package qualified as part of the government's "fiscal framework" (ibid., 11), it provided an opportunity for a confidence vote. The discussions between the three parties led to an agreement whereby the Liberals and NDP would form a coalition government, supported by the Bloc, following the defeat of the Conservative minority government. At a press conference on December 1, Liberal Party leader Stéphane Dion, New Democratic Party leader Jack Layton, and Bloc Québécois leader Gilles Duceppe outlined the plan for a Liberal–NDP coalition government. Six of the 24 Cabinet positions would be given to the NDP. The coalition agreement would last until June 2011, with the BQ pledging its support for a minimum of 18 months. Dion would serve as prime minister until May 2009, when the Liberal Party would select a new leader to replace him (Taber et al. 2008). Dion had been expected to resign because the 2008 election, his first as leader, was seen as nothing short of a catastrophe for the federal Liberals. They went from 103 seats to 77 and won only 26 percent of the popular vote—an all-time low until the devastating results of the 2011 election, where the party was reduced to a mere 34 seats and 19 percent of the popular vote.

The three opposition leaders also signed an accord that publicly confirmed their intentions and Dion sent a letter to Governor General Michaëlle Jean, stating: "I wish to inform you that my party and the other two opposition parties have lost confidence in this Conservative government" (Letter from Stéphane Dion to Governor General Michaëlle Jean 2008). For a short time the defeat of the Harper government seemed inevitable, but the Conservatives managed to create an escape hatch. The prime minister's first course of action was to delay the confidence vote by pushing the scheduled Liberal opposition day back from December 1 to December 8. Then the government withdrew the three controversial new policies, including its plan to cancel public funding for political parties—the very proposal that had most angered the opposition parties in the first place. The delayed opposition day gave Harper's

Conservatives the time they needed to launch an effective campaign impugning the proposed coalition.

By Tuesday, December 2, the government had made its strategy to further postpone a confidence vote in the House of Commons clear: it would ask the governor general to prorogue Parliament until January 26, which would suspend the work of Parliament by bringing the session to an end, thereby rendering the opposition majority in the House powerless for the next seven weeks. On the evening of December 3, Harper and Dion hit the airwaves. Each leader used a brief televised video clip to explain his side of the story to Canadians. Harper attacked the democratic legitimacy of the proposed coalition, calling it an "unholy alliance" (Whittington, Campion-Smith, and McCharles 2008). He claimed that the opposition had no right to "impose" a partnership "with the separatists" without first obtaining the consent of Canadians by way of an election. He insisted that only voters could choose the government. He claimed that a Liberal–NDP coalition, with BQ support, would overturn the results of the October 2008 election, which Harper saw as a clear victory for his Conservatives, even though only 37.65 percent of voters supported the Conservatives, and voter turnout, at 59.1 percent, was the lowest in Canadian history. For his part, Dion explained that coalitions are a normal and legitimate outcome in parliamentary systems around the world. Voters choose a parliament and then the parliament chooses the government. Near the end of his video, Dion mentioned Harper's plan to request a prorogation and asked the governor general not to grant it unless and until Harper demonstrated that he still commanded the confidence of the House. Both in the video and in other public presentations, Dion argued that Harper had in fact lost the confidence of the majority of members of Parliament, as evidenced by the letter to this effect signed by the MPs of all three opposition parties.

Dion's position, that Harper had to demonstrate that he had the confidence of the House before obtaining a prorogation, directly spoke to the convention that requires the governor general to exercise the Crown's prerogative powers only after advice from the prime minister.

However, many experts say that the governor general is not bound by the advice of the prime minister when he or she has lost the confidence of the House. If Harper did not have that confidence when making his request for prorogation or if, as Heard (2009) argues, there were "serious doubts" about this issue, then, according to this interpretation of the confidence convention, the governor general would have every right to refuse him.

So, when Harper asked for a prorogation on December 4, 2008, did he have the confidence of the House? As noted, days before he made this request, the three opposition party leaders gave verbal and written confirmation of their plans to defeat the government. And Dion, as the leader of the official Opposition, had proclaimed publicly and in a letter to the governor general that the government had lost the confidence of the majority of MPs: 161 members of the House, a clear majority, signed a public document stating that the Conservative government had lost confidence (ibid., 58). Because the prime minister had delayed the scheduled Liberal opposition day, the opposition could not vote non-confidence explicitly on a confidence motion on the floor of the House of Commons. The opposition MPs were thereby forced to express their intent outside the House. Heard (ibid., 54) describes the Harper government's actions as abusive and unprecedented among modern democratic systems. He explains that the governor general's "normal duty simply to act on the prime minister's advice was suspended by the impropriety of that advice and by the signed commitment of a majority of MPs to vote non-confidence in the government" (ibid., 60).

Heard's conclusion is that legitimate and valid expressions of non-confidence can be raised by MPs and opposition party leaders outside the walls of the House of Commons. However, there is no precedent to suggest that a government—or a governor general—is bound by expressions of non-confidence made outside the House. But the fact that Governor General Michaëlle Jean prorogued the House, after Harper asked her to do so, does not necessarily mean that she felt bound by his advice, nor does it mean that she felt that Harper still had the confidence of the House. In fact, we cannot conclude anything from what she did, because she did not give an account, other than making some general remarks about deciding in the best interests of the country. Her meeting with the prime minister, which was also attended by a top professional public servant, Clerk of the Privy Council Kevin Lynch, and the secretary to the governor general, Sheila-Marie Cook, lasted for more than two hours. At one point, Jean excused herself to speak with one of her constitutional advisers, Peter Hogg. This could suggest that she was indeed making a decision and exercising her discretion rather than merely rubber-stamping the prime minister's advice (Franks 2009, 36). But if that were the case, it means that the constitution is whatever the governor general decides—whatever happens!

Silencing the House of Commons

As noted earlier, both prorogation and dissolution involve bringing the work of the House of Commons to an end, thereby temporarily suspending its operations. The break between sessions allows the government to begin with a new agenda, as outlined in the throne speech, which starts the next session. Normally, prorogation is then used to end a parliamentary session when a government completes the agenda established in the Throne Speech. The length of time between the sessions following the prorogation has varied but can be as short as a day.

As we have recently experienced, however, prorogation can be used by the prime minister in an attempt to avoid or postpone political defeat or embarrassment. Harper's request to suspend Parliament to avoid a confidence vote in December 2008 was a blatant abuse of that power for political reasons that served no public purpose.

A year later, he did it again. The political reason this time around was to avoid the scrutiny of a House of Commons committee into allegations that government officials had "misled the House of Commons in denying knowledge that detainees handed over to the local authorities by Canadian troops in Afghanistan were being tortured" (*Economist* 2010). This prorogation lasted from December 30, 2009 until March 3, 2010

(left) On December 4, 2008, Prime Minister Stephen Harper visited Rideau Hall, the governor general's residence, to request that Parliament be prorogued. (right) Governor General Michaëlle Jean.

SOURCES: (left) Adrian Wyld/Canadian Press. (right) MCpl Jean-François Néron. © Office of the Secretary to the Governor General of Canada 2009. Reproduced with the permission of the Office of the Secretary to the Governor General.

and drew the ire of constitutional experts, pundits, and politicians. In a rare moment of Canadian political outrage, anti-prorogation rallies were even organized and held across the country, bringing thousands of protestors into the streets to oppose Harper's actions. A stinging *Globe and Mail* (2010) editorial entitled "Time to Stand Up for Parliament" accused Harper of purging Parliament "for the purposes of political convenience and to escape accountability." The editorial called for "greater knowledge and understanding about the unwritten rules of the constitution, and more legislative control over some of those rules" as checks on the hubris of the prime minister and the consequent decay of parliamentary democracy in Canada. Even the international press weighed in on the prime minister's behaviour. An editorial in the top-ranked British newsmagazine, *The Economist* (January 2010), noted that Harper was "subjecting Parliament to prime-ministerial whim." The article described Harper as a "competent tactician with a ruthless streak," citing his willingness to silence government watchdogs as well as his own ministers in his efforts to cling to power, control information, and avoid accountability. His requests for prorogation in 2008 and 2009 fit this profile.

Harper's prorogation has been described as unprecedented, but this is not entirely accurate. Prime Minister Jean Chrétien also used prorogation for political purposes. For example, he obtained a prorogation of Parliament in November 2003 when the Liberal Party leadership and the office of prime minister transferred from Chrétien to Martin. This same prorogation also had the political advantage for the Liberals of forestalling the public release of the auditor general's report on her investigation into the Liberal government's sponsorship program, a report that played a major role in bringing the so-called sponsorship scandal to public view. Chrétien had always led a majority government, so there was never any doubt about whether he had the confidence of the House when he requested prorogation. Nonetheless, his control over the operations of the House via party discipline does not excuse his misuse of the Crown prerogative for exclusively partisan purposes. The same can be said for a 19th-century Canadian prime minister who used prorogation for a purely partisan purpose. In 1873, Sir John A. Macdonald sought to avoid a vote of non-confidence over the Pacific Railway scandal (Russell 2010). Lord Dufferin, the governor general, did not reject his request, although he did put a ten-week limit on the break between sessions. In that case, the prorogation merely postponed the end of the Macdonald government. When Parliament returned, Macdonald resigned in anticipation of a vote on a motion of censure.

If nothing else, Prime Minister Harper's controversial prorogations gave the country a unique opportunity to become aware of the importance of the unwritten parts of the constitution as well as the uncertainty about them. The first prorogation was more controversial and provoked far more heated and partisan discussion than the second. It allowed the government to do an end run around a non-confidence vote and avoid losing power to a coalition government-in-waiting, and it demonstrated clearly that there was no consensus about the confidence convention and its implications. As events unfolded in Ottawa, it became clear that not only were journalists, citizens, and politicians divided, but experts also disagreed among themselves on whether the governor general was bound by the prime minister's advice.

In response, the University of Toronto Press published a volume entitled *Parliamentary Democracy in Crisis*, in which prominent political scientists and constitutional lawyers weighed in on the matter. As noted in Chapter 1, the book revealed significant differences of opinion on fundamental aspects of Canada's unwritten constitution. C.E.S. (Ned) Franks (2009), for instance, argued that the governor general had a choice. In his essay, Franks cited conflicting precedents relating to dissolution and prorogation, which made it difficult to predict what the governor general would do in December 2008 or to be clear about what she ought to do. No governor general had ever denied a prime minister's request for prorogation, so precedent suggests that Jean ought not to have denied Harper's request either. However, this was no ordinary request to suspend Parliament. It was a request by a prime minister in whom the confidence of the House had already been declared as withdrawn by a majority of MPs, although there had been no chance to vote non-confidence in the House. It was also a request whose only purpose was to avoid losing the anticipated non-confidence vote once a vote was taken in the House. Franks (2009) insists that it would be inconsistent with constitutional convention for a governor general to grant a request for *dissolution* that was plainly motivated by the desire to avoid defeat in the House. Why, then, should the precedent for this convention, clearly established in the King–Byng case, not have been decisive in Governor General Michaëlle Jean's decision (Franks 2009, 33)? The answer is not at all clear, unless one concludes that the misuse of prorogation is less damaging than the misuse of dissolution.

In the same volume, Andrew Heard (2009) agrees with Franks that the governor general had a choice to make and therefore was not bound by Harper's advice, but says that she got it wrong. In Heard's (2009, 60) view, Harper's advice was improper in light of the plenitude of evidence to confirm that he had lost the confidence of the majority of MPs in the House. Heard writes: "Her decision to suspend Parliament … amounted to a serious intervention in the political process that stymied our elected representatives' ability to resolve the crisis." This is in direct contrast to Franks's view that the governor general's decision to prorogue effectively "tossed the government's fate back into the hands of the politicians, where it belonged" (Franks 2009, 45).

Heard also says that we need to decide how the governor general ought to have acted because "the repercussions of her decision will likely be felt for many years to come" (Heard 2009, 47). In other words, her decision is a precedent. But what is the precedent? What is the take-home message here? Merely that the governor general had a choice, as she herself has insisted publicly? That the governor general alone decides what the constitution is? Or that governors general have neither the constitutional authority nor the political legitimacy to refuse a prime minister's advice?

Since some experts are of the view that the governor general should, or at least could, have refused Harper's request for a prorogation, the question of what then would or should happen became an issue of intense discussion and debate. Would or should Harper resign as prime minister immediately, that is, even before the non-confidence vote was held, on the ground that Governor General Michaëlle Jean had, in effect, accepted that the written expression of non-confidence by the majority of MPs meant that the Harper government had already lost the confidence of the House? But even if this were not the case and Prime Minister Harper met the House and was then defeated on December 8, would he be required to resign so that the Liberal–NDP coalition could be formed, or could he have a dissolution and election?

Given that Canadians had gone to the polls only seven weeks earlier, that the October election had been called by the prime minister himself, and that an alternative government had already identified itself, some experts thought it highly unlikely that Governor General Jean would have agreed to a dissolution following a vote of non-confidence. But this too is an issue of constitutional significance on which there is no clear consensus. There is no agreement on how recent the prior election has to be in order for it to be too recent to justify a refusal of dissolution. Some people argue that the election would have had to have been in the previous six months, while others say nine months. In the debate that followed the 2008 prorogation, a new element of disagreement arose. Some now claimed that the governor general should never be expected to ask that an alternative government be formed from the same Parliament following a defeat on confidence. Those who advanced this argument instead claimed that only the people have a right to decide which party leader forms the government and that this always requires dissolution and another election, no matter how recent the last election and no matter who called it. These differences of opinion are explored in greater detail in Chapter 5.

In her memoirs, former Governor General Adrienne Clarkson waded into these murky waters by suggesting that six months after an election is an appropriate minimum shelf life for a parliament. Therefore, a prime minister who loses confidence within that time frame after a general election ought not be granted a dissolution (Clarkson 2007). Clarkson did not get the opportunity to make her opinion a precedent and thus more than just an opinion. Her opinion, however, was in accord with that of the late constitutional expert Eugene Forsey, perhaps the leading authority on dissolution in the Westminster systems. Forsey wrote: "One of the biggest threats to parliamentary democracy in Canada is the dogma that any government, regardless of circumstances, always has a dissolution in its pocket: that an appeal to the people is always proper" (see H. Forsey 2008). Forsey defended the propriety and utility of the Crown's reserve power to refuse to dissolve Parliament as the safeguard against a prime minister willing to send voters to the polls in order to avoid responsibility to the House.

At any rate, in this instance a refusal of a request to dissolve Parliament would have paved the way forward for the proposed coalition government. Had this occurred, Franks assumes that Stephen Harper, now from the opposition side of the House, would have "continued his in-flammatory and constitutionally incorrect but popularly supported ... rhetoric" (Franks 2009, 46), slamming the legitimacy of both the new government and the governor general's role in allowing it to assume office.

The December 2008 incident, in other words, exposed many consti-tutional problems, but solved none of them. There is now undoubtedly even more uncertainty, disagreement, and confusion in Canada regard-ing the meaning and requirements of our constitutional conventions. And it is clear that neither of the two tests for establishing constitu-tional conventions—the Jennings test and the explicit agreement test—is able to resolve questions about the unwritten constitution.

In Chapter 4, we discuss further the implications of prime ministers' use and abuse of the prerogative powers to achieve political ends along-side their powers over the operations of parliamentary government, including through their role as party leader. The reality of the prerogative powers reverses and perverts the logic of responsible government, which dictates that the House of Commons is supreme. Prime ministers, in fact, control the operations and workings of the legislative branch, whether their party holds a majority of the seats or not. In this light, there is no particular reason for defenders of Parliament to rejoice at the prospect of a minority government; the prime minister's powers are formidable still.

References

Brun, Henri, and Guy Tremblay. 1982. *Droit constitutionnel.* Cowansville, QC: Editions Yvon Blais.

Canada. House of Commons. 2005. *Journals*, November 28.

Canada. House of Commons. 2006. *Journals*, September 18.

CBC News. 2010. Little support for proroguing Parliament: Poll. *CBC.ca*, January 7. http://www.cbc.ca/news/canada/story/2010/01/07/ ekos-poll-prorogue.html.

Clarkson, Adrienne. 2007. *Heart matters: A memoir.* Toronto: Penguin Group Canada.

Conacher v. Canada (Prime Minister). 2009 FC 920.

Conacher v. Canada (Prime Minister). 2010 FCA 131.

CTV News. 2002. Chretien calls Kyoto accord vote "a great day." *CTV.ca*, December 11.

CTV News. 2008. For a dysfunctional place, Parliament's been busy. *CTV.ca*, August 18. http://www.ctvbc.ctv.ca/servlet/an/local/CTVNews/ 20080818/parliament_output_080818?hub=EdmontonHome.

Dawson, R.M. 1948. *The government of Canada.* Toronto: University of Toronto Press.

Desserud, D. 2006. *The confidence convention under the Canadian parliamentary system.* Ottawa: Canadian Study of Parliament Group.

Dicey, A.V. 1885. *An introduction to the study of the law of the constitution.* London: Macmillan.

Dion, Stéphane. 2008. Public letter to the Right Honourable Michaëlle Jean from Stéphane Dion, leader of the Opposition. December 1. http://xfer.ndp.ca/coalition/2008-12-01-DionLetter_en.pdf.

Economist. 2010. Canada's Parliament: Harper goes prorogue. Editorial. January 7.

Forsey, Eugene A. 1984. The courts and the conventions of the constitution. *UNB Law Journal* 33: 11.

Forsey, Helen. 2008. Defeating a government doesn't have to trigger an election. Canadian Centre for Policy Alternatives, December 4. http://www.policyalternatives.ca/publications/commentary/ defeating-government-doesn%E2%80%99t-have-trigger-election.

Franks, C.E.S. 2009. To prorogue or not to prorogue: Did the governor general make the right decision? In Peter H. Russell and Lorne Sossin, eds., *Parliamentary democracy in crisis.* Toronto: University of Toronto Press.

Globe and Mail. 2010. Time to stand up for Parliament. Editorial. January 22. http://www.theglobeandmail.com/news/politics/article724889.ece.

Heard, Andrew. 1991. *Canadian constitutional conventions: The marriage of law and politics.* Toronto: Oxford University Press.

Heard, Andrew. 2007. Just what is a vote of confidence? The curious case of May 10, 2005. *Canadian Journal of Political Science* 40: 395–416.

Heard, Andrew. 2009. The governor general's suspension of Parliament: Duty done or a perilous precedent? In Peter H. Russell and Lorne Sossin, eds., *Parliamentary democracy in crisis*, 47–62. Toronto: University of Toronto Press.

Heard, Andrew. 2010. Conacher missed the mark on constitutional conventions and fixed election dates. *Constitutional Forum* 19 (1): 21–32.

Jennings, I. 1959. *The law and the constitution.* London: University of London Press.

Mallory, J.R. 1984. *The structure of Canadian government,* rev. ed. Toronto: Gage.

Marleau, R., and C. Montpetit. 2000. *House of Commons procedure and practice.* Ottawa: House of Commons.

Marleau, R., and C. Montpetit. 2009. *House of Commons procedure and practice,* 2nd ed. Ottawa: House of Commons.

McWhinney, E. 2006. Constitutional guidelines for a governor general in minority government situations. *Canadian Parliamentary Review* 29 (3): 66–67.

Russell, F. 2010. PM abuses prorogation. *Winnipeg Free Press,* May 26, A13.

Taber, J., B. Curry, C. Campbell, and S. Chase. 2008. Opposition sets coalition terms. *The Globe and Mail,* December 1.

Valpy, Michael. 2009. The "crisis": A narrative. In Peter H. Russell and Lorne Sossin, eds., *Parliamentary democracy in crisis.* Toronto: University of Toronto Press.

Whittington, L., B. Campion-Smith, and T. McCharles. 2008. Liberals, NDP and Bloc sign coalition pact. *The Toronto Star,* December 1. http://www.thestar.com/news/canada/article/546315.

CHAPTER FOUR

The Prime Minister and the House of Commons: The Democracy Deficit

Introduction

The great strength of the Westminster system of parliamentary democracy is that it concentrates executive power in the prime minister and Cabinet, allowing for efficient and accountable governance. This means that the government is able to implement its program if, and once, it is approved by Parliament. In turn, it is accountable to the people for its program at the next election. Between elections, the government is responsible to, and should be held to account by, the House of Commons for its administration of public affairs. But the Canadian prime minister also has significant powers to direct and manage the operations of the House. These powers include, but are not limited to, the powers to summon, prorogue, and dissolve Parliament as well as the powers of party leaders in Canada.

The great weakness of the Westminster system as practised in Canada is that it lacks firm rules and thus must rely on the prime minister to act in good faith and not abuse those powers merely for partisan advantage. It also relies on public opinion as virtually the only deterrent to abuse. When the prime minister abandons good faith and public opinion does not constrain his or her actions, the weaknesses of the system are quickly revealed.

Many have come to expect the prime minister to have strong control over governance and public administration. This expectation makes it all the more important that the media and citizens be able to distinguish between (a) instances where the prime minister centralizes direction and control as a means of dealing with the demands of permanent campaigning as a modern partisan strategy and the invasive 24-hour media cycle; and (b) instances where the prime minister abuses power.

Accordingly, the issue addressed in this chapter is not whether some degree of concentration of powers in the prime minister and Cabinet is an essential prerequisite of contemporary parliamentary democracy. Clearly, the prime minister is the leader of the government and therefore must lead it. But excessive centralization of executive powers by the prime minister can damage good democratic government. And, beyond a certain point, centralization increases the likelihood of inappropriate politicization of public administration that goes well beyond a government's legitimate pursuit of its partisan policy agenda. Many observers have concluded that recent Canadian governments have too often improperly politicized public administration. For example, the public administration of the sponsorship program by Jean Chrétien's Liberal government clearly suffered from this politicization effect. The result was the scandal that eventually brought down the government of his successor, Paul Martin. The Harper Conservative government's politicization of public service advertising and public opinion surveys, as well as the improper conduct of some of his political staff in directing public servants, follows the same pattern.

Instead, the issue of concern addressed in this chapter is that power can be concentrated beyond what is required for responsible government to work effectively. The important question then is whether Canada suffers from an unnecessary and excessive—and thus dangerous—level of prime ministerial power over the House. This point is reached, we suggest, when a prime minister can abuse power with little or no fear of being effectively constrained by the House, including by the government's own MPs in the party's caucus or in the Cabinet. Is there a democratic deficit at the heart of our system? In our opinion, there is.

We begin by briefly considering the factors that give the prime minister power over his Cabinet and caucus colleagues and note the developments that have enhanced these powers. We next outline, also briefly, the reforms over time that have diminished the powers of the prime minister to act in ways that put important public interests at risk of partisan manipulation. We then look at the reform agenda that the Harper Conservatives brought with them when they gained power in 2006. This noble aim had the potential of going a long way to addressing the democratic deficit, had it been implemented in whole and in the original spirit. Finally, we note some of the salient differences in the conventions and practices of the political systems of Australia, Britain, and New Zealand, which help us to understand what is distinctly Canadian about our own system.

The Prime Minister: The Power to Control

On February 6, 2006, Stephen Harper was appointed prime minister of Canada, two weeks after Canadians had elected a new House of Commons. The Conservatives had won more seats than the second-place Liberals (124 to 103), but not a majority of the 308 seats in the House of Commons. However, the fact that Prime Minister Harper led a minority rather than a majority government in no way diminished the powers at his disposal as prime minister.

As the head of the government, in practice Prime Minister Harper had virtually full authority and discretion to exercise the powers of the governor general to summon, prorogue, and dissolve Parliament. These are prerogative powers beyond the control of the House. As outlined in Chapter 3, the prime minister also has considerable discretion to decide what constitutes a non-confidence vote and to manipulate the opportunities available to the opposition parties to propose a vote of non-confidence. Of course, a majority in the House (and the Senate) must approve the government's legislative proposals for them to become law, and for the government to have the money to carry them out as well as to deliver existing public services. But just because a majority of MPs in a minority government context have the power to reject the government's legislative proposals does not imply that they have the power to constrain the prime minister's use of executive powers.

We should also point out that the Canadian federal system, because it distributes legislative powers between the federal Parliament and provincial legislatures, limits the policy areas over which the federal government can seek to have Parliament legislate. But the federal system does not constrain the prime minister's executive powers or powers over the operations of the House of Commons or the Senate. Nor does the constitutional capacity of the courts constrain the prime minister's executive powers vis-à-vis the operations of the House of Commons or the Senate. The courts can declare invalid legislation and executive actions that violate a citizen's constitutional rights and freedoms as set out in the *Canadian Charter of Rights and Freedoms*. But these are not constraints on the prime minister's constitutional powers. They are constraints on the federal Parliament and government.

The reasons why the Canadian prime minister is subject to so little constraint have much to do with his or her capacity both to act independently of the government ministers and the party's backbench MPs and to keep them in line by deploying various rewards and sanctions, and with the relative powerlessness of either group to address what they consider to be abuses of executive power. The sections that follow demonstrate these claims. Before turning to them, it is very important to repeat here that not all the resources available to the prime minister are inherent in the Westminster constitution of responsible government. Some are merely Canadian political practices, as indicated below.

Status as Party Leader: Selection and Removal

Only the leaders of the Conservative and the Liberal parties have ever become prime minister. Beginning with the Liberals in 1919 and then the Conservatives in 1927, both parties have selected their party leader by means of a national leadership convention (Courtney 1995). Before this development in 1919, the duty of selecting the party leader was left to the party's MPs, organized informally as the party's parliamentary caucus. At the time, this practice was the norm for the major parties in Australia, Britain, and New Zealand and, as discussed later in this chapter, is still the case everywhere but Britain. The national convention method enables party delegates, selected from local party associations across Canada, to join the party's MPs and other *ex officio* delegates, such as executive members of the party's national association, in electing their leader. Since the first Liberal convention in 1919, an average of about 1,500 persons have voted at these conventions.

The Liberals chose the national convention method because their parliamentary caucus was dominated by MPs from Quebec. The convention method allowed for a nationally representative set of party electors. It also made it easier for someone not an MP, and thus not a member of the party's caucus, to win the leadership, as Mackenzie King did at that first convention. In making this change, the Liberals were aligning themselves with public demands for greater democracy within political parties.

The most significant effect of this change, intended or not, was to provide the party leader with greater security as leader by eliminating the caucus's ability to remove a sitting party leader, including one who was prime minister. Indeed, amidst a confrontation with his caucus, Mackenzie King is reported to have reminded his MPs that they had not selected him and so could not remove him. The governing party caucus, in short, was bereft of one of its chief instruments to constrain the prime minister.

Approving Party Candidates

The most important power of local constituency associations has been the selection of the party candidate for federal elections (Carty and Erickson 1991). Until 1970, candidates' affiliation with their political party was not officially recognized on the ballot, the assumption being that local constituency associations were able to informally regulate who was recognized as the party's candidate in their constituency. In 1970, the party affiliation of candidates was added to the ballot by an amendment to the *Canada Elections Act*. To avoid the chief electoral officer getting dragged into any intra-party disagreements over who actually was the party's official candidate in a constituency, the Act gave the party leader the power to approve or not approve the official party candidates for election. That power could not be given to the officials representing the local party constituency association because these associations were not recognized in the amended election statute at that time.

Samara's recent "exit interviews" with former MPs have made clear that this power is often exercised in an ad hoc and arbitrary fashion, with "little consistency in the nomination process across ridings" and the prime minister and the national party apparatus taking "very little interest in local nomination races, except to occasionally overturn them" (Samara 2011, 24; see also Samara 2010).

Yet, as events have unfolded, this power has become an additional measure available to the prime minister, as party leader, to reward or sanction MPs who wish to seek re-election. As Michael Chong, a Conservative MP from Ontario, puts it: "If you know that the leader may not sign your papers in the next election or may in fact kick you out of caucus [*see next section*], that's going to colour your judgement about whether or not you're going to support the party on a particular vote" (Wherry 2011, 9). The prime minister's leverage over the party's MPs can also affect whether an MP is allowed to collect the generous gold-plated government pension that awaits those who have served at least six years in office.

Expelling MPs from the Government Caucus

MPs are elected as the party's candidates in the local constituency and are expected to act as part of the party team in the House. Occasionally, an MP will take a position on one or more issues that differs from the party's position. When the MP in question is a member of the governing party, voting against the party's policy is voting against government policy, even when the vote is not a vote of confidence. Depending on the circumstances, the MP might cross the floor of the House to the opposition side and either sit as an independent MP or seek to join an opposition party caucus. Or the prime minister, as party leader, can expel the MP from the party caucus.

Given the self-disciplining behaviour of MPs on the government side of the House, a prime minister does not frequently expel MPs. However, he can and has, Prime Minister Harper being the latest example. The threat of expulsion deters MPs who might otherwise be tempted to put their consciences or the views of their constituents ahead of party policy. In 2007, for instance, Bill Casey, a Nova Scotia Conservative MP, was expelled from the caucus by Harper when he took what he declared was a principled stand and voted against his government's position on the province's agreement with the federal government on offshore resources. He then sat as an independent MP. Casey was a popular and respected MP, and the Conservative local constituency association nominated him in 2007 as the Conservative candidate in the next election. Harper promptly rejected the nomination. The party parachuted another candidate into the riding to compete on its behalf. Casey was re-elected, but had to continue to sit as an Independent in the House—a lonely experience indeed.

Organizing and Staffing the Ministry

For MPs of the governing party, the most sought-after rewards, in descending order of importance, are as follows: Cabinet ministers, ministers of state, and parliamentary secretaries. In Canadian government, the prime minister has complete control over who is appointed to these positions. In almost all cases, a Cabinet minister will head a government department, although there are exceptions, such as the government leader in the Senate, who has non-departmental-focused responsibilities. The prime minister may also appoint MPs to the second-order positions called "ministers of state." These junior ministers are assigned to assist a Cabinet minister in managing a government department. In the Canadian system, parliamentary secretaries are not part of a ministry and do not have executive responsibilities. Instead, each assists a Cabinet minister with a department in the conduct of the minister's parliamentary duties—hence the title.

There are no formal constraints on the manner in which the prime minister organizes his or her government, the number of ministers in the Cabinet, or the number of ministers of state and parliamentary secretaries. Nor does a prime minister face any formal restrictions on his or her discretion to change the individuals who occupy these three sets of positions or to determine the scope of their responsibilities and duties. In February 2011, for instance, Harper had made the most of his powers of appointment. He had 63 of 124 Conservative MPs serving as either Cabinet ministers (26, including himself), ministers of state (11), or parliamentary secretaries (27). All have extra pay and various other perks and benefits.[1] The large number of Cabinet, minister of state, and parliamentary secretary appointments has become standard practice. When Paul Martin's government lost power in November 2005, it numbered 68 MPs serving as Cabinet ministers (32, including Martin), ministers of state (6), and parliamentary secretaries (30), out of a total of 133 Liberal MPs at dissolution, just slightly more than 50 percent of the Liberal caucus. Following his 2011 election victory, Harper

---

1. An MP's base salary, at the time of writing, is $157,731 per year. On top of this, a parliamentary secretary earns an additional $15,834, a minister of state gets an additional $56,637, and a minister earns an additional $75,516 per year (Akin 2011; Parliament of Canada 2011).

appointed 39 individuals to his Cabinet (28 ministers and 11 ministers of state), creating the second largest federal Cabinet in Canadian history, following Brian Mulroney's Cabinet of 40. He also appointed 28 parliamentary secretaries. While this amounts to a slightly smaller percentage of the Conservative caucus, given its new majority status, the number of appointments in absolute numbers remains inflated.

One cannot overemphasize the degree to which Canadian prime ministers have been able to use "Cabinet shuffles," entailing some mix of promotions, demotions, lateral transfers, and dismissals, to keep ministers in line with the prime minister's agenda. It is a contributing factor to the diminished importance of Cabinet as a decision-making body and the increased importance of the prime minister and the political staff of the Prime Minister's Office, a trend that began with Trudeau (Savoie 1999).

Assigning Members and Chairs to Commons' Committees

For MPs on the government side who do not become ministers or parliamentary secretaries, the next order of status is to chair a House of Commons committee, preferably one that carries some degree of prestige, or at least be appointed to a committee of one's choice. As leader of the governing party, the prime minister controls the appointment of MPs to committees and appoints the chairs of committees that are headed by a government MP.[2] A government MP chairs all but a handful of committees. The committees of the House mirror the party standings in the House, so that a majority government will have a majority on each committee and a minority government will have a minority. But even when the government is a minority government and thus has

---

2. Technically, committees choose their own chairs but the governing party, as directed by the prime minister, can easily manipulate this formality by directing its MPs on every committee chaired by a government MP to vote for the MP whom the prime minister wants as chair.

fewer MPs on each committee than the combined opposition parties, the prime minister selects the chairs of the committees that are chaired by a government MP. The committees chaired by an opposition MP are those whose primary or even exclusive function is to scrutinize and hold government to account for its administration of public affairs. The Public Accounts Committee, which reviews the government's financial management and management practices and is assisted by the audits conducted by the independent Office of the Auditor General, is the best example of this.

Prized committee assignments enhance an MP's status, often generating more media coverage, and in some cases providing various perks, such as international travel. In the case of committee chairs, the assignment also comes with an increase in pay.[3] As with the other powers of the prime minister over the government party's MPs, committee appointments are used to reward loyalists and sanction those who do not toe the line. As discussed later, when he was opposition leader, Harper cleverly engineered a surprise change whereby Prime Minister Chrétien agreed to let Commons committees select their chairs.

Patronage Appointments for Post-MP Life

The prime minister has the power to make other significant appointments that can be, and are, dangled before MPs as future rewards—on retirement or after defeat in an election—for good behaviour now. These appointments include senators, judges of the superior and federal courts, and ambassadors. For most defeated politicians, the Senate is a marvelous reward that features tenure to age 75,[4] a good salary and

---

3. The additional payment for committee chairs is $11,165 per year (Akin 2011).

4. It should be noted that in the appointments that Prime Minister Harper made to the Senate, he has asked new senators to voluntarily step down after eight years, in keeping with his stated intent to reform the Senate. It should also be noted that this is a voluntary measure and there is no mechanism to either enforce it or to sanction those who choose not to step down.

pension, and life in politics regardless of which party is in power. For example, after they were defeated as Conservative candidates in the 2011 election, Fabian Manning, Larry Smith, and Josée Verner were appointed to the Senate by Prime Minister Harper. Both Manning and Verner had previously been MPs.

The prime minister also can and does appoint retired or defeated MPs to the boards of various non-departmental government corporations, agencies, and commissions that, at least in theory, operate at various degrees of arm's length from ministers. These include, for example, the Canadian Radio-television and Telecommunications Commission (CRTC), which regulates radio and television broadcasting, and Canada Post.

Enforcing the Prime Minister's Power

The prime minister's power in relation to MPs, including ministers, has been enhanced in recent decades by the significant expansion of two institutions that directly serve the prime minister: the Prime Minister's Office (PMO) and the Privy Council Office (PCO). The prime minister staffs the PMO with partisans from the governing party and personal supporters. These individuals serve at the pleasure of the prime minister. They are not public servants, although they are paid from the public purse.

The PMO and the partisan political staff in each Cabinet minister's own office constitute the political arm of government, in contrast to the non-partisan public service. The PMO directs the political staffs of the ministers on all matters of priority to the prime minister. Total political staff now number approximately 500, with roughly 100 in the PMO alone. Under a prime minister set on intensive micro-management and political control over public policy issues, administration, and communications, the scope of PMO power is extensive (Aucoin 2010).

The powers of the prime minister over the non-partisan public service have also been enhanced since the 1970s (Aucoin 1995, 2008). This can be seen not only by the increase in the last five decades in the number of departments and agencies for which there must be deputy ministers, but also through the creation, then gradual expansion in the number, of associate deputy ministers. All of these officials, roughly 75 in total, are appointed by and serve at the prime minister's pleasure, meaning that they can be dismissed, demoted, or transferred by the prime minister at any time. Ministers of departments do *not* appoint or dismiss their own deputy ministers or associate deputy ministers even though they are personally responsible for the management of their individual departments.

The Canadian tradition has been for the prime minister to appoint career federal public servants from the ranks of the non-partisan public service,[5] based on recommendations from the Clerk of the Privy Council (and from advisers in the PMO, at least for some positions) (Aucoin 2006). However, the constant shuffle of senior officials over the past few decades has given prime ministers considerable leeway in shaping the culture of the public service. Some say that the clearest example of this occurred under the Liberal government of Jean Chrétien in the sponsorship scandal that brought down Chrétien's successor Martin's Liberal government. And under the Harper government, concerns emerged in the weeks leading up to the May 2011 election that public servants were inappropriately involved in government-sponsored media advertising campaigns and public opinion polling that were, at least partly, serving the governing party's political interests (Cheadle 2011). These and related concerns give rise to serious questions about the capacity and willingness of the public service to maintain the oath all public servants must take to act impartially.

Constraining the Prime Minister and Government

The history of democratic government in Canada has not witnessed a uniform increase in the power of the prime minister over the House of

---

5. Public servants at the assistant deputy minister level and below, who number in the tens of thousands, are appointed and promoted on the basis of merit by the Public Service Commission, an agency that is not subject to direction by the prime minister or Cabinet. It reports directly to Parliament and is discussed below.

Commons or even over the executive branch of government. Democratic reforms, large and small, have been adopted since the first decade of Confederation.

Democratic reforms were necessary in the first decades of Canada to remove the powers of the government to manage elections in ways that could be, and were, easily deployed to benefit the governing party. For example, a decade after Confederation, the practice of the party in power to stagger the date of individual constituency elections across the country over several weeks was eliminated. This reform removed the capacity of the prime minister to first hold elections in what were considered safe seats for the government side in the hope of establishing momentum for his party. A second reform was the adoption of the secret ballot, which was intended to help eliminate government intimidation of voters when they had to vote orally.

The biggest reform in democratic election administration, a reform that put Canada on the map of the Western democracies, came 53 years after Confederation. In 1920, the authority to administer elections was assigned by statute to the newly established chief electoral officer (CEO), an officer of Parliament designed to be independent of the government. The CEO is appointed by way of a resolution of the House of Commons and heads the election administration agency now referred to as Elections Canada. The CEO's independence has placed Canadian election administration in the top ranks of impartial election administration in the democratic world.

An equally significant democratic reform was initiated a decade earlier in 1908, when the powers of the prime minister to make appointments to the public service were substantially constrained, reducing the capacity of the prime minister to make partisan patronage appointments of party loyalists and supporters. That reform was initiated by the creation of the Civil Service Commission and the assignment of statutory authority to the commission for staffing the public service below the level of deputy minister (and, for some time, some positions outside Ottawa). Although the effectiveness of the commission (now the Public Service Commission [PSC]) has waxed and waned over the years, its very existence had become an effective reform by the end of the Second World War. Since 2000, the commission, as an independent executive agency reporting to Parliament, has adopted a role that is more independent of the leadership of the deputy minister community. The commission has also restored its capacities to audit and review departmental practices. These capacities are especially critical now that most staffing authority has been delegated from the commission to deputy ministers (who then delegate the authority to managers within their own departments). This delegation means that deputy ministers are then held to account by the commission for how they apply that authority.

The powers of the prime minister and government to control information about financial and administrative practices and behaviour have also been diminished by several developments over the past century. One was the establishment of the Office of the Auditor General, another independent officer of Parliament. This agency has evolved considerably over time. Suffice to say that since a major set of legislative amendments to the office in the mid-1970s, the auditor general has been a significant presence in scrutinizing government administration and in helping the House of Commons to hold government to account. The auditor general has the responsibility and the powers to audit and report to the House not only the financial accounts of the government—covering all expenditures of public monies approved by Parliament on an annual basis—but also the financial and associated management practices used to achieving economy and efficiency and effectiveness ("results," to use the current term). At present, the Office of the Auditor General is a very strong and independent institution. It is widely considered to be the most effective check on government even though it is equipped only with the power to publish and publicize its audits and review—it has no authority to demand changes.

Alongside the auditor general, the information commissioner, also an independent officer of Parliament, is another basic building block of the Canadian system of ministerial and government accountability. Legislation enacted in 1985 established the public's right of access to government information on a wide range of governmental subjects (the so-called access to information law). The Canadian access to information regime has been an important asset in securing public accountability, despite its shortcomings from the standpoint of its Canadian critics (see, for example, Roberts 2005, 2010). Canada's record on freedom of information was once very good by international standards, since the country was one of the first national governments to adopt this constraint on government secrecy. Since that time, its effectiveness has eroded terribly, and in 2011 Canada was judged the worst in a five-country study that compared it with Australia, Britain, Ireland, and New Zealand (Hazell and Worthy 2010).

Reforming the Democratic Deficit: The Harper 2006 Agenda

The Harper Conservatives earned their victory in the 2006 general election in large part by default. As was the case in the 2004 election, when the majority government of Liberal Prime Minister Paul Martin was reduced to a minority government, many Canadians were disgusted with the Liberals. They blamed the Liberal governments of Martin and his predecessor, Jean Chrétien (1993–2004), for one of the most infamous and highly publicized scandals in Canadian political history, the so-called sponsorship scandal, referred to earlier in Chapter 1. In brief, the scandal referred to the maladministration and corrupt expenditures of money for pro-Canada advertisements at cultural and sporting events in Quebec. By sponsoring these advertisements, the federal government hoped to counter the pro-separatist forces that had almost won the 1995 Quebec referendum on separation from Canada. Under the program, funds were directed to ad firms that, it turned out, provided little or no work, often fraudulently invoicing the government while directing funds back to the Liberal Party. The prime minister's political staff was involved with the public servants responsible for administering these monies and, unfortunately, the management controls were lax or non-existent. In the end, one public servant was tried and convicted of criminal offences, as well as a few advertising company executives and Quebec federal Liberal Party officials (see Commission of Inquiry into the Sponsorship Program and Advertising Activities 2005).

For the Liberals, it was a political disaster; for the opposition, a gift from the electoral gods. Unfortunately for the Liberals and to the delight of the opposition, the scandal unfolded slowly and dramatically over two long years. This period encompassed daily and extensive TV and newspaper coverage of the event. It included a long stream of witnesses—among them Prime Minister Martin and former Prime Minister Chrétien—who were examined and cross-examined daily on the live televised public hearings of the Gomery commission, the independent inquiry established by Martin to examine the scandal. By 2006, even more voters had turned against the Liberals, making the 2006 election a classic "throw the bums out" election. At the same time, the lack of sufficient enthusiasm for the Harper Conservatives meant that the new government did not win a majority of the seats in the House of Commons.

The Conservatives had focused their election campaign on the scandal. They promised reforms to "clean up" and bring about "accountable government" in response to the Liberals' scandal. They also had a plan to establish a "better democracy" to address what Paul Martin had called the "democratic deficit" of Canadian parliamentary government.

The promise of democratic reform could not help but fall on receptive ears. For at least a half century, beginning with the Liberal government of Pierre Trudeau, the "decline of Parliament" thesis had gained momentum in Canadian academic, political, and media circles. It was usually accompanied by the charge that successive prime ministers, again beginning with Trudeau, were "presidentializing" the parliamentary system. These twin ideas appeared to resonate with the public. Even though political historians could not identify a golden age of parliamentary government in Canada, there was widespread agreement

Prime Minister Pierre Trudeau (left, seen here in 1972 with Cabinet minister and future prime minister Jean Chrétien). Many observers trace the "decline of Parliament" to the Trudeau era.

SOURCE: Peter Bregg/Canadian Press.

that the prime minister had become less constrained over time by Cabinet ministers and caucus. The reasons commonly noted were those listed in the first part of this chapter.

In 2002, before he became Liberal Party leader, Paul Martin had made headlines with his criticism of what he labelled Canada's "democratic deficit." The language here was useful to Martin in two ways. First, it played to his campaign to revitalize parliamentary democracy after several years of criticism of what was said to be the dictatorial management style of his predecessor, Jean Chrétien. Second, it played to his own greatest achievement as Chrétien's minister of finance, namely, eliminating the enormous fiscal deficit the Liberals had inherited when they came to office in 1993. In these two ways, Martin hoped to overcome the fact that he was not only the minister of finance from 1993 to 2002, a period that overlapped with the sponsorship abuses, but also arguably, after the prime minister, the most powerful minister in the Chrétien Cabinet.

According to Martin, the democratic deficit was the gap between how the system of parliamentary democracy was supposed to work in principle and how it actually worked in practice (Aucoin and Turnbull 2003). In Martin's view, a gap came into being because the people's elected House of Commons was too weak and the prime minister was too strong. The democratic deficit had to be overcome if the original spirit of parliamentary democracy was to be restored. Martin promised to introduce the British practice of three-line votes, distinguishing between:

1. votes that are declared confidence votes by the prime minister (or, of course, non-confidence motions from the opposition) and discipline is enforced on all ministers and government MPs alike;
2. votes that are so-called free votes where MPs can vote as they wish, and no discipline is applied because no government position is declared; and,
3. most important, votes where all ministers are expected to take a collective stance but where backbench government MPs are allowed to decide on their own.

Martin had plenty of company for his view of the democratic deficit. As noted in Chapter 1, in 2001 Jeffrey Simpson of the *Globe and Mail* had published a book on Jean Chrétien, whom he portrayed as the "friendly dictator." And, in 1999, political scientist Donald Savoie had characterized the concentration of power under the prime minister as a governance structure resembling a powerful monarchy. According to his description, the prime minister is the king and is surrounded by a cabal of courtiers, each dependent for their status and influence in the king's court on the personal whims of the prime minister. And, in 1997, at a time when he was not an elected politician, Stephen Harper had co-authored an article with his one-time adviser, political scientist Tom

Flanagan, entitled "Our Benign Dictatorship." According to Harper and Flanagan (1997), "We persist in structuring the governing team like a military regiment under a single commander with almost total power to appoint, discipline and expel subordinates." The Reform Party, established in 1988 and for which Harper had been an MP from 1993 to 1997, had pledged to change the balance of power between the prime minister and MPs in the House of Commons by freeing MPs from the grip of party discipline imposed by traditional party leaders, especially Liberal and Progressive Conservative prime ministers, in controlling their party's MPs.

In the 2006 election campaign, the Conservative plan for a "better democracy" and "accountable government" that would affect the balance of power between the prime minister and Parliament included the following measures, of direct relevance to the democratic deficit as defined above:

- legislation requiring fixed election dates every four years, except when a government loses the confidence of the House and an election follows, with the next election to be scheduled four years later;
- the idea of making all votes in Parliament, except the budget and main estimates, "free votes" for ordinary MPs;
- an increase in the power of Parliament and parliamentary committees to review the spending estimates of departments and hold ministers to account;
- the establishment of a Public Appointments Commission to set merit-based requirements for appointments to government boards, commissions, and agencies, and to ensure that competitions for these positions are publicized and fairly conducted;
- the establishment of a Parliamentary Budget Authority to provide objective analysis directly to Parliament about the state of the nation's finances and trends in the national economy;
- the strengthening of the *Access to Information Act* and the powers of the information commissioner; and

- the establishment of an accounting officer system that would distinguish between the accountabilities of deputy ministers and ministers.

These proposed reforms addressed many of the key deficiencies that have distorted the balance of power between the prime minister and Parliament and given rise to the democratic deficit. Unfortunately, as laudable as these proposals were, they have all fallen short of the mark in implementation.

Fixed Election Dates: Absent Good Faith

Fixing elections for a set date is meant to prevent prime ministers from calling an early election to coincide with what is perceived, accurately or not, as an advantageous time for the governing party to head to the polls. As noted in Chapter 1, the maximum length of time of a parliament in Canada is established at five years in the *Constitution Act, 1982*. Since elections are held after the governor general dissolves Parliament, the prime minister has always had the ability to call an election within that five-year limit. These so-called snap elections have happened many times.

In recent years, the ability of the prime minister to call snap elections became the subject of much political criticism. Prime Minister Jean Chrétien, on two successive occasions, initiated snap elections in attempts to solidify his grasp on power. The first came in 1997, barely three and a half years after the 1993 election. Chrétien's election call derived from his Liberal Party's favourable position in the polls and the split between the two conservative parties of the day—the Progressive Conservative Party and the new Reform Party. With the opposition divided and unable to mount much of a challenge, it was thought likely that the Liberals would revel in a landslide victory.

Chrétien was widely criticized for the early election call, and while the Liberals managed to hold onto power, they lost 22 seats and saw their share of the total vote decrease as well. Undeterred by this outcome, Chrétien triggered another snap election in 2000, little more than three years into his new mandate. This time, the election was seen as an attempt to maintain power before the divided conservative opposition parties could unite and mount a greater challenge. After the 1997 election, the Reform Party had morphed into the Canadian Alliance, a party dedicated to uniting small "c" conservatives into a single party that stood a greater chance of achieving electoral success. Chrétien seized the moment, both to capitalize on the Liberals' rise in popularity and the government's new budget surplus after years of deficits, as well as to exploit the Canadian Alliance's lack of election preparedness and doubts about the electoral appeal of its newly minted leader, Stockwell Day. In this election, Chrétien won a third straight majority government, increasing both the Liberal share of seats in the House and the total popular vote.

Notwithstanding the mixed results of these two snap elections, observers and opposition parties can usually be counted on to object strenuously to the ability of prime ministers to call an election simply when it is politically advantageous. These objections led to the campaign commitment of the Conservatives in the 2006 election to establish a fixed election date law as part of its proposed package of democratic reforms.

Once elected, Prime Minister Harper professed: "Fixed election dates prevent governments from calling snap elections for short-term political advantage. Fixed election dates stop leaders from trying to manipulate the calendar. They level the playing field for all parties. The rules are clear for everybody" (Meissner 2006). This promise was made into law in 2007 as an amendment to the *Canada Elections Act*. In less than a year and a half, Harper himself flouted the reform. On September 7, 2008, he called an early election for no other reason than his thought that the timing was politically favourable to his party, with what came to be known as the global financial crisis looming.

Following dissolution, Harper claimed: "We are clear. You can only have certainty about a fixed election date in the context of a majority government" (Martin 2010, 157). As a factual statement of probabilities, the statement is an accurate one. A majority government has never been defeated on a confidence vote at the federal level in Canada, whereas minority governments have been defeated on several occasions. However, as a statement intended to convey the idea that the law did not, and could not, apply to minority governments, it is sheer nonsense. Both the purpose of the law's fixed election date and the purpose of the provision allowing for an early election are clear. Neither justified Harper's own snap election. And, by ignoring the law, he forced the governor general to wade into partisan politics, since either a positive or a negative response to the prime minister's request for an election could be seen as favouring one party over another, especially in the absence of any firm rules to guide the governor general in exercising discretion. Harper's only concern about ignoring the law was the possibility of negative public reaction to his action (Martin 2010, 157), but the calculation was that it would not be a significant factor for voters when casting their ballots.

Free Votes: A Promise Buried Deep

Although Stephen Harper's original party home was the Progressive Conservative Party, he left it early in his political career to join Preston Manning in the formation and building of the Reform Party of Canada. Manning and his Reformers were ardent critics of what they saw as excessive party discipline in the House of Commons, especially prime ministerial control over the governing party's MPs (Smith 1999). Instead, they enthusiastically supported reforms to secure greater freedom for MPs to vote as their conscience or constituents demanded. The 2006 Conservative Party election platform maintained this connection to its Reform Party roots. It promised to "make all votes in Parliament, except the budget and main estimates [the government's spending proposals], 'free votes' for ordinary members of Parliament."

Party discipline has been a fact of parliamentary democracy in Canada from the outset of responsible government. Although responsible government does not require disciplined political parties in any constitutional sense, the logic of responsible government implies them. Party discipline arises from the practical necessity of organizing a team of MPs to form a government with a realistic chance of maintaining the confidence of a majority of all MPs. In Canada, as elsewhere in the Westminster democracies, there are at least two competing parties, ensuring that there will be one party that forms the government with the confidence of a majority of MPs and another that forms the opposition. The opposition party or parties also have political incentives to act in a disciplined manner in order to present themselves as an alternative government.[6] By design, the accountability process of responsible parliamentary government is adversarial and thus partisan.

At the same time, responsible government does not require absolute or excessive party discipline. MPs do not have to be completely under the thumb of their party leader, even when the party leader is the prime minister. On the contrary, the logic of responsible government as parliamentary democracy assumes, even requires, just the opposite (Franks 1997). As is discussed further in Chapter 5, if responsible government is not to degenerate into a process simply for electing the government, then MPs cannot be merely voting robots controlled by party leaders. Parliamentary democracy assumes that MPs, including those on the government side of the House, will fulfill their primary obligations for debating legislative proposals, scrutinizing the government's administration of public money and services, and holding the prime minister and other ministers to account for their decisions and actions as the government, including withdrawing confidence if deemed necessary (Smith 2007).

On the positive side, party discipline is critical insofar as the House of Commons is one of the forums for conducting a continuous election campaign between elections. It is also critical because the institutional logic of responsible government assumes that the major responsibility

---

6. Or they may wish simply to be an effective opposition, as must be the case with the Bloc Québécois, since this party runs candidates only in Quebec. Even if the Bloc won every seat in Quebec, they would have only 75 seats.

for scrutinizing and holding the government to account falls squarely on the shoulders of opposition MPs, both in the House itself and in its committees. Undisciplined opposition parties are far less likely than disciplined parties to be able to perform these critical parliamentary functions.

Disciplined parliamentary parties require at least two things. First, the party's MPs must have a degree of self-discipline. These MPs were elected as the recognized candidates of their party against the recognized candidates of other parties. They thus have a responsibility to their party leader, their party colleagues in the House, and those who voted for them as the candidate of their party. In each case, it is assumed that they will accept, at least for the most part, their party's policies and positions in the House and in other political arenas, including the media. Second, the prime minister is required to discipline MPs who break ranks on matters of priority to the government, especially those that challenge its survival. A significant measure of self-discipline and leader control, then, has been a critical feature of responsible government from the outset. But prime ministerial control over the party's MPs need not be absolute for responsible government to work as the democratic foundation of parliamentary democracy. We need to be reminded of Lord Acton's aphorism that absolute power is always a threat to democracy, because absolute power corrupts absolutely.

When he was president of the National Citizens' Coalition, however, Harper reminded an American audience of this very point. He gave the Americans a "civics" lesson in which he mocked the Canadian system of government in comparison with the American system. His description is worth quoting at some length:

> On the surface, you can make a comparison between our political system and yours. We have an executive, we have two legislative houses, and we have a Supreme Court.
>
> However, our executive is the Queen, who doesn't live here. Her representative is the Governor General, who is an appointed buddy of the Prime Minister.

... [The] Senate, our upper house, is appointed also by the Prime Minister, where he puts buddies, fundraisers, and the like. ... [Our] Supreme Court ... is also appointed by the Prime Minister. Unlike your Supreme Court, we have no ratification process.

So if you sort of remove three of the four elements, what you see is a system of checks and balances which quickly becomes a system that's described as unpaid checks and political imbalances. ...

What the House of Commons is really like is the United States electoral college. Imagine if the electoral college which selects your president once every four years were to continue sitting in Washington for the next four years. And imagine its having the same vote on every issue. That is how our political system operates. (Harper 1997)

Harper's opportunity to make good on this analysis was the 2006 Conservative campaign promise to reduce enforced party discipline by having votes deemed to be "free votes," except for the government's budget and its main estimates. However, nothing at all was heard about it after the election. The Harper Conservatives dropped it like a stone.

Harper was not the first prime minister to ignore a campaign promise to reform excessive party discipline. Jean Chrétien promised to do so in the 1993 election campaign and it all came to naught when his Liberals won the election. In his decade in power (1993–2004), he did not seek to address the issue in any meaningful way. As noted above, Paul Martin sought to adopt the British three-line whip system.

Martin's failure to adopt this approach as a principal method for addressing the problem of excessive discipline during his tenure as prime minister was regrettable. Harper's approach—free votes on everything but the budget and main estimates—was untenable from the start. Harper failed to understand the necessity for party discipline on votes other than these two exceptions, and thus refused to see the obvious merit in the three-line voting system. In any event, excessive party discipline has been the order of the day under his leadership.

Beginning with the Chrétien government and extending to the Harper government, Canada's problem with excessive party discipline has been exacerbated with the practice of the government introducing omnibus bills, especially omnibus budget implementation bills. The bills encompass what should be several separate bills, since some are certainly not part of a budget implementation bill. The practice of tying several pieces of legislation together, especially to the budget, virtually guarantees that some matters will not be given proper scrutiny and MPs will not be given a chance to vote against some of the included legislation based on its merits. The abuse of Parliament by prime ministers here is closely related to excessive party discipline. Party discipline is always applied to budget bills because votes on these bills have always been deemed to be confidence votes.

With excessive party discipline the reigning practice, the only circumstance in which the government is likely to change its mind and allow amendments to its legislative proposals is when there is widespread revolt in the government caucus or public outrage. Both are rare occurrences but can happen. For instance, Chrétien once had to change a budget implementation bill when his MPs and even almost all his ministers, except he and the finance minister, revolted when they discovered that the Liberal government planned to give hundreds of millions of dollars to an independent board to decide on government infrastructure projects (Aucoin 2003). The allocation across the country of infrastructure funds from the federal government has, politically, always been a hugely important matter for all ministers and for government MPs. It is one of the few matters of public administration on which individual government MPs might expect to have some influence. Chrétien relented to fend off a revolt.

Equally important, the assumption that party discipline must be applied to all votes because all votes are confidence votes displays a complete disregard for the logic of responsible government. If one wishes to reject that characterization, while acknowledging that completely "free votes" will be rare, then acceptance by politicians, media, and citizens that the government will not win all votes is imperative. Only by accepting some such system can we expect the House of Commons to make changes to bills that improve them as they make their way through the legislative process.

Parliamentary Budget Officer

The Conservative government kept its promise to establish a parliamentary budget officer (PBO), and it has turned out to be a welcome reform to those who favour greater scrutiny of government. The first officer, Kevin Page, has been a thorn in the side of the government, consistently publishing analyses of government finances and projections of spending and revenues that dispute the government's figures. However, the status of the office is not as independent as it might have been. Instead of being a parliamentary agency in its own right, it was placed under the management authority of the Librarian of Parliament. And it has had to struggle with what it considers inadequate funding and access to necessary information from the government.

Parliamentary Committee Reform

The Conservative Party (2006, 44) promise to "increase the power of Parliament and parliamentary committees to review the spending estimates of departments and hold ministers to account" was partially fulfilled by the establishment of the parliamentary budget officer. In virtually every other respect, however, the momentum has been not to reform but to undermine the capacity of parliamentary committees to perform their functions.

Parliamentary committees are an essential part of a modern Parliament's capacity to scrutinize proposed government legislation, examine the administration of government, and hold the government and its individual ministers to account. For the most part, the logic of responsible government has the opposition playing the most critical roles in all these respects. For the same reason, government MPs most often play a defensive role on behalf of the government, because it is the government's proposals and performance that are under review. This is especially likely in the federal Parliament, where ministers do not sit as members of parliamentary committees, although they are required to appear before committees to explain and justify their proposals and performance and to be held to account for both. Excessive party discipline by the prime minister, however, makes a mockery of the fundamental purposes of parliamentary committees as central to the spirit of review, debate, scrutiny, and reaching agreements on all those matters that do not require strict compliance with the government party line.

Of the two dozen or so House of Commons committees in existence at any given time, even when the government is a minority and has only a minority of the seats on each committee, most are chaired by a government MP. Prior to the 2011 election, there were five exceptions chaired by an opposition MP: Access to Information, Privacy and Ethics; Government Operations and Estimates; Public Accounts; Status of Women; and the Standing Joint (House and Senate) Committee for the Scrutiny of Regulations. Having opposition MPs chair these five committees is justified on the grounds that the roles of these committees are primarily to review and assess the government's compliance with its statutory obligations and its financial management performance.

Committee chairs are technically elected by secret ballot of committee members. The traditional practice, however, was for the prime minister to select which MPs would chair which committees for the government side, with government MPs voting accordingly. As Opposition leader, Stephen Harper rejected the practice, and then in a surprise development was able to embarrass Prime Minister Chrétien into allowing Liberal MPs to vote on their own. Once in power, Harper reversed that position by appointing Conservative MPs as committee chairs. Not wanting to draw attention to his own about-face, he did not announce the change. He was only caught out when one of his MPs inadvertently announced that he had been appointed the chair of a committee before the committee had voted!

Given the tight control Harper had over his caucus after the 2006 election, this reversal may not have made much, if any, difference in any event. It stretches the imagination too much to think that any Conservative committee chairs would have acted contrary to instructions issued by the prime minister or his political staff. Indeed, as part of this tight control, the PMO issued a handbook to Conservative chairs that instructs them how to advance the government's agenda, how to secure government-friendly witnesses and advise them on what to say, and how to obstruct and undermine committee proceedings, including filibustering meetings or stopping them entirely (Martin 2007). Conservative committee chairs and members took these missives to heart (see O'Malley 2009a, 2009b).

Committees are an extension of the House and its partisan divisions, but committee chairs are a pale imitation of the Speaker of the House, who functions with a responsibility to preside over House proceedings impartially. Committee chairs who run roughshod over impartiality display a deep lack of appreciation of the democratic requirements of responsible government. If the opposition cannot perform its functions adequately because of partisan chairs, the parliamentary process is undermined.

Merit-Based Public Appointments: Patronage Regained

The Harper government did create a Public Appointments Commission that would constrain a prime minister's power to make partisan appointments. But the statute that created it gave the prime minister the discretion to decide whether to implement the reformed process. After a parliamentary committee rejected his nominee of the chair of the commission, the prime minister abandoned the commission.

Appointments to two to three thousand boards of directors and commissions of the government thus remain the prerogative power of the prime minister, and the processes of selecting candidates for the prime minister to consider are not independent of the government. Along with Senate appointments, these are the main patronage powers available to the prime minister, and the qualifications of those appointed are often well down the list of criteria for making or approving an appointment, if they are there at all. Personal loyalty and support for the prime minister or the prime minister's party are often the key, even only, criteria.

It should be noted that even if the Public Appointments Commission had been established and made operative, the prime minister would still have retained the power to make appointments. The British model on which the Canadian system was based has in large part improved the quality of appointments in Britain by requiring persons to apply for these positions and then having the applicants screened for competence and qualifications by committees that are not themselves political. Nonetheless, the British system has not eliminated political patronage altogether, because the prime minister still gets to choose the successful applicant, even if he or she has to select someone from short lists of qualified candidates presented by these non-political committees.

The Accounting Officer System

As part of their proposals to strengthen accountability, the Conservative Party (2006, 13) pledged to "[d]esignate the deputy minister of each government department or agency as the Accounting Officer for that department. The deputy will be responsible to Parliament for the departmental spending and administrative practices of his or her department." The Conservatives considered this a way of responding to concerns that "the lines between ministers and non-partisan civil servants have been blurred, and clear lines of accountability need to be re-established" (Conservative Party 2006, 13). But in implementing the reform after being elected, the Conservatives only muddied matters even more, opening deputy ministers to further risk of politicization.

The promise of the accounting officer system is that designating particular areas of responsibility and accountability to be solely the domain of deputy ministers would have the effects of clarifying who is accountable and diminishing political interference in areas of responsibility that are formally recognized as being the statutory authority of deputy ministers. After the reform was adopted, the Harper government issued a "guidance" to support the reform that backed away from the stated intent of the reform. The guidance effectively argued "that formal adoption adds no new responsibilities and no change to the existing accountability relationships—essentially suggesting that nothing has changed, despite [related] new legislation and amendments to existing legislation" (Jarvis 2009, 526; see also Franks 2007). The result is to both elevate the deputies' accountability to Parliament and do nothing to protect them from political interference in the relevant areas of responsibility.

A Moderate Commencement

Many will decry the government's handling of its reform program as starkly disappointing, if not outright cynical, especially since many Canadians across a wide spectrum of political loyalties, not just Conservative supporters, welcomed the promises of reform in all these areas. But the change of heart, from being enthusiastic reformers while in opposition or during an election campaign to less than ardent implementers of reform after a successful election, is not unique to the Harper Conservatives.

Further, it is hardly realistic to expect such a broad reform agenda to usher in such hefty changes overnight. Notwithstanding Harper's disappointing reform effort to date, the ideas at the heart of the reforms were both good and noble and addressed the key issues, even if, in implementation, they did not turn out as hoped. This observation is not meant to justify Harper's choices or to minimize the defects of the reforms as implemented. Many of them were included in a so-called *Federal Accountability Act*, a bundle of several diverse measures rushed through the legislative process with indecent haste, which was nothing more than political posturing by the Conservative government. In some cases, subtle changes to proposed reforms occurred once the government took office, such as the changes in the personal accountability of deputy ministers before parliamentary committees. In other cases, the changes turned out to be merely rhetorical compared with what had been promised, such as the fixed election date promise. Other changes amounted to virtually nothing, such as promises to reform the access to government information regime. Or, as in the case of the PBO, they became the subject of government backtracking once they were in place.

Nevertheless, the adoption of these measures constitutes an important first step toward addressing real problems. No government is going to eliminate the PBO or get rid of fixed election dates, for example, even if it ignores or contravenes them. Over time, all of these reforms can be bolstered from their current state to become more meaningful.

Comparing Westminster Systems

It is commonly asserted by scholars and media commentators that the Canadian prime minister's power to enforce party discipline on MPs, including ministers, is the tightest and toughest in the Westminster systems. The result is a House of Commons where the governing party's MPs are permitted virtually no independence in the House or its committees. However, as discussed earlier and in more detail below, party discipline is part and parcel of responsible government in all of the parliamentary democracies.

Here we outline some of the important variations across the Westminster systems in the status and powers of prime ministers vis-à-vis their party caucus and the House of Commons. One must be cautious in interpreting comparative analyses, for practices in one system may not be easily transferable to another, even if the systems share the same basic structure. Comparative analyses, nonetheless, can be especially helpful in sorting out what is inherent in a particular type of system, such as the Westminster model of parliamentary democracy, and must be accepted, in contrast to what is a non-essential practice that could be reformed to improve the democratic foundation.

Great Britain

In Great Britain, the political culture gives high priority both to maintaining the prerogative powers of the Queen as "the Crown" separate from the powers of the prime minister, and to keeping the Queen separate from partisan politics. This culture has political effects because acting in good faith is widely accepted as a requirement of the unwritten British constitution. The contrast with Canadian political culture and experience is dramatic.

British prime ministers from both the Conservative and Labour parties have long had to tolerate a good deal of independence from their party's MPs. It has been quite normal in both parties to see important differences between two or more factions within their party emerge over contentious issues. The size of the British House of Commons, at 650 MPs, also contributes here in two ways. First, there are large numbers of MPs who know that they are never going to be ministers, even junior ministers. These are often experienced MPs who take their parliamentarian role quite seriously. Second, when the government has a large majority, as Tony Blair did, a significant number of government MPs can vote against government legislation, knowing that the legislation is still likely to pass. Consequently, prime ministers have developed and used the three-line voting system, described earlier in this chapter, which distinguishes between actual confidence votes and "free votes," and votes where the government takes a collective stance but allows its MPs to determine their own position. In the third case, the threat of the government being defeated on non-confidence if the government position fails to obtain a majority of MPs voting is understood by the House as a whole to have been removed. In this instance, a government's loss is a loss of face rather than a loss of confidence.

As a result of this system, British prime ministers have had to pay closer attention to the diversity of views among their caucus members or opposition members whose support is necessary to pass their legislative agenda. This evolution has reduced the prime minister's control over his or her party MPs, even though the norms of party solidarity remain as strong as ever, especially when the confidence of the House in the government is at stake. By using this threefold category of votes the government is able to allow its MPs more freedom than is found in Canada. Equally important, and unlike the Canadian media, the British media do not portray every vote against the prime minister's government by its own MPs as a failure of leadership on the part of the prime minister. The system has gotten them used to losses on government votes that are not about critical issues.

Many observers of British politics lament what they have long taken to be a decline of Parliament, in contrast to expanded prime ministerial and Cabinet control over governance. In fact, though, Britain has experienced a reinvigorated Parliament over the past two decades. This has occurred despite the fact that, as in Canada, prime ministers have increasingly centralized power under their personal control, reducing the importance of the Cabinet as a collective executive body. Even two long-serving and highly control-oriented prime ministers—Conservative Margaret Thatcher (1979–1990) and Labour Tony Blair (1997–2007)—experienced large numbers of their own party MPs consistently voting against government legislative proposals in the 650 MP-strong House of Commons. In Thatcher's case, this meant that a good deal of proposed government legislation never became law. In Blair's case, his parliamentary majority was so large that he could suffer the defection of dozens of Labour MPs on any one piece of legislation and still get a majority vote in the House, in some instances with opposition support. That British prime ministers must accept the fact that they cannot make all votes matters of confidence obviously requires them to tolerate a degree of MP independence as long as it does not bring down the government.

Even the British House of Lords has been refurbished. The details are complicated, given the historical evolution of the House of Lords, which at one time comprised only hereditary peers and bishops of the Church of England. Now there are also appointed peers, who constitute roughly 85 percent of the current membership of nearly 800 peers. Unlike the Canadian practice in Senate appointments, where all but an occasional token appointment are partisan appointments, one quarter of the British upper house consists of peers who are appointed for life by an independent House of Lords appointment commission and sit as non-partisan peers (that is, not as members of a political party). The result is that the governing party cannot expect to possess a majority in the House of Lords.[7]

It is also important to note that British prime ministers no longer possess unilateral patronage powers for appointments to the governing boards of a wide variety of non-departmental government agencies, commissions, and corporations. An independent Public Appointment Commission now plays the lead role in selecting persons for these positions, although the final decisions remain with the prime minister or another minister.

Finally, it should be noted that the caucus of the British Conservative Party has changed from a system whereby the caucus alone had the power to select and remove its leader, to a system that can involve the full party membership. Under the old rules, the caucus had the power to remove its party leader and select a new leader from the caucus, even when the party leader was the prime minister, as happened to Prime Minister Margaret Thatcher in 1990 when the caucus replaced her with John Major. The rules governing the selection of the party leader were altered in 1998. Now, while the Conservative caucus retains the power to dismiss a prime minister, the process is considerably more complicated and can take several weeks.

The Labour Party uses an even more complicated and drawn-out process for removing a party leader, with even more barriers to removing a leader who is prime minister. These rules effectively insulated Tony Blair from threats by Labour MPs who wanted to remove him. Even when Blair became highly unpopular in his caucus, he was as safe as any Canadian Conservative or Liberal prime minister.

---

7. The Conservative–Liberal Democrat government that came to power in 2010 has promised to pursue further reform of the House of Lords to make it an elected body.

Australia

The Australian experience is important to Canada for a number of reasons. It too has a Senate because, like Canada, it has a federal system of government. There the states (counterparts of the Canadian provinces) are represented equally by 12 senators. This principle of equal state representation in the Senate is counterbalanced, as one would expect, by the principle of representation by population in the lower house, called the House of Representatives.

Three factors have made the Australian Senate a powerful institution of Parliament. First, senators are elected, not appointed as in Canada. This effectively eliminates the prime minister's chief means of bestowing patronage upon those loyal to him or her. It also gives the Senate the required democratic legitimacy to effectively constrain the government. Second, the term of each senator is six years, with half the Senate elected every three years. This compares with the Australian House, which must be dissolved for a new election at least once every three years (compared with the Canadian written constitutional limit of five years).[8] Senators thus tend to be both more experienced than members of the House and relatively more independent of their party leadership. Third, the Senate is elected using a form of proportional representation, with the expected result that when there are three or more political parties contesting elections, the numbers of elected senators from each political party will be a reasonable approximation of the actual distribution of all votes for each party. In a competitive multi-party system, as has been the experience in Australia for almost all of the past four decades, this usually also means that no single party will obtain a majority in the Senate. When the government party does not have a majority in

8. Under a so-called double dissolution, where both the House and the Senate are dissolved, some senators may end up serving only three years before facing another election. Double dissolutions are used to resolve impasses between the House and the Senate under limited conditions set out in section 57 of the Australian constitution. It is quite a rare occurrence.

the Senate, it is inclined to pay greater attention to the views of senators, including those from its own party.

The relative power of the prime minister is affected by two further factors. First, both the government parties, the Liberal and Labor parties,[9] have retained the power of the party caucus of MPs to select and depose the party leader, including when he or she is prime minister, and then to select a new party leader who immediately becomes prime minister. This process unfolded in 2010 when Prime Minister Kevin Rudd was effectively deposed by the Labor caucus and replaced by the new Labor party leader and prime minister, Julia Gillard, all within 24 hours.[10]

Second, the Australian political culture has reinforced the tradition of Cabinet government as a collective executive. By contrast, recent prime ministers in both Canada and Britain have seriously diminished their Cabinets as important institutions of government. Even under Liberal Prime Minister John Howard (1996–2007), viewed by his opponents as a highly centralizing prime minister, the Cabinet system of collective decision making prevailed. It was not until his final year in office that Howard's efforts to stay in power by outflanking his own finance minister (called treasurer), and his chief rival within the government, led him more and more into the realm of a one-man government. Indeed, the downfall of his successor, Prime Minister Kevin Rudd, a short three years later in 2010, was due in large part to the fact that he ran a one-man government, bypassing the Cabinet on most important issues. A strong Cabinet system normally provides an important constraint on the prime minister from within the governing party.

---

9. The Australian Liberal Party is the main conservative party in Australia. It is usually aligned with the National Party, a smaller conservative party. In government, the two are often referred to as the coalition government, although "composite" party might be a more appropriate term since the two parties, once elected, tend to operate as a single party, with the prime minister in charge.

10. Rudd actually resigned because he knew that he did not have support in the party caucus to defeat the Gillard challenge.

New Zealand

In New Zealand, prime ministers had been as autocratic as recent Canadian prime ministers until 1996, when the country decided to adopt a system of proportional representation as its electoral system. Since then, there has not been one single-party majority government. Single-party minority governments and, more commonly under this new electoral system, coalition minority and majority governments, have changed the political dynamics between prime minister, caucus, and the House of Representatives.

The new semi-proportional voting system means that no single party has a realistic chance of getting the 50 percent of the total vote necessary to form a single-party majority government in a competitive multi-party system. This is unlike the Canadian system, where a single party in a competitive multi-party system can win a majority government with much less than a majority of the total vote, as the Liberals did in three successive elections, 1993, 1997, and 2000, and as the Conservatives did in 2011. In 1993, the Liberals elected 57.1 percent of the MPs with only 40.8 percent of the total vote; in 1997, 51.5 percent of the MPs with only 38.5 percent of the total vote; and, in 2000, 60 percent of the MPs with only 41.3 percent of the total vote. In 2011, the Conservatives elected 54 percent of the MPs with 39.6 percent of the vote. This is discussed in further detail in Chapter 5.

The end of single-party majority governments has revitalized the New Zealand House of Representatives. Its committees, for example, are stronger than they once were, no longer dominated by a government party majority that functions on the command of the prime minister. The Cabinet has also been strengthened vis-à-vis the prime minister by virtue of the fact that almost all Cabinets since 1996 have been composed of members from two or more parties, eliminating the ability of the prime minister to simply demand greater party discipline. As in Australia, the party caucuses of each of the two primary parties that have formed governments, National and Labour, have retained the power to remove their party leader even when prime minister. This last happened in 1997 when the conservative National Party caucus moved to dismiss Prime Minister Jim Bolger and replace him with Jenny Shipley. As did Prime Minister Kevin Rudd in Australia in 2010, Bolger resigned to avoid being voted out by his caucus.

New Zealand also has the most effective system of freedom of information among the Westminster systems (Hazell and Worthy 2010). Further, the prime minister's control over the public service was substantially reduced in 1988, when the effective power to appoint, supervise, and dismiss the chief executives of departments (the equivalent of Canadian deputy ministers) was assigned to the state services commissioner, an officer who operates separately from political direction. The senior ranks of the New Zealand public service are thereby staffed using the most politically independent appointment and dismissal system in the Westminster systems.

Conclusion

In Chapters 2 and 3 we described how Canadian prime ministers over time have come to be able to use the absence of clear and explicit rules in our unwritten constitution to abuse executive powers to whatever ends they think they can get away with electorally that will benefit their governing party. What some see as the flexibility in our constitution has never been anything more than the discretion of the prime minister to use the powers of the governor general to do whatever benefits the governing party. In this chapter, we have described how a prime minister's other executive powers, and powers as party leader (including over the careers, even the future careers, of the governing party's MPs, including ministers), combined with a prime minister's insulation from removal by the party caucus, have removed any effective constraint on him or her by the caucus or Cabinet. The personal and partisan interests of these MPs are too intertwined with those of a prime minister to produce opposition from this quarter. Rare indeed has been the MP willing to confront a prime minister on a matter of principle. Rarer still has been the MP who has had much of a career after any attempt to do so. The result of all of this is that there are few, if any, constraints on a prime minister running roughshod over the House of Commons and undermining parliamentary government—effectively turning the House into what one columnist recently described as a "sham" (Wherry 2011).

Public opinion as a constraint on a prime minister is a limited constraint at best. Indeed, politically informed prime ministers know very well that they can get away with abusing power and imposing excessive party discipline. The risk is minimal. Experts disagree on what the Canadian constitution means and thus render themselves collectively of no political consequence whatsoever. Too much of the media treat the abuse, including the abuse of the House of Commons, as merely part of a game, usually a dirty game at that, increasingly portraying abusive behaviour as simply tough leadership, if they pay attention at all. In any event, the public usually pays no attention, especially to what's happening in Parliament and its committees. Even on those few occasions when there appears to be a ripple of discontent, the lessons from history are that it passes quickly and has no lasting electoral effect. This has been the case even when the discontent is over an early election call that is seen as a cynical exploitation of the prime minister's power to call an election at a time favourable to the governing party. And it is especially so when the government is able to use public funds, rather than party funds, to launch advertising and campaigns promoting its policies.

In almost all respects, the Canadian prime minister has greater constitutional and political power than is the case in Great Britain, Australia, and New Zealand to abuse the democratic structure of responsible government and undermine its basic assumptions and foundations, namely, to scrutinize government legislation, administration, and performance and to hold it to account accordingly. The constitutional conventions and political practices of these jurisdictions demonstrate that the Canadian way is not the only or even the best way to realize the principles of responsible government. Our constitutional evolution and political practices have degenerated over time into a poorly defined doctrine and practice of what we can call "electoral democracy," in which the electorate decides on who forms the government and the prime minister then governs as a virtual autocrat until the next election. In this scheme, responsible government simply means counting party standings in the House after an election to see which party will be the government and providing for the rare occasion when the government loses the confidence of the House and the prime minister is able to call an immediate election. It is not surprising then that we have a less than robust system of parliamentary democracy between elections. As discussed in the next chapter, elections let the people decide who forms the government, but that decision is not enough to qualify the system as a democratic one.

References

Akin, David. 2011. Parliamentary secretaries compared: Some veteran MPs out; some rookies are in. May 25. http://davidakin.blogware.com/blog/_archives/2011/5/25/4824686.html.

Aucoin, Peter. 1993. The politics of electoral reform. *Canadian Parliamentary Review* 16 (1): 7–13.

Aucoin, P. 1995. *The new public management: Canada in comparative perspective.* Montreal: Institute for Research on Public Policy.

Aucoin, P. 2003. Independent foundations, public money and public accountability: Whither ministerial responsibility as democratic governance? *Canadian Public Administration* 46 (1): 1–26.

Aucoin, P. 2006. The staffing and evaluation of Canadian deputy ministers in comparative Westminster perspective: A proposal for reform. In Commission of Inquiry into the Sponsorship Program and Advertising Activities (Gomery Commission), *Restoring accountability: Research studies, Volume 1—Parliament, ministers and deputy ministers.* Ottawa: Public Works and Government Services Canada.

Aucoin, P. 2008. New public management and new public governance: Finding the balance. In D. Siegel and K. Rasmussen, eds., *Professionalism and public service: Essays in honour of Kenneth Kernaghan.* Toronto: University of Toronto Press.

Aucoin, P. 2010. Canada. In C. Eichbaum and R. Shaw, eds., *Partisan appointees and public servants: An international analysis of the role of the political adviser.* Northampton, MA: Edward Elgar.

Aucoin, P., and Turnbull, L. 2003. The democratic deficit: Paul Martin and parliamentary reform. *Canadian Public Administration* 46 (4): 427–449.

Carty, R.K., and L. Erickson. 1991. Candidate nomination in Canada's national political parties. In Herman Bakvis, ed., *Canadian political parties: Leaders, candidates and organisation*, Royal Commission on Electoral Reform and Party Financing Research Studies, 13:97–190. Toronto: Dundurn Press.

Cheadle, B. 2011. Tories re-brand government in Stephen Harper's name. *The Globe and Mail*, March 3. http://www.theglobeandmail.com/news/politics/tories-re-brand-government-in-stephen-harpers-name/article1929175/.

Commission of Inquiry into the Sponsorship Program and Advertising Activities. 2005. *Phase 1 report: Who is responsible?* Ottawa: Canadian Government Publishing.

Conservative Party of Canada. 2006. *Stand up for Canada: Conservative Party of Canada election platform.* Ottawa. http://www.cbc.ca/canadavotes2006/leadersparties/pdf/conservative_platform20060113.pdf.

Courtney, John. 1995. *Do conventions matter? Choosing national party leaders in Canada.* Montreal and Kingston, ON: McGill-Queen's University Press.

Foot, Richard. 2010. Only in Canada: Harper's prorogation is a Canadian thing. *National Post.* http://www.nationalpost.com/Only+Canada+Harper+prorogation+Canadian+thing/2446705/story.html.

Franks, C.E.S. 1997. Free votes in the House of Commons: A problematic reform. *Policy Options* (December): 33–36.

Franks, C.E.S. 2007. The unfortunate experience of the duelling protocols: A chapter in the continuing quest for responsible government in Canada. Paper prepared for the conference in honour of J.E. (Ted) Hodgetts, University of Guelph, September.

Harper, Stephen. 1997. Text of Stephen Harper's speech to the Council of National Policy, June. http://www.ctv.ca/CTVNews/SpecialEvent7/20051213/elxn_harper_speech_text_051214.

Harper, Stephen, and Tom Flanagan. 1997. Our benign dictatorship. *Next City* 2 (2) [Winter 1996–97].

Hazell, R., B. Worthy, and M. Glover. 2010. *The impact of the Freedom of Information Act on central government in the UK: Does FOI work?* Basingstoke, UK: Palgrave Macmillan.

Jarvis, M.D. 2009. The adoption of the accounting officer system in Canada: Changing relationships? *Canadian Public Administration* 52 (4): 549–568.

Martin, D. 2007. Tories have book on political wrangling. *National Post*, May 17. http://www.canada.com/nationalpost/news/story.html?id= 16b42ac1-56a5-429c-a013-d9464dce3de1&k=0.

Martin, Lawrence. 2010. *Harperland: The politics of control*. Toronto: Viking Canada.

Meissner, D. 2006. *Prime Minister Stephen Harper wants fixed dates for federal elections*. http://www.cnews.canoe.ca/CNEWS/Canada/2006/05/26/1599832 -cp.html.

New Zealand. 2008. *Cabinet manual*. http://cabinetmanual.cabinetoffice .govt.nz/node/68.

O'Malley, K. 2009a. Part one—Unprecedented or not? Memories of committee meltdowns past. *CBC Inside Politics Blog*. http://www.cbc .ca/news/politics/inside-politics-blog/2009/12/unprecedented-or- not---memories-of-committee-meltdowns-past-part-one.html.

O'Malley, K. 2009b. Part two—So, is this the death of the committee system as we know it? *CBC Inside Politics Blog*. http://www.cbc.ca/news/ politics/inside-politics-blog/2009/12/part-2---so-is-this-the-death-of- the-committee-system-as-we-know-it.html.

Parliament of Canada. 2011. *Indemnities, salaries and allowances: Members of the House of Commons*. April 1. http://www.parl.gc.ca/Parlinfo/Lists/ Salaries.aspx?Menu=HOC-Politic&Section= 03d93c58-f843-49b3-9653-84275c23f3fb.

Phillips, R. 2010. Young people disenfranchised in Australia's snap election. *World Socialist Web Site*, July 30. http://www.wsws.org/articles/2010/ jul2010/snap-j30.shtml.

Roberts, A.S. 2005. Spin control and freedom of information: Lessons for the United Kingdom from Canada. *Public Administration* 83 (1): 1–25.

Roberts, A.S. 2010. Right to information: Need for an enforcement strategy. *Accountability Forum*, January 13. http://accountabilityindia.blogspot .com/2010/01/right-to-information-need-for.html.

Samara. 2010. *The accidental citizen?* http://www.samaracanada.com/ downloads/Samara_Report_The_Accidental_Citizen.pdf.

Samara. 2011. *"It's my party": Parliamentary dysfunction reconsidered*. http://www.samaracanada.com/downloads/ItsMyParty.pdf.

Savoie, Donald. 1999. *Governing from the centre: The concentration of power in Canadian politics*. Toronto: University of Toronto Press.

Simpson, Jeffrey. 2001. *The friendly dictatorship*. Toronto: McClelland & Stewart.

Smith, D.E. 2007. *The people's House of Commons: Theories of democracy in contention.* Toronto: University of Toronto Press.

Smith, Jennifer. 1999. Democracy and the Canadian House of Commons at the millennium. *Canadian Public Administration* 42 (4): 398–421.

United Kingdom. Cabinet Office. 2010. *Coalition agreement for stability and reform.* http://www.cabinetoffice.gov.uk/sites/default/files/resources/coalition-agreement-may-2010_0.pdf.

Wherry, Aaron. 2011. The House of Commons is a sham. *Maclean's,* February 18.

CHAPTER FIVE

Letting the People Decide: When Elections Aren't Enough

Introduction: Toward a Robust Democracy

Elections are a necessary, but not sufficient, condition of a robust democracy. Where the government—with the prime minister and Cabinet as the political executive—is not elected directly, the people's directly elected representatives in the House of Commons must select the government. In the Canadian democratic system, MPs determine who forms the government by deciding which political party (or parties, if the government is a coalition) has the confidence of a majority of MPs. In parliamentary democracy, a government must have the confidence of the House to govern. The responsibility of the people's elected MPs to perform this vital function is an essential and necessary element of the parliamentary system of responsible government; it is the mechanism that grants a government democratic legitimacy and it reflects what should be an immutable principle: the House must decide. This role cannot be replaced by a reliance on elections alone. As we will demonstrate, doing so would turn our democracy into the worst possible form of elected dictatorship. If we desire the direct election of the government as the political executive, change is possible, but institutional changes that establish a system akin to the American presidential–congressional system would be necessary.

The processes of parliamentary democracy associated with selecting a government function with limited challenge when a single party wins a majority government. By virtue of having won the majority of seats in the House, and assuming the normal operation of party solidarity, the governing party will enjoy the confidence of the House until the next election. Yet even under majority government, the situation can be far from ideal in terms of democratic legitimacy. This is the case when the governing party has won a majority of the seats in the House but has secured less—and at times far less—than 50 percent of the total votes cast. In this case, the issue in terms of democratic legitimacy is not the fairness of the system, as many electoral system reformers argue. All parties, after all, are competing within the same rules. Instead, the issue is the inaccuracy inherent in the first-past-the-post voting system when there are more than two competitive parties. The same inaccuracy can occur with minority governments, but it is most blatant when a party with less than 40 percent of the total or *popular* vote has a secure majority in the House, as occurred with Liberal Prime Minister Jean Chrétien's second majority government in 1997 (38.5 percent) and Prime Minister Stephen Harper's majority in 2011 (39.6 percent).

In minority government, the matter of commanding the confidence of the House and the legitimacy to govern can be more complicated, both following an election and between elections. Canadians have rarely experienced major problems immediately following an election when the party with the most seats does not have a majority. In every instance but one, the party with the most seats either stayed on as the government, as the Martin Liberal government did in 2004, or replaced the government that had been in power, as the Harper Conservatives did when they replaced the Martin Liberals in 2006.

Notwithstanding this pattern, convention actually has it that the government at the time of dissolution has the right to meet the House to determine whether it can command confidence. The sole exception to the standard practice occurred following the 1925 election when Liberal Prime Minister Mackenzie King stayed on as prime minister, despite his Liberals coming in second to the Conservatives, who had won the most seats, though not a majority. King secured sufficient support from the MPs of a third party, the Progressives, and a few independent MPs, to govern for several months.

The more serious problem with minority government, as practised in Canada, concerns the operation of the confidence convention. In Chapter 3, we discussed the obstacles facing MPs in removing confidence in a sitting government, even in a minority government. These obstacles include the capacity of the prime minister to manipulate the parliamentary calendar to postpone votes of non-confidence. Even if opposition MPs do vote, the prime minister has the power to obfuscate whether the opposition's vote is actually recognized as a vote of non-confidence. The prime minister can achieve the former by controlling the schedule of so-called opposition days. If shuffling opposition days isn't enough,[1] the prime minister can, more draconically, prorogue Parliament. And, of course, the prime minister can also call a snap election to shut down Parliament altogether.

Beyond these opportunities to create obstacles and confusion, a new challenge to the traditional understanding of the confidence convention has emerged: a challenge to the possibility of a change of government between elections—in other words, a change of government without

---

1. During the 39th and 40th Parliaments, the Standing Orders were amended to constrain the government's capacity to reschedule opposition days. The changes required at least one opposition day for any 10-day sitting period, inhibiting the ability of the government to put off all opposition days to the end of a supply period. It should be pointed out, however, that this arrangement expires at the end of 2011. See Standing Order 81(10)(a): http://www.parl.gc.ca/information/about/process/house/standingorders/chap10-e.htm.

an election. This position has not been outlined in any great detail, but Prime Minister Harper and other Conservatives, as well as some academics and other observers, have staked out a claim to deny the legitimacy of any party seeking to form a government when it has not "won an election." The basis of their position is that voters must grant democratic legitimacy to the prime minister and government, and that voters can do this only through elections. If we are to accept this, it also follows that a prime minister who has lost the confidence of the House some time after an election and the start of a new Parliament—even on the Speech from the Throne—should never resign but always call an election. This would effectively alter the confidence convention in two ways. First, the governor general would lose the discretion of the Crown's prerogative powers to refuse dissolution. Second, the primacy of the confidence convention and the House's primary function, to form and terminate governments, would be diluted.

The appeal of this election-only perspective is reinforced in part by the failure of constitutional experts, pundits, and politicians to agree on how and when to use the governor general's reserve powers in protecting and upholding the constitution of responsible government. They also, increasingly, even if unintentionally, accept the virtual right of the prime minister to dissolve Parliament, and to call an election, when the prime minister's government has lost the confidence of the House.

This chapter provides a brief overview of why elections in a parliamentary system are necessarily an indirect mechanism of selecting the government. It then reviews how elections function with single-party majority governments and single-party minority governments. This includes a brief discussion of the limits of the Canadian voting system in providing the best possible degree of democratic legitimacy for the prime minister and government. The chapter next discusses differing opinions on the democratic and constitutional legitimacy of changes in government between elections. Finally, it considers the implications for the theory and practice of responsible government in a parliamentary democracy of relying exclusively on elections for government formation.

The Canadian Single-Member-Plurality Electoral System

Under the Canadian system of parliamentary government, citizens do not directly elect the prime minister and the government. This is not unique to Canada. Parliamentary systems worldwide rely on elections during which citizens elect parliamentarians who then determine who will be the prime minister and government. Only in some presidential systems is the chief executive—usually called the president—directly elected.[2]

Our electoral system is called the *single-member-plurality* (SMP) system. It has two components: MPs compete in single-member constituencies and the candidate with the most votes (a plurality) is elected. It is more popularly known as the *first-past-the-post* system to indicate that the winning candidate only has to get the most votes, not a majority of votes. (This term leaves out the single-member component by simply taking it for granted.)

In directly electing their members of Parliament to the House of Commons, voters in the 308 constituencies across Canada vote overwhelmingly for the candidates representing the main political parties in the House. They do this for a good reason. As discussed earlier, the standing of parties in the House after an election has come to be the means whereby voters select, albeit indirectly, the party that forms their

---

2. Even in the American system, where the president and two houses of Congress (the House of Representatives and the Senate) are elected separately, voters do not directly elect the president. While American citizens may consider themselves to be voting directly for the presidential candidate of their choice, in casting their ballots they are actually electing the members of an Electoral College, who *then* elect the president. The system appears to be one of direct election because the members of the Electoral College vote according to the votes cast by citizens. In some rare cases, including the 2000 presidential election, the Electoral College vote may not reflect the popular vote. But for our purposes here, it is important to note that the Electoral College could be replaced by direct election without distorting the relationship between the executive and legislative branches of American government. That would not be the case in a parliamentary system.

government, either in terms of which party first attempts to form government or how the House will extend or withdraw confidence. With the exception of one election, no more than 5 percent of voters have ever voted, in a single election, for parties that did not elect at least one MP.

The one exception was the 2008 general election, when the Green Party received nearly 7 percent of the popular vote across Canada without electing a single MP. We also need to note that, until the 2004, 2006, and 2008 elections, the parties represented in the House gained at least 95 percent of the total vote in every election since 1867. The success of the Green Party in achieving popular support but not winning seats in these recent elections points to the inevitable effect of the current electoral system. In each constituency, only one candidate can win. When, as in Canada at present, there are as many as five competitive parties, the effect is highly likely to result in disproportionate seat distribution for each party in comparison with the total votes received for all a party's candidates across the country.

The Democratic Legitimacy of Election Outcomes

Of the Westminster parliamentary systems in Australia, Britain, Canada, and New Zealand, the SMP system is used in Canada at both the federal and provincial levels and in Britain for elections to the House of Commons. Great Britain soundly rejected altering the first-past-the-post system for the House of Commons in a referendum held May 5, 2011. In contrast, Australian parliamentary elections for the federal House of Representatives and Senate, and state legislative bodies, as well as for New Zealand parliamentary elections, do not use the SMP system. They use different electoral systems that seek to provide a greater degree of proportionality between the party preferences of voters and the parties' share of seats in the various parliamentary bodies.

The results of the SMP system can be controversial for the democratic legitimacy of the government in a competitive multi-party system such as Canada's. The reason is that the electoral success of the government party is partly due to the distorting features of the SMP voting system itself. The governing party may win a secure majority of the seats but not come close to obtaining even a simple majority of the total votes cast across the country. Since the end of the Conservative and Liberal two-party system in 1921, only 3 of the 16 majority governments that have been elected have actually held a majority of the popular vote:

- the Conservatives in 1984 won 75 percent of the seats with 50.03 percent of the total vote;
- the Conservatives in 1958 won 78 percent of the seats with 53.7 percent of the total vote; and
- the Liberals in 1949 won 73 percent of the seats with 50.1 percent of the total vote.

In the other 14 cases, the elected majority government failed to win the majority of the total vote. Critics of SMP call these results "false majorities." The SMP system exaggerated the electoral success of the winning party in each instance. For example, the Liberals under Jean Chrétien won three successive majority governments:

- in 1993, they won 60 percent of the seats with only 41.3 percent of the total vote;
- in 1997, they won 51.5 percent of the seats with only 38.5 percent of the total vote; and
- in 2000, they won 57.1 percent of the seats with only 40.8 percent of the total vote.

And with Canada's most recent majority, in 2011, Stephen Harper won a majority government with 54.1 percent of the seats and only 39.6 percent of the total vote. An increase of less than 2 percent of the total vote in the 2008 election, which led to a Conservative minority government, delivered 23 additional seats, an increase of 16.8 percent.

In one extreme case—the 1979 election—the SMP system even reversed the relationship between the number of seats won by two parties and the percentages of their total vote. In that election, the Conservatives won 136 seats, 22 more than the Liberals' 114 seats, even though the

Liberals won a greater percentage of the total vote (40.1 percent to 35.9 percent) than the Conservatives.

A more recent example of the distorting effect of SMP, this time for a party other than the governing party, occurred in the 2008 election with the Green Party case noted earlier.

While one could draw on numerous examples of this phenomenon, one of the most profound, for its longer-term implications, was the 1993 election. The Reform Party, led by Preston Manning, was able to capitalize on its western Canada concentration to turn its nearly 2.6 million votes into 52 seats, mainly in BC and Alberta. In contrast, the Progressive Conservatives were decimated in the same election, retaining only 2 seats in the House, even though the party received nearly 2.2 million votes spread across the country.

In the 1997 election, the emergent Reform was able to use the momentum from 1993 and their time as an opposition party to vault into the role of official Opposition, just crossing the 2.5 million vote threshold, and increasing their seat count to 60. Again, in contrast, the PCs increased their popular vote tally by nearly three times the amount the Reform Party had, falling slightly short of 2.5 million votes. Yet, while the PCs significantly increased their share of seats in the House in 1997, they only managed to increase the total to 20 seats. The results marked a dynamic shift in the balance of power among parties of the right in Canadian electoral politics and had significant implications for "uniting the right" in 2003, which resulted in the creation of the Conservative Party of Canada.

Critics are unmoved by the argument of SMP defenders that the system secures majority government better than all other electoral systems used by other parliamentary democracies. They also usually point out that the record of SMP in producing majority governments in Canada, even with false majorities, is not that great, given the number of minority governments we have had in the past 50 years (these include 1962, 1963, 1965, 1972, 1979, 2004, 2006, and 2008).

We do not need to engage in a debate over the merits of different electoral systems here to highlight a serious problem for parliamentary democracy when the effects of SMP come under attack. The problem is that when a minority of voters elects a majority government, the democratic legitimacy of the resulting government is less than what it would be when a majority of voters elects a majority government. When the difference is not great and the governing party comes close to winning 50 percent of the vote (that is, in the mid to high 40 percent range), SMP's effects can be deemed acceptable, even welcomed by some. However, the greater the difference between the total percentage of the vote for the majority party and the number of seats it has won, the lower its democratic legitimacy.

Forms of Party Government

When a single party has won the majority of seats in the House, the formation of government is straightforward. After a general election, if the prime minister's party "wins," there is no change of government. The "re-elected" government simply carries on. On the other hand, if the prime minister's party loses to another party that has won a majority of the seats, the prime minister resigns and the governor general invites the party leader with a majority to form the government and become prime minister. As we commonly say, the old government has been "defeated," and a new government "elected." In both cases, the practice of party solidarity means that a government party with the majority of MPs on its side has the confidence of the House, and it can be assumed that it will not lose this confidence.

When no single party wins a majority of seats, the situation can be more complicated. If the prime minister's party holds the most seats but not a majority, the government can stay as government and seek to govern in one of two ways. First, it could govern as a single-party minority government as long as it secures sufficient support from one or more opposition parties (and/or independent MPs if there are any) to have the confidence of a majority of the House. This is what Prime

Minister Stephen Harper did after the 2008 election. It is what every Canadian prime minister in this situation has done.

The second option, never taken up by a Canadian prime minister, is to form a multi-party coalition government with one or more other parties, which becomes part of the government. If, together, the parties in the coalition have a majority of MPs, the coalition government would be a majority government, as was recently formed after the 2010 election in Great Britain. How secure the coalition would be depends on the willingness of the two or more parties to compromise and collaborate with one another. If the combined number of MPs in the coalition were less than a majority, the coalition government would then be a minority government, with the insecurity that minority government entails. The advantage of a minority coalition government in this instance is that it would be stronger than a single-party minority government, though it would still require support from other parties or independents in the House. Both kinds of coalition governments—minority and majority—have been formed in New Zealand over the past two decades. (See the accompanying table for a summary of all the governments formed in New Zealand since the adoption of a system of proportional representation.) It is important to emphasize the option of *coalition minority government*, since both the media and academics in Canada, at least before the 2008 proposed Liberal–New Democrat coalition that would have been a coalition minority government, have assumed that coalition governments are, by definition, majority governments.

When no single party wins a majority and the prime minister's party comes second, the norm in Canada has been for the prime minister to resign and the leader of the party with the most seats to form a single-party minority government. This is what happened after the 2006 election when Prime Minister Martin's Liberals came second to the Conservatives under Harper. Again, no incoming prime minister in this situation has ever sought to form a coalition government.

But, as previously discussed, one prime minister refused to resign. In 1925, Prime Minister King's Liberals came second to the Conservatives,

NEW ZEALAND GOVERNMENTS UNDER MIXED-MEMBER PLURALITY

Years	Government	Type	Time needed to form	Notes	Mode of termination
1996–1998	National–NZF	Majority coalition	8 weeks	• Coalition only held 61 of 120 seats	Coalition broke down Aug 1998
1998–1999	National	Single-party minority	N/A	• After coalition breakdown, National Party governs as single-party minority	Scheduled election
1999–2002	Labour-Alliance	Minority coalition	Within 2 weeks	• Minority coalition government with support of non-coalition Green Party • Government triggers election several months earlier than required, leading to some consternation when Alliance Party splinters and Green support for government falters	Early election called
2002–2005	Labour–PC	Minority coalition	2 weeks	• Minority coalition government with support of non-coalition United Futures Party results in stable minority	Scheduled election
2005–2008	Labour–PC	Minority coalition	1 month	• Minority coalition government with support of non-coalition United Futures and New Zealand First parties results in stable minority	Scheduled election
2008–	National	Single-party minority	11 days	• After winning 58 of 122 seats, National Party elects to form single-party minority, support from the ACT, United Future, and Maori parties	TBD

Adapted from Yong (2010).

yet were able to continue to govern by gaining the support of a sufficient number of opposition MPs to have the confidence of a majority in the House.

As the practice has evolved in Canada, confidence in a single-party minority government, whether continuing or new, has simply been assumed until the minority government opens the new parliamentary session with the Speech from the Throne. The Speech presents the government's plan for governing for the parliamentary session to follow. How specific and detailed the plan is will vary from government to government. The debate on the Speech from the Throne has always been subject to a confidence vote, and this vote is the first de facto opportunity to signal the House's confidence, or lack of confidence, in a new government. No minority government in Canada has ever been defeated on its initial Speech from the Throne; however, six minority governments have been defeated at a later point in their tenure: in 1925, 1963, 1974, 1979, 2005, and 2011.

We will return to the issue of what happens after the defeat of minority governments later in this chapter. Here we simply conclude by noting that since voters in Canada do not directly elect the government, elections cannot be expected to always resolve the issue of who should form the government. Voters may elect no one party with a majority of MPs. In such a case, there is no outright "winner." In the absence of a method for electing the government directly, and thus separately from the election of MPs to the House of Commons, the "will of the people" can only be understood in terms of to whom the House awards its confidence. Of course, the standing of each of the parties that represents the decisions of the people will play a significant role in how confidence is exercised, but any interpretation other than how the House awards its confidence demands speculative interpretation of electoral results. The House must decide. Everyone, including the prime minister of a minority government, should respect the fact that the people have not chosen to have one party constitute a single-party majority government and the different governing arrangements that may follow.

Minority Government in Canada

Canada's experience with single-party minority government has been varied. The two Diefenbaker Progressive Conservative minority governments in 1957–58 and 1962–63 are best categorized as the bookends of his 1958–1962 majority government. The 1979–80 Clark Progressive Conservative minority government was barely out of the starting gate when it lost confidence through the defeat of its first budget. The Pearson Liberal minority government of 1963–1968 and the Trudeau Liberal minority government of 1972–1974 are regarded as more substantial experiences, not just because they lasted longer but also because they produced a considerable number of important and lasting public policies, including universal health care and the Canada Pension Plan. In contrast, the Martin Liberal minority government of 2004–2006 and the Harper Conservative minority government of 2006–2011 have been characterized as dysfunctional and were certainly fractious. All these portraits are relative but they illustrate that minority government can produce quite varied results depending on the political dynamics at play.

Although the performance of governments and parliaments is always, in some measure, in the eye of the beholder, the Pearson and Trudeau cases are clearly preferable to the Martin and Harper cases for those who see democratic virtue in minority government. Proponents of single-party minority government consider it preferable to single-party majority government because, as Peter Russell (2008, 161) argues, "Under minority government, the leaders of the governing party must take parliament seriously *all* the time." The range of potential benefits cited by proponents of minority government include:

- compromises by the government on items included in its main governing agenda in order to secure passage of legislation and maintain the confidence of the House;
- responsiveness to proposals emanating from one or more opposition parties that the government deems it can live with;
- enhanced government responsibility and accountability so as to maintain its public support;

- greater space for individual MPs to fulfill a role as legislators; and
- greater chance that the work of committees will be consequential in scrutinizing the conduct of government and in reviewing government legislation. (See Russell 2008.)

Taking Parliament seriously can mean a variety of things to different people, including acting in line with its principles and practices, such as those noted above. Or it can mean just the opposite. It can mean engaging in tactics designed to limit the effectiveness of Parliament, such as withholding necessary information. It can also mean playing chicken or brinkmanship with the opposition through the lingering threat of an election as a means of furthering the government's agenda. That threat is constant if it is assumed that the prime minister can call an election whenever the timing looks good for the government or whenever the opposition defeats the government on a vote of non-confidence. As is discussed later in this chapter, the "games" that can be played by the prime minister and the opposition depend at least in part on the rules. Most important, if the prime minister knew that an alternative government could be formed from the opposition without an election any time following the defeat of the government, the games to be played by the prime minister would be dramatically riskier and, quite likely, altered and/or reduced.

The politics of minority government are also determined in part by the political complexion of the competing parties in government and in opposition, and the fragmentation of the opposition. (See the accompanying graph for a summary of the composition of the House of Commons in Canada between 1968 and 2011 following general elections.) In the Pearson and Trudeau minority government contexts, for example, the Liberals needed only the support of the NDP for a majority in the House. In Martin's case, the support of the NDP was not sufficient for a majority. While the Liberals and NDP have hardly been bedfellows over the years, they are at least better able to find a common point of reference on a range of policy matters than parties from opposite ends of the political spectrum.

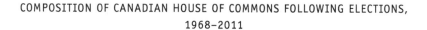

COMPOSITION OF CANADIAN HOUSE OF COMMONS FOLLOWING ELECTIONS,
1968–2011

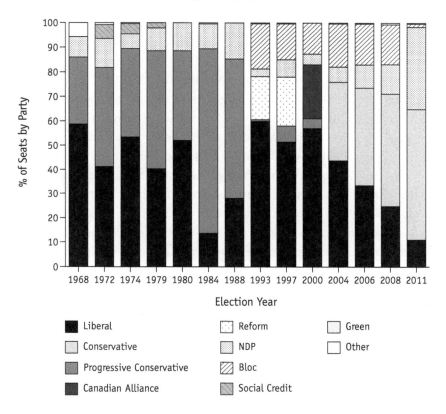

By contrast, prior to the 2011 Harper majority, the Harper minority context was one where the Conservatives had no natural bedfellows. Ironically, the closest party in terms of ideology was the Liberal Party, but it is also the perpetual adversary of the Conservatives, and was seen, before the 2011 election, as the only other contender capable of forming a single-party alternative government (Flanagan 2010). Further, between 2006 and 2011, the Liberals and the NDP did not have enough MPs between them to defeat the government. They needed the Bloc Québécois to join them to bring down the Harper Conservatives, as happened in March 2011. From 2006 to 2008, the Conservatives required either the Liberals or the Bloc to vote with them—or at least not against them—in order to maintain the confidence of the House. To stay in power from 2008 to March 2011, the Conservatives required any one of the three opposition parties to vote with them or at least not vote against them.

Without a natural bedfellow, however, almost all accommodations between the Harper Conservative government and the opposition parties during that time occurred on a case-by-case basis. In this context, especially given Canadian prime ministers' de facto constitutional powers, including the power to dissolve Parliament even after losing confidence, the likelihood of a productive minority government experience is diminished. Compromise is not required. Another election can always be called to attempt to pound the other parties into submission.

Notwithstanding the appeal minority government holds for some as an antidote to the spectre of single-party majority government running roughshod over Parliament and parliamentary processes, the recent Canadian minority government experience made clear the limits of minority government for constraining a government. In part, the ineffectiveness of minority government as a constraint reflects the continued treatment of minority government by politicians, especially Conservatives and Liberals, as an occasional exception to a majority government norm. This ignores the fact that Canadian elections have resulted in eight minority governments over the past half century; indeed, Canada is above average internationally in this regard (Russell 2008). Kaare Strøm (1990), in a 15-country study of minority governments between 1945 and 1987, found that the relative frequency of minority government in Canada was higher compared with the other countries in the study.[3]

Nonetheless, politicians still tend to see minority government as a temporary situation, one election away from a majority government. This explains why Pearson called a snap election in 1963, following the

---

3. It should be noted that neither New Zealand nor Australia was included in Strøm's study.

Liberal win over the Progressive Conservatives in 1962; why Trudeau called an election in 1968 as soon as he took over from Pearson (in addition to the fact that he was the new Liberal prime minister); why Trudeau engineered his own defeat in the House in 1972 so that he could then call an election; and why Harper called the 2008 election. Of course, not all these political moves were successful: both Pearson in 1965 and Harper in 2008 failed to secure a majority.

On the other side of the House, the expectation of easily defeating a languishing minority government, after having fallen from being a majority government, can bring the leader of the Opposition to seek to dismiss the government in the House on a confidence vote. This was the case when the Pearson Liberals in opposition moved to bring about the defeat of the Diefenbaker Progressive Conservative government in the House in 1963, resulting in the election that brought Pearson to power. The same thing occurred in 2005 when Conservative opposition leader Harper moved to bring down the Martin government, resulting in the 2006 election that brought Harper to power.

Recently, University College London's Constitution Unit, which specializes in comparative constitutional reform research, issued a report drawing on the minority government experiences of Canada, New Zealand, and Scotland, as well as the historical experience of Britain. As the title *Making Minority Government Work* suggests, the report was intended to provide practical advice to a range of actors in anticipation of a potential "hung parliament" (as the British call a parliament in which no single party has a majority) in the May 2010 British general election. As it turned out, the election did produce a result where the British Conservatives won the most seats but not a majority. Following the resignation of Gordon Brown, the Labour prime minister, whose party came second, David Cameron, the Conservative leader, opted to form a coalition majority government with the Liberal Democrats rather than try his hand at single-party minority government.

The report notes that Canada stands in stark contrast to the experience elsewhere. As University College London's Constitution Unit put it:

> A strongly majoritarian culture still treats minority administrations as the exception to the rule, … [even though] the party system has diverged from two-party dominance. … As a majoritarian system manqué, Canada therefore offers important lessons to the UK, though given the perceived failure of the most recent minority administrations, this may be more in the form of cautionary tale than exemplar. (Paun 2010, 15)

Even if there is plenty of blame to be shared by all four parties for the state of parliamentary behaviour in Canada, since 2006 Prime Minister Harper bore much of the blame for the lack of collaboration between the government and opposition parties. Brinkmanship, tight party discipline, and unilateralism have been described as his dominant modes of governance (see, for example, Martin 2010; Flanagan 2010). Harper declared nearly all government legislative proposals to be matters of confidence despite his 2006 campaign promise to diminish the scope of confidence votes and allow government MPs to vote according to their conscience or constituency interests. And, in 2011, Harper's Conservative government was found in contempt of Parliament for having withheld the financial details of its "tough on crime" agenda. Harper later dismissed the historic contempt finding as merely part and parcel of "the game of democratic politics," suggesting that "you win some, you lose some," even though no government in any of the Westminster systems, whether minority or majority, had ever been held in contempt before (Gardner 2011).

Most curiously, in October 2007, Harper declared the novel view that the government would consider the opposition's having allowed the government's Speech from the Throne to survive a confidence vote to be "an endorsement of its agenda." He went further by insisting that the opposition had to allow the government's legislation to pass without having seen its details. The logic he offered was that, "This Parliament must get done what it was elected to do" (Prime Minister of Canada 2007), ignoring the reality that voters had elected a majority of MPs who did not belong to the Conservative governing party, and that it was the duty of those MPs to scrutinize the government's decisions, actions, and legislation, and to reject them where they thought it was in the country's best interest.

In any event, Harper provoked a continuous game of chicken, because each opposition party had to calculate the political risks of opposing government legislative proposals. One of the things that the government had wanted to avoid was being portrayed as triggering an "unnecessary election." It especially did not want to cause an election at any point in time when public opinion polls were less than optimal. For the most part, Harper's tactics worked well for him: the three opposition leaders continuously took the bait. While there was no guarantee that a minority government would get to implement its agenda, the opposition leaders, at the same time, engaged in their own game of chicken by threatening non-confidence, only to be forced later to back down at the last moment for fear of public opinion, leaving themselves open to being (rightfully) criticized for not fulfilling their role in scrutinizing the government responsibly.

Changing Governments Between Elections

In the Westminster model of responsible parliamentary democracy, changing the government without an election has always been considered a possible outcome following the defeat of a government on a vote of confidence. If the prime minister resigns following a defeat in the House, the Queen or the governor general must ensure that another government is formed. The expectation is that the Queen or governor general calls on the leader of the official Opposition to form a government. If the new government can secure the confidence of the House, it carries on as government until the next election, whenever that might occur. If the new government cannot secure the confidence of a majority, an election has to be held immediately. When this occurs, the new government formed from the opposition remains as the government, pending, of course, the election outcome in the normal manner.

Other than mid-19th century British experiences in the early evolution of responsible government, and the King–Byng case in 1926, changes in governments between elections have become essentially theoretical. In the Canadian experience, with one exception, no prime minister has ever resigned following a defeat on confidence. Instead, they have all opted to call an election, with the approval of the governor general. Again, the noted exception was that of Liberal Prime Minister King in 1926, although he had not been defeated in the House. Rather, he re-signed after Governor General Byng denied his demand for an election, to escape being defeated. The governor general then asked the leader of the Opposition, Arthur Meighen, to form a new government with-out an election.

In the absence of recent experiences with the conventions regarding changes of governments between elections or clear rules whether and in what circumstances it is ever acceptable for a governor general to refuse the dissolution request of a prime minister who has lost the confidence of the House, allowing for a change of government between elections has become subject to the most disagreement and controversy.

The near defeat of the Harper Conservative government on a vote of non-confidence in December 2008—a vote ultimately postponed by Harper's first controversial prorogation—immediately brought what had been a theoretical possibility to the level of a pressing, practical question of constitutional democracy. The reason was twofold. First, although the government had secured the confidence of the House when the House did not defeat it on the Speech from the Throne, this first parliamentary session since the 2008 election had begun only weeks earlier. Second, and more critical, the three opposition parties had joined forces not only in stating their intention to defeat the government, but in calling on the governor general to ask the Liberal leader of the Opposition, Stéphane Dion, to form a new government without an election. The NDP had agreed to be a partner in a Liberal–NDP coalition government and the Bloc Québécois had agreed to support the pro-posed coalition on matters of confidence for 18 months. In this circum-stance, another election would not be necessary for a change in government to take place; however, in all likelihood, this would have required the governor general to refuse a call by Harper, as the defeated prime minister, for an election instead of a change of government.

Threatened with losing power, Harper not only prorogued Parliament but also launched an aggressive campaign to turn public opinion against the coalition effort. The hyperbole hit its peak when Conservative MP Daryl Kramp pronounced on the proposed coalition's effort to unseat the government and to seek the approval of the governor general to govern in its place:

> This is over the top now. *This is a coup d'état.* It makes us look like a banana republic. The only difference here is there's no blood, thank goodness. (Whittington, Campion-Smith, and MacCharles 2008; emphasis added)

Other Conservative MPs sang from the same song sheet. Professor Tom Flanagan, a former Conservative campaign manager, supplied the scholarly rhetoric. Flanagan (2009, 13) is worth quoting at length to outline the basic tenets of the Conservatives' version of the constitution:

> The coalition's apologists glory in the supposed fact that Canada's Constitution is not democratic. Responsible government, they say, means only that the cabinet has to maintain majority support in the House; it doesn't mean the voters have a voice. ...
>
> Canada has inherited the antiquated machinery of responsible government from the pre-democratic age of the early 19th century, when most people couldn't vote and political parties were only parliamentary cliques. ...
>
> Canada changed from a constitutional monarchy to a constitutional democracy as the franchise was extended to all adults and political parties became national in scope. ...
>
> The most important decision in modern politics is choosing the executive of the national government, and democracy in the 21st century means the voters must have a meaningful voice in that decision. Our machinery for choosing the executive is not prescribed by legislative or constitutional text; rather, it consists of constitutional conventions— past precedents followed in the light of present exigencies. ...

That means that, in the area of choosing the executive, the Constitution, for all practical purposes, is whatever the Governor-General says it is; there is no appeal from vice-regal decisions. But that doesn't mean the Governor-General is a free agent; she has a responsibility to make her decisions within the Constitution, including those "underlying principles" identified by the Supreme Court.

How, then, should Michaëlle Jean decide if the government is defeated over the budget? Arguably, a new election would be called for, even though it would only be five months after the last election. Gross violations of democratic principles would be involved in handing government over to the coalition without getting approval from voters. ...

The Governor-General, as the protector of Canada's constitutional democracy, should ensure the voters get a chance to say whether they want the coalition as a government. They haven't yet had that chance.

Beyond the political rhetoric intended to keep the Conservatives in power, something else was evident in the reaction that followed the events leading up to the 2008 prorogation, and not just from the Conservatives. That reaction exposed the gaping holes of the Canadian constitution: the absence of a few clear, firm, and binding rules guiding the most fundamental aspects of the Canadian constitution has led to a high level of disagreement on our constitutional conventions for determining what the governor general should or should not decide and under what conditions.

Among the contested terrain, a debate among experts and commentators has broken out over the constitutional and democratic legitimacy of a new government assuming power without an election. Setting aside the question of the legitimacy of the Bloc Québécois having a say about who governs Canada, Conservative rhetoric declared that a change of government without an election was illegitimate (a *coup d'état*) and undemocratic (a banana republic).

The debate persisted even after the expected defeat of the Conservative government did not occur. One group of scholars was called together by University of Toronto professors Peter Russell and Lorne Sossin, who produced an edited volume of their individual papers under the title *Parliamentary Democracy in Crisis*. The group did not include anyone making the case that the Conservatives advanced, that the only people who could decide who forms the government are voters. Even still, there was no agreement among this group of experts on some critical questions, including the appropriateness of the governor general's granting of prorogation. Andrew Potter (2009b), *Maclean's* columnist and blogger and former *Ottawa Citizen* national news editor, took the group to task for failing to offer an explanation of the crisis that recognized the perspective that voters should play a more direct role in selecting the government. In a post on his *Maclean's* blog and later in a review he penned for the *Literary Review of Canada* of *Parliamentary Democracy in Crisis*, Potter argued (2009a, 2009c) that two clear positions had emerged in midst of this crisis. He labelled them the *parliamentarians* and the *democrats*.

The *parliamentarian* position—a group he suggested "includes almost every academic in the country"—was said to be premised on a strict and literal commitment to the basic tenets of the Westminster parliamentary system:

> that we elected a parliament, not a party or a president; that parliamentary coalitions are unremarkable in all sorts of civilized countries; and that Harper's Conservatives had clearly lost the confidence of the House, with a stable government waiting to take over.

Potter contrasted this position with what he termed the *democrat* position:

> that while the coalition may be constitutionally ok in a narrow, legal sense, it violates basic principles of democratic legitimacy. (Potter 2009a)

While Potter may well have captured the sentiments at the core of the opposition to the idea of a change in government without an election, his designation of the opposing sides as *parliamentarians* and *democrats* constitutes a false dichotomy. To accept that the *parliamentarians* are not democrats requires interpreting the tradition of British parliamentary democracy as undemocratic. Like Flanagan, Potter has to assume that responsible government is, in principle and in practice, fundamentally flawed, deficient, or lacking in some critical democratic respect.

Differing Opinions

Nonetheless, Potter's distinction between *constitutional* and *democratic* legitimacy offers a valuable means of systematically considering the differing perspectives on changes of government between elections. It is possible to compare the differing opinions through a basic framework based on two dimensions, reflecting two questions that allow us to better understand the actual arguments being made.

The first dimension represents a dichotomy: *Can a governor general constitutionally refuse the request for dissolution of a prime minister who has lost the confidence of the House, thus allowing for a change of government between elections?*

The second dimension asks the question: *Democratically, should a governor general refuse a prime minister's request for dissolution, allowing for a new government to be formed from the opposition parties without a new election?* This dimension is most appropriately understood as a continuum, so it is possible to plot a number of differing perspectives along this horizontal axis.

The accompanying chart offers a visual representation of these two dimensions and the array of opinions.

It is important to note that the framework is not merely a theoretical construct; it is driven by expressed opinions. While the boundaries between the two dimensions are at times blurred, mostly due to the fiery rhetoric with which opinions on the matter have been expressed, the framework still allows for a more refined understanding of the differing perspectives on this issue.

As can be seen, few individuals actually occupy a position in the lower half of the framework, arguing, in effect, that the governor general *constitutionally cannot* refuse the advice of the prime minister, even after the prime minister has lost the confidence of the House. Among these individuals are constitutional scholars Henri Bruni (2008), Edward McWhinney (2009), and Guy Tremblay (2008) (see also Cyr 2011 and

DIFFERING OPINIONS ON CONSTITUTIONAL AND DEMOCRATIC LEGITIMACY

Constitutional Legitimacy: *Can a governor general refuse a prime minister's request for dissolution?*

Democratic Legitimacy: *Should a governor general refuse a prime minister's request for dissolution?*

		Democratic Legitimacy		
		Should Not	**Could Under Unclear Conditions**	**Should Under Specified Conditions**
Constitutional Legitimacy	Can	Flanagan (2009) Bliss (2008) Potter (2009)	Hogg (2008) Coyne (2008, 2011) Fox (2011)	Forsey (1953) Heard (2009) Franks (2011)
	Cannot	Bruni (2008) McWhinney (2009) Tremblay (2008)		

MacDonald and Bowden 2011). To accept this position is to assert that the governor general does not possess the prerogative power to refuse the prime minister's request for an election or to call on an opposition leader to form government.

Nearly all other academic experts, pundits, and politicians allow that changes in government between elections are *constitutionally* legitimate. But perspectives differ as to whether and when they are also *democratically* legitimate. At least three distinct positions can be identified in the Canadian context.

On the upper left of the continuum, or axis, are those who argue that, while the governor general *constitutionally can* refuse the request for dissolution of a prime minister who has lost the confidence of the House and invite the leader of the Opposition to form a government if he or she can command the confidence of the House, the governor general *democratically should not* do so. This category best accommodates the perspective—that we must have elections to select governments—shared by Tom Flanagan (2009), as discussed above, and Michael Bliss (2008), who argued that the coalition would require "some kind of electoral mandate from the Canadian people." It also accommodates Andrew Potter's view that only outcomes that are supported by the people are democratically legitimate, which implies that we must have elections to change governments.

Potter (2009b) asserts the coalition's lack of public support by citing public polling conducted at the time of the crisis suggesting that Canadians disapproved of the coalition taking power without an election. It goes without saying that we cannot—in any formal way—rely on polls to assess the legitimacy of governments formed through democratic elections and in accordance with the constitution. Polling results can be very different from pollster to pollster, invite questions and criticism of methodology and can be—indeed, as discussed below, have been—quite volatile. Short of introducing a referendum to ensure support for any government formed following an election, the only way to ensure legitimacy in accordance with this view is to treat elections—as Flanagan and Bliss directly endorse—as mechanisms for choosing *governments* rather than *parliaments*. Potter's view empowers parties, rather than individual MPs or Parliament as a whole, by seeing government as the entitlement of the party that has won the most seats. It only follows logically from this line of argument that if the party loses confidence, then the people must elect a new "party."

Most Canadian academics, pundits, and politicians can be grouped in a third category slightly to the right of the middle of the continuum. They argue that while a governor general *constitutionally can* refuse a request for dissolution and allow for a change in government between elections, he or she *democratically could* only under certain circumstances. However, they do not indicate any clear requirements to guide this practice. Those included in this category cite a range of factors that would determine

whether such a change in government would be democratically legitimate. Because of the circumstances, many of the relevant comments were
made with reference to the proposed Liberal–NDP coalition of 2008.
For example, both Peter Hogg (2010) and Andrew Coyne (2008) have
raised the issue of stability. Hogg has said that while former Governor
General Michaëlle Jean could have refused the prime minister's request,
she ultimately made the correct decision, given how quickly the coalition
fell apart following prorogation. Coyne (2011) has also expanded his list
of considerations: "There's nothing wrong with coalitions in principle.
But not every coalition is the same. What made the coalition of 2008 so
dubious were the particulars of the situation: the weakness of the Liberals,
the absence of a credible leader, the potential for blackmail given the
Liberals' palpable fear of another election, and most of all, the involve-
ment of the Bloc." Others have been considerably murkier in their
thinking, suggesting, as Graham Fox does, that the governor general
needs to consider whether a potential government enjoys sufficient
legitimacy and public support, without indicating how the governor
general should make that kind of calculation (quoted in Scoffield 2011).

Setting aside the issue of the Bloc, we argue that this approach is
untenable. Beyond the basic reality that there is not, and has not been,
a constitutional demand for such considerations, without firm rules the
governor general, likely in the midst of political drama, is required to
arbitrate on an ad hoc basis what is and is not politically appropriate,
directly inserting himself or herself into partisan politics and opening
the office of the governor general to partisan attack. Further, issues like
stability and others cited by many of those in this category invite speculation and subjective interpretation. For example, there is no way to
know how long a Liberal-led coalition with the NDP would have lasted
and how good or poor the resulting governance would have been (what
would be the baseline for such a judgment?).

In the absence of binding rules or guidelines, there is no way to
govern the behaviour of the prime minister or governor general or to
establish clear expectations among the public. This approach falls short

of the New Zealand *Cabinet Manual*, which has effectively removed the governor general from the negotiations that determine who forms the government. Even more important, this approach is inherently undemocratic. It will be left to the personal discretion of an appointed governor general to decide when a change in government is acceptable.

Moving more to the right on the upper half of the continuum, a fourth position can be identified: that a governor general *constitutionally can* and *democratically should* refuse a request for dissolution and allow for a change in government between elections under at least one specified condition. This encompasses the positions of experts, including the late Eugene Forsey (1953), Andrew Heard (2009), and Ned Franks (quoted in Scoffield 2011), who have advocated a much clearer rule to guide this practice. They stipulate that they think it is both constitutionally permissible and democratically legitimate to refuse the request for dissolution of a prime minister who has lost confidence shortly after the most recent election. However, of those that accept this position, the commonly accepted standard is suggested to be within six to nine months (Cyr 2011), which still means the governor general must exercise discretion to decide on the outer time limit.

While, collectively, these four categories represent the main positions held in the ongoing Canadian debate, they do not canvass the entire waterfront in Westminster or other parliamentary democracies. Both the British government's proposed fixed parliamentary term legislation and the New Zealand *Cabinet Manual* go further. Both suggest that not only constitutionally *can* a new government be formed without an election, but indeed a new government *should* be formed between elections after a loss of confidence when an alternative government could garner the support of majority of MPs. The UK bill, currently at the "Ping Pong" stage, fixes the terms of Parliament at five years with elections to fall on a specified day. The bill allows for two ways in which an early election could be triggered: if a motion of no confidence is passed and no alternative government is found within two weeks; or if a motion for an early dissolution is approved by two-thirds of MPs (or without division). Four principles comprise the protocols prescribed by the New Zealand *Cabinet Manual*:

1. The prime minister has no virtual or actual right to a dissolution of Parliament and new election on loss of confidence in the House.
2. The governor general should ask the opposition party leaders whether they can form a government that can gain the confidence of the majority of the House.
3. The governor general should not intervene politically in any negotiations between these opposition leaders or exercise discretion in the formation of a new government.
4. An election should only result where no alternative government can be formed with the support of the majority in the House.

When a government loses confidence, there is no logical reason to dissolve the entire House since, in this circumstance, we do not need a new House of Commons; rather, we need a new government. Parliamentary systems allow elected representatives to choose a new government on their own when they no longer have confidence in the incumbent. The principle is that neither the prime minister nor the governor general should decide: the House must decide.

The Election-Only Option: The Logic and Consequences

If there is a significant distinction to be made here, it is not between Potter's two categories of parliamentarian and democrat. It is between those who adhere to the classic view of parliamentary democracy and those who advance an essentially *populist* critique and alternative. The classic view of parliamentary democracy is that popular sovereignty lies with the people, who elect their representatives to the House of Commons, with the government being formed from and by the House, and the crucial role of political parties, both in elections and in the House, is acknowledged.

For their part, populists would share Potter's complaint that there is "a founding defect in the Canadian constitution, which is that 'the people' do not get a mention, and much of the functioning of Parliament amounts to the executive and our elected representatives doing what they will and simply inviting the public to 'trust us'" (Potter 2009a). This sentiment echoes classic populism in the long-standing Canadian tradition of popular discontent with the status quo: a distrust of elites (political, economic, and judicial) and, in particular, a disdain for disciplined political parties in the legislature, which are subject to tight control by party leaders, especially the prime minister. For example, Aucoin (1993, 8) notes that Canadian populism, "with its conception of a 'true democracy, government by "the people,"'" was never entirely extinguished however. It regained its status as a contending reform movement in the first part of this century, particularly on the prairies, and has once again re-emerged as a vital political force. As with the first wave of democratic populism earlier in this century, this pole of political thought extends across the partisan political spectrum, encompassing elements of what otherwise would be considered both the left and right spectrums of Canadian politics." Historically, these "radical reformers" have pushed for proposals, including:

- MPs voting freely, as their constituents wish or their consciences demand;
- MPs being subject to "recall" elections when they stray from the interests and views of constituents who elected them as their "delegates" to the legislature;
- the use of binding referendums and "citizen initiatives" so that citizens themselves get to vote on matters of proposed legislation; and
- procedures that allow citizens to put their proposals on the political agenda. (See Smith 1999.)

The dispute between parliamentarians and populists simply comes down to competing visions of democracy. Parliamentarians accept that a new government may be formed between elections because every government, including those formed or maintained immediately after an election, achieves its legitimacy from the people through the MPs that the people directly elect. Populists demand a more direct measure of legitimacy, relying exclusively on the standings of the political parties in the House of Commons, which result directly from the election.

It is critical to understand that the principle that underlies the "election-only" method for deciding which party leader will become the prime minister—that the will of the people must be strictly adhered to if the government is to be legitimate—demands more than just elections as the basis for determining which party will form the government. Within the parliamentary system, this principle would be predicated entirely on the people electing MPs who are the officially recognized candidates of registered political parties, because political parties would constitute the mechanism that enables voters to directly choose the prime minister as the head of the government. No other intervening players, such as the governor general or MPs (individually or as a party), could deviate from the election result by calling on or expressing confidence in anyone but the party leader with the most seats to form government.

To this end, political parties would be required to have absolute party discipline in order to ensure that party candidates, once elected as MPs, not be permitted, individually or collectively, to change the decisions of voters in any way. The House of Commons would not be able to bring about a change of government following a loss of confidence by the government, with a new government that had the support of a majority of MPs. Further, if the principle that a government can gain the legitimacy to govern only through elections is to be truly meaningful, a number of other fundamental departures from traditional and current practices ought to follow. They would include, for example:

- under no circumstance would MPs be permitted to cross the floor because that would change the result of the voters' choice of a party's candidate in their constituency;

- MPs would be required to vote their party's position whenever it is enunciated by their party leader in order to adhere to the electoral choice of those who voted for their party; and
- MPs who failed to vote as required would need to be expelled from the House, thereby causing a new election to be held in their constituency.

But this is where the capacity of the parliamentary system to provide such a direct measure of democratic legitimacy breaks down: confidence votes would always have to adhere to the electoral choices of voters so that the prime minister's government is not supported by opposition parties. If a party with a plurality did not have a majority, it could not garner confidence, except in cases where parties campaigned on forming a multi-party coalition government and had already designated a prime minister. In any other circumstance, the MPs of other parties who were supporting a minority government would be ignoring the voters' electoral choices. They would thus contravene the ability of voters to "choose" who governs them, in the same way as forming a coalition without having campaigned for it would. Likewise, a coalition of parties that campaigned with the intention of forming a coalition government if their parties elected the most MPs would be required to form such a government if they won, unless they did not intend to follow the will of those who voted for them.

Of course, those who demand elections as the only way of earning democratic legitimacy presumably do not intend all these changes. Since none of the proponents of the elections-only position has produced an explicit outline of what it would require in practice, we do not know precisely what they have in mind. However, since they build their case on voters voting for parties, we must assume that absolute party discipline would then become the primary feature of Canadian parliamentary democracy, locking party leaders, their parliamentary parties, and all MPs into the straitjacket of election results. In which case the party leaders might as well be casting the votes of their party's MPs.

What else could the election-only option mean in a parliamentary democracy? If MPs, individually, and/or collectively as parties, are allowed the room to respond to changing circumstances as they see fit, we are simply left where we are now: that MPs are able to exercise discretion as our representatives, with the exception of being able to decide who should govern between elections. This substantially waters down the basic principle that gives the election-only option its claim to democratic legitimacy—the requirement that prohibits MPs and parties from departing from what voters have decided, expressed in the number of seats or votes awarded to parties.

If one were willing to compromise the democratic integrity of the election-only option, a rule could still be enacted stating explicitly that a government defeat in the House required an immediate election. This would mean that the prime minister could not resign following the defeat of the government, even if he or she wanted to do so. The electorate would have to have the right to choose its government.

Harper himself has embraced this watered-down version of the election-only option. Speaking in London at a press conference on June 3, 2010, along with newly installed UK Prime Minister David Cameron, whose own Conservative Party formed a coalition government with the Liberal Democrats following the 2010 election, Harper held forth:

> David and I were discussing this—I think the debate in Britain was instructive. There was an interesting period of a few days when people discussed the various constitutional issues that were involved and the various constitutional options but I think in the end, the verdict of public opinion was pretty clear which was that losers don't get to form coalitions. Winners are the ones who form governments. ... The coalition in Britain—I think it's important to point out—was formed by the party that won the election and, of course, this coalition in Britain doesn't contain a party dedicated to the breakup of the country. And these were the two problems in Canada. The proposition by my opposition was to form a coalition for the purposes of excluding the party that won the election and for the purposes of including a party dedicated to breaking up the country. (Akin 2010)

Since then, Harper "has argued repeatedly that if his party has the most seats, his party should form the government" (Scoffield 2011). Of course, as a description of past practice Harper has been playing fast and loose with the facts here: one of the "losers" (the Liberal Democrats) was included in the British coalition government; the British coalition government was formed immediately after the 2010 election, whereas the proposed Liberal–NDP government would have replaced a government defeated in the House; and the Bloc Québécois was never intended to be a party in the Liberal–NDP coalition government. Further historical Canadian and international parliamentary experience makes clear that there exists no requirement that only the party with the most seats or votes forms the government. But Harper's statement wasn't just intended as description; it was a normative statement intended to influence future practice. His emphasis on his Conservative Party as the "winning party" and the government being formed by "the party that won the election" made it clear that he regarded the democratic legitimacy of the government as deriving exclusively and directly from voters.

How Public Opinion Changes

There is an obvious logic to Potter's (2009b) point that nobody stays happy for very long with a system that consistently produces outcomes that do not have widespread support, regardless of how much tradition that system represents. This is the same sentiment felt by those who advocate for a change from our SMP electoral system to some type of "proportional representation" electoral system so that the number of MPs elected by each party is reasonably proportionate to each party's actual share of the total vote.

The question of legitimacy will always be determined in part by the politics of the day. For example, Potter argued (2009b) that our biggest problem was "not that Canadians didn't understand how their system works; it is that a large number of Canadians saw how their system works and recoiled in horror." He pointed to public opinion polls conducted at the time of the 2008–9 crisis suggesting that Canadians strongly disapproved of the coalition. One polling company, Ipsos (2008b), released polling results on December 5, 2008 that reported that: "Six in ten Canadians (60 percent) 'oppose' the newly declared Coalition of the Liberal, New Democratic and Bloc Québécois Parties, compared with 37 percent who support the coalition" and "almost two thirds (62 percent) of Canadians indicate that they are 'angry' (39 percent very/23 percent somewhat) with the coalition's attempt to take over power from the governing Conservatives."

The politics of the day in this instance included the Conservatives' success in convincing some citizens that the coalition government would include the Bloc Québécois, that the Bloc was not a legitimate partner in a government coalition (or even a supporter of a minority government), and that the formation of a new government without an election was either unconstitutional or undemocratic or both. As Prime Minister Harper argued, "The Opposition has been working on a back-room deal to overturn the results of the last election without seeking the consent of voters. They want to take power, not earn it" (Fitzpatrick and O'Neill 2008; see also Franks 2009). This serious misrepresentation of our parliamentary system presumably had its intended effects, result-ing in considerable concern among the electorate. Looking back, it is easy to forget how tumultuous the period actually was at the time. In-deed, "almost three quarters (72 percent) of Canadians indicate that they are truly scared for the future of the country with what is going on in Ottawa" (Ipsos 2008b).

Given Canadians' feelings of unease about the idea of a new gov-ernment taking power without an election, support for the populist position that an election should be required—however fleeting that support might be—should come as little surprise. First, there has not been a mid-term change in the governing party since 1926, and that instance, as we have discussed, was controversial then and is still the subject of disagreement today. Second, notwithstanding Potter's asser-tion that Canadians' lack of knowledge of the parliamentary system was not influential in their reaction, polling at the time suggested that 51 percent of Canadians believed the prime minister is directly elected (Ipsos 2008a), which is hard to reconcile with Potter's claim. Third, constitutional experts have not provided a clear and unambiguous declaration on what is constitutionally possible and proper when the opposition proposes a change of government without an election, following the defeat of the government in the House.

In addition, of course, there has never been a coalition government as was proposed by the Liberals and NDP in 2008. At the federal level, Canadians have experienced only single-party government, whether a majority or a minority government. And, finally, Stéphane Dion, the Liberal leader who would have become the prime minister of the Liberal–NDP coalition government, had already agreed to step down as party leader, and mere months before had promised not to enter into a coalition with the NDP.

In this context, Prime Minister Harper was only too happy to deride the coalition's efforts as nothing short of an unconstitutional and undemocratic coup designed to hand power to the separatist Bloc Québécois. For their part, the Liberals and the New Democrats struggled mightily to counter all of these obstacles, but any hope of securing much in the way of democratic or social legitimacy had already gone up in flames.

Not long after the resumption of Parliament, however, new polls suggested Canadians' feelings had "evolved, with 50 percent of respondents favouring a coalition government, while 43 percent are happier with the current Conservative government" (Leblanc 2009). Approximately six months later, another poll report stated that "despite the apparent weariness with minority governments, the poll suggested that slightly more Canadians—45 percent versus 42 percent—would support the idea of a coalition government after the next election" without having to make clear the possibility of a collaboration prior to an election or any stipulations about its membership (Canadian Press 2009). And by the 2011 election campaign, those in favour of and those opposed to a coalition were statistically tied, with slightly more individuals preferring a Liberal–NDP coalition than a Harper majority (Ipsos 2011). This hardly affirms the view that "a large number of Canadians saw how their system works and recoiled in horror."

To the degree that we are dissatisfied with the parliamentary process for determining who forms the government or the capacity of MPs to change governments without an election, we require fundamental changes in the institutional designs of our democratic system. And this, of course, should require a rethinking of our understanding of democracy in Canada as a parliamentary system. As Harper himself once suggested, we should perhaps consider the direct election of the government in a manner akin to the American system. The direct election of its president is separate from the election of Congress—in order to create "a more powerful and independent executive, not dependent on the short-term whims of the legislative parties" (Harper 2000, 48). We do not come to this conclusion, or endorse it, because we think that our parliamentary system can be reformed to meet the requirements of modern democracy and contemporary governance.

Elections and Parliamentary Governance

As discussed earlier in this chapter, in a parliamentary system elections serve only as an indirect mechanism for selecting governments, but they are a direct means of selecting a parliament, whose primary task is to select a government. In this way, elections build the basis for parliamentary governance as representative democracy. The system provides for a government that is formed by and from the House of Commons but that operates as the executive branch of government, with some considerable independence from the legislature to manage the affairs of state. At the same time, the prime minister and Cabinet have the responsibility to propose to Parliament new or amended legislation to address public policy issues and to develop and present to Parliament fiscal and expenditure budgets for raising and spending public money in order to administer and deliver public services and enforce the law and regulations.

For their part, the House of Commons and Senate have the responsibility to review and report on all government proposals and give or withhold approval; to scrutinize government administration; to question ministers on their conduct as well as the conduct of their political staff and public servants; to hold ministers to account; and thus to pass judgment on the performance of the government, ultimately providing or withdrawing their confidence in the government. These responsibilities fall primarily on the opposition parties and their MPs in the House of Commons and its committees. Although there is a long tradition of some Senate committees doing excellent work, the fact that the Senate is not an elected body diminishes its democratic legitimacy, especially when it passes judgment on the government or rejects its legislation.

As important as the free press and mass media, a vigilant citizenry, and well-organized interest groups are to a modern democracy, there is no substitute for a well-performing legislature. Even with our written constitution and the power of courts to strike down legislation and executive action as unconstitutional, including infringing on the rights prescribed by the *Charter of Rights and Freedoms*, the courts can only react when citizens or governments bring cases before it. It is only the legislature that has the constitutional authority to constrain, check, and control the government on a continuous basis. That is why tyrants are so quick to shut down the legislative branch of government, with its official opposition to the government, whenever they can.

And as critical as legislatures are to democratic government, it does not automatically follow, even in developed parliamentary democracies such as Canada's, that parliaments at work are necessarily edifying or inspiring spectacles. No one in Canada seems impressed by the House of Commons at work—in Question Period, in Commons' debates, or in Commons' committees. Indeed, the House is subject to much public disdain (see, for example, Wherry 2011a; Samara 2011).

There are several reasons why the House performs its critical functions so poorly, but partisan politics in the House is not one of them. Partisanship is to robust democratic politics what competition is to an open economic marketplace. Partisanship flows from the fundamental democratic right to have one's own political views, to organize politically with others of similar views, and, most important, to stand in opposition to others, whether these others are in power or not, and in the majority or not. This is why the opposition to the government in the British parliamentary system is called the "Loyal Opposition." In opposing the government, it is not committing sedition, treason, or subversion against the state. On the contrary, it is performing a crucial democratic function. The opposition is recognized as legitimate in its criticism of the government.

Partisanship inherently entails criticism of other parties and their members. And criticism is usually, if not always, negative. It is invariably personal, at least when one is criticizing another person's views, positions, actions, and/or conduct. Emotions are involved when views are strongly held and strong words are used. Further, it is not the opposition's responsibility to help the government achieve its partisan policy objectives. Partisans disagree not only on methods but also on objectives. Occasionally, when partisans agree on a policy objective, but differ on how best to achieve the objective, there can be an effort on all sides to reach a compromise that will enable the government to pursue its policy objective. On most matters, however, policy objectives are themselves in dispute, or the objectives and the methods are too interconnected to be separated, and the opposition will oppose them, as it should. It is offering the public another option.

As we argued in the first chapter, any efforts to improve democracy by eliminating partisanship are doomed to failure. The entire parliamentary process is predicated on partisan politics, which sees institutionalized adversarialism as the best means of securing democracy. Partisanship is an essential dynamic of public accountability in our democratic system.

However, it should be noted that partisanship does not require the mindless squabbling, nasty name calling, mean-spirited personal attacks, deliberate punching below the belt, and blatant misrepresentation of what others have said or done that has come to mark the common perception of Parliament at work in Canada, and that is ultimately discrediting the institution. Demonstrating one's rudeness, incivility, absence of manners, narcissism, and, invariably, lack of sense of humour has nothing to do with partisanship. Question Period and other House business, as currently enacted, are derided as time wasted by MPs and any citizens or media watching or listening, with good reason.

What is much more damaging to democracy occurs when one or more parties and their leaders deliberately, as a matter of partisan strategy and tactics, seek to discredit the parliamentary process in order either to stop citizens and the media paying attention or to impede parliamentary scrutiny. When strategies or tactics are used to this end, it is almost always the prime minister and government at fault. The government is the party that benefits when the principal public forum of the opposition is in disarray, dismissed as dysfunctional or merely a venue of "partisan" games or "bickering," and/or ignored by citizens. From this partisan vantage point, the ideal is to have the House and its committees meet as infrequently as possible, accomplish as little as possible, and, ultimately, to have Parliament itself lose credibility. Proroguing Parliament for partisan advantage is merely an extension of this strategy.

The effectiveness of the House is undermined by a flawed constitutional arrangement that, applied in the context of minority government, allows the prime minister to effectively act on a political incentive to keep the House in a state of permanent election campaigning. Beyond proroguing Parliament to escape scrutiny, the prime minister is able to call an election whenever the timing appears good. The prime minister has two options: (1) call an election, not having been defeated in the House, or (2) engineer the government's own defeat by provoking the opposition parties to unite against the government with one or more measures that they cannot possibly support. The advantage of the first option is that the prime minister totally controls the timing; its disadvantage is that the prime minister risks being criticized for intentionally causing what might be an unwelcome election.

Of course, the permanent election campaign of the minority government context also includes the possibility that the opposition parties can bring about an election by voting non-confidence in the government.

And, as stated earlier, recent opposition parties have only been too happy to engage in their own version of brinkmanship. They have threatened non-confidence votes conditioned according to their own interpretation of "good timing," given that the prime minister gets to call an election if defeated and would invariably do so, as opposed to any firm judgment of the propriety and performance of the government. As Aaron Wherry (2011b) has noted: "If there's one thing that has most made a mess of the last three years it is this. That an election might result becomes the dominant factor in every discussion and every debate. It is the prism through which the events around Parliament are understood. It defines and dictates news coverage. Political leadership becomes a test of manhood based on one's ability to force his rivals into difficult spots."

The point here is that since parliamentarians' primary responsibilities include scrutinizing government performance and administration and extending and withdrawing confidence as they see fit (that is, holding government to account), the government's ability to disrupt their ability to do so, including through calling early elections, undermines parliamentary governance. Elections have long been celebrated as the ultimate accountability mechanism—the chance, as they say, to "throw the rascals out."

While elections are an important mechanism of accountability, accountability also requires investigation, and forcing the government of the day to provide information about its decisions, behaviour, and policies—an account. In their role as opposition, members of Parliament have an obligation to not only extract those accounts, but also to scrutinize them. The problem with an overreliance on elections as a mechanism of accountability is that they often disrupt the opposition's ability to fulfill this duty, with potentially grave consequences for the efficacy of our parliamentary system:

> Without robust parliamentary scrutiny the system can easily slide into what commentators like to label an "elected dictatorship," namely, a parliamentary government where the Prime Minister operates without

significant checks and balances from the legislative assembly of the people's representatives. (Aucoin and Jarvis 2005, 72)

When the House of Commons is able to be sidelined—in addition to normal concerns about opposition incompetence or ineffectiveness—in scrutinizing the government's administration and conduct, the government is able to operate in greater secrecy. As Harper (2005) put it so clearly when leader of the Opposition:

> Information is the lifeblood of democracy. Without adequate access to key information about government policies and programs, citizens and parliamentarians cannot make informed decisions, and incompetent or corrupt government can be hidden under a cloak of secrecy.

Voters rarely, if ever, have full information when they cast their ballots. That means people are forced, at times, to vote in the dark, which inhibits their ability to fully hold the government to account. Worse still, they can be seen as having afforded it legitimacy, when, had they been better informed, they might well have voted differently, even to the point of electing a different government.

Conclusion

Normally, elections are held only once every few years to allow citizens to decide who should represent them in the House of Commons and thereby determine who forms the government. In doing so, voters also hold the government to account and pass judgment on the government, its policies, and its conduct in governing. Elections are the foundation of democracy. In the Westminster system, elections, traditionally, are an indirect mechanism of selecting a government. Instead of directly electing a prime minister or governing party, Canadians vote for local party candidates, and the government is formed by, and from, the House, either as a single-party majority or minority, or as a majority or minority multi-party coalition.

Beyond legitimate complaints about how the first-past-the-post electoral system translates voter intentions into disproportionate party seat counts, this system of selecting governments works with little complaint when a single party is awarded a majority of seats in the House and holds a firm grip on power. However, in cases where no single party wins a majority of seats—a common, and increasing, reality in Canada—the selection of governments is more complex and has become much more contested, especially in regard to the legitimacy of governments formed between elections.

Unlike New Zealand, Australia, and Britain, the option of the opposition forming a government with the backing of a majority of MPs but without an election occurring has likely become the most hotly contested aspect of the constitution. Even what might or should happen in Canada if the government were ever defeated on confidence on the Speech from the Throne—the first opportunity for a confidence vote—is completely uncertain, because there is no Canadian rule, no agreed upon Canadian convention, and therefore no convention. There is no definitive guidance from any Canadian source. Nor, despite much heaping of praise on the Canadian constitution's supposed "flexibility" and "evolutionary character," is there even a clearly stated principle, democratic or otherwise. Instead, a range of opinions has emerged as to what should happen, and under what conditions.

Prime ministers have come to exercise excessive control over the formation and dismissal of governments, in order to protect or advance the partisan political interests of the governing party. Relying on the personal discretion of an appointed governor general to constrain a prime minister from abusing those powers, as some continue to advocate, is an equally problematic solution, given the high level of disagreement on our constitutional conventions for determining what the governor general should or should not decide and under what conditions.

In failing to invest these powers concretely in the House, we weaken its ability to fulfill its role of scrutinizing the government and extending or retracting its confidence in the government as it sees fit. Instead, the prime minister is not only able to decide when the government has lost the support of the House of Commons, as discussed in earlier chapters, but also to dissolve Parliament and seek a new election at his or her discretion, even when he or she no longer has the confidence of the House. Concentrating those powers in a single individual does not belong in a robust democracy.

The best that the parliamentarians or so-called traditionalists can agree to is that whatever happens is presumably what should have happened! On the other hand, the election-only view is clear: an election would have to be held.

Minority government, in recent experience, is inherently incapable of providing for effective parliamentary government. The 2011 Conservative majority government obviously altered the scene but it merely returned us to the pre-2004 status quo. It did not address the capacity of the prime minister to abuse the powers of prorogation or dissolution. And, barring other reforms, it did not address the long-standing problem of the government majority in the House and in committees of abusing majority rule to diminish the effectiveness of parliamentary governance, especially in committees. A change to our electoral system might help, if New Zealand is a case from which to learn, but even then proportional representation and the embracing of coalition governments have not completely removed the power of the PM to secure an early dissolution solely to serve partisan interests. More, then, is required. In Chapter 6, we turn to how the current imbalance in power between government and Parliament might be corrected.

References

Akin, David. 2010. In his own words: Harper on coalition governments. June 3. http://davidakin.blogware.com/blog/_archives/2010/6/3/4543939.html.

Aucoin, Peter. 1993. The politics of electoral reform. *Canadian Parliamentary Review* 16 (1): 7–13.

Aucoin, Peter, and Jarvis, Mark D. 2005. *Modernizing government accountability.* Ottawa: Canada School of Public Service.

Brun, Henri. 2008. La monarchie réelle est morte depuis longtemps au Canada. *Le Soleil*, December 4. http://www.cyberpresse.ca/le-soleil/opinions/points-de-vue/200812/04/01-807282-la-monarchie-reelle-est-morte-depuis-longtemps-au-canada.php.

Canadian Press. 2009. Canadians growing weary of minority governments: poll. July 13. http://www.ctv.ca/CTVNews/QPeriod/20090713/minority_govenment_090713/.

Cheadle, Bruce. 2011. Big bucks: Harper government's ad buy costs taxpayers $26 million. *Winnipeg Free Press*, March 13. http://www.winnipegfreepress.com/breakingnews/harper-governments-latest-ad-campaign-costs-taxpayers-26-million-117897189.html.

Coyne, Andrew. 2008. Notes on a crisis: The coalition is not illegitimate, just ill-advised. *Macleans.ca*, December 3. http://www2.macleans.ca/2008/12/03/notes-on-a-crisis-the-coalition-is-not-illegitimate-just-ill-advised/.

Coyne, Andrew. 2011. Iggy's coalition problem. *Macleans.ca*, March 25. http://www2.macleans.ca/2011/03/25/iggys-coalition-problem/.

Cyr, Hugo. 2011. *The dissolution of Parliament: Memo for workshop on constitutional conventions*. David Asper Centre for Constitutional Studies, February 3–4. http://www.aspercentre.ca/Assets/Asper+Digital+Assets/Events+and+Materials/Constitutional+Conventions+Workshop/Workshop+Papers/Cyr-article.doc.

Fitzpatrick, Meagan, and Juliet O'Neill. 2008. Harper pushes back confidence motions. *National Post*, November 28. http://www.nationalpost.com/news/story.html?id=1001273.

Flanagan, Tom. 2009. Only voters have the right to decide on the coalition. *The Globe and Mail*, January 9, A13.

Flanagan, Tom. 2010. A Canadian approach to power-sharing. *Policy Options* 31 (8): 31–36.

Forsey, Eugene. 1953. Professor Angus on the British Columbia election: A comment. *Canadian Journal of Economics and Political Science* 19: 226–230.

Franks, C.E.S. 2009. To prorogue or not to prorogue: Did the governor general make the right decision? In Peter H. Russell and Lorne Sossin, eds., *Parliamentary democracy in crisis*. Toronto. University of Toronto Press.

Gardner, Dan. 2011. Are we going to reward contempt of Parliament? *Ottawa Citizen*, April 8. http://www.ottawacitizen.com/news/decision-canada/Gardner+going+reward+contempt+Parliament/4564215/story.html.

Harper, Stephen. 2000. Comment on Johnston, "Canadian Elections at the Millennium." *Choices* [Institute for Research on Public Policy] 6 (September): 44–51.

Harper, Stephen. 2005. Cleaning up the mess in Ottawa: Transparency is key to preventing scandal. *The Montreal Gazette*, June 7, A21.

Heard, A. 2009. The governor general's suspension of Parliament: Duty done or a perilous precedent? In Peter H. Russell and Lorne Sossin, eds., *Parliamentary democracy in crisis*, 47–62. Toronto: University of Toronto Press.

Hogg, Peter W. 2010. Prorogation and the power of the governor general. *National Journal of Constitutional Law*, 193–203. Toronto: Carswell.

Ipsos. 2008a. In wake of constitutional crisis, new survey demonstrates that Canadians lack basic understanding of our country's parliamentary system. December 15. http://www.dominion.ca/ DominionInstituteDecember15Factum.pdf.

Ipsos. 2008b. Majority (68%) of Canadians from every part of country supports governor general's decision to prorogue parliament. December 5. http://www.ipsos-na.com/news-polls/pressrelease.aspx?id=4201.

Ipsos. 2011. Split decision: Half of Canadians support coalition (48%), half oppose coalition (52%). April 2. http://www.ipsos-na.com/news-polls/ pressrelease.aspx?id=5180.

Leblanc, Daniel. 2009. Liberals gain steam as economy sputters. *The Globe and Mail*, January 20. http://www.theglobeandmail.com/news/ politics/article966687.ece.

MacDonald, Nicholas A., and James W.J. Bowden. 2011. No discretion: On prorogation and the governor general. *Canadian Parliamentary Review* 34 (1): 7–16.

Martin, Lawrence. 2010. *Harperland: The politics of control*. Toronto: Viking Canada.

McWhinney, Edward. 2009. The constitutional and political aspects of the office of the governor general. *Canadian Parliamentary Review* 32 (2): 2–8.

Paun, Akash. 2009. Introduction. In R. Hazel and A. Paun, eds., *Making minority government work: Hung parliaments and the challenges for Westminster and Whitehall*, 10–19. London: Institute for Government. http://www .instituteforgovernment.org.uk/pdfs/making-minority-gov-work.pdf.

Potter, Andrew. 2008. Two concepts of legitimacy. *Macleans.ca*, December 3. http://www2.macleans.ca/2008/12/03/two-concepts-of-legitimacy/.

Potter, Andrew. 2009a. The madness: Democrats vs parliamentarians. *Macleans.ca*, January 7. http://www2.macleans.ca/2009/01/07/the-madness-democrats-vs-parliamentarians/.

Potter, Andrew. 2009b. Still talking about the madness. *Macleans.ca*, July 7. http://www2.macleans.ca/2009/07/07/still-talking-about-the-madness/.

Potter, Andrew. 2009c. Unbalanced thoughts. *The Literary Review of Canada* 17 (July/August): 3–4.

Prime Minister of Canada. 2007. *Prime minister says passage of Throne Speech will be mandate to govern.* Press release. http://www.pm.gc.ca/eng/media.asp?category=1&featureId=6&pageId=26&id=1862.

Russell, Peter H. 2008. *Two cheers for minority government: The evolution of Canadian parliamentary democracy.* Toronto: Emond Montgomery.

Samara. 2011. *"It's my party": Parliamentary dysfunction reconsidered.* http://www.samaracanada.com/downloads/ItsMyParty.pdf.

Scoffield, Heather. 2011. Harper's vision of how to form a government undermined by constitutional facts. April 12. http://ca.news.yahoo.com/harpers-vision-form-government-undermined-constitutional-facts-20110412-193240-015.html.

Smith, Jennifer. 1999. Democracy and the Canadian House of Commons at the millennium. *Canadian Public Administration* 42 (4): 398–421.

Strøm, Kaare. 1990. *Minority government and majority rule.* Cambridge, UK: Cambridge University Press.

Tremblay, Guy. 2008. Libre-opinion—La gouverneure générale doit accéder à une demande de prorogation ou de dissolution. *Le Devoir*, December 4. http://www.ledevoir.com/non-classe/220782/libre-opinion-la-gouverneure-generale-doit-acceder-a-une-demande-de-prorogation-ou-de-dissolution.

Wherry, Aaron. 2011a. The House of Commons is a sham. *Maclean's*, February 18.

Wherry, Aaron. 2011b. The House: Considering reform. *Macleans.ca*, May 24. http://www2.macleans.ca/2011/05/24/the-house-considering-reform/.

Whittington, L., B. Campion-Smith, and T. McCharles. 2008. Liberals, NDP and Bloc sign coalition pact. *The Toronto Star*, December 1. http://www.thestar.com/article/546315.

Yong, Ben. 2009. New Zealand's experience of multi-party governance. In R. Hazell and A. Paun, eds., *Making minority government work: Hung parliaments and the challenges for Westminster and Whitehall*, 38–53. London: Institute for Government. http://www.instituteforgovernment.org.uk/pdfs/making-minority-gov-work.pdf.

CHAPTER SIX

Conclusion: Reforming Responsible Government

Introduction

Why is the Canadian parliamentary system failing? As we have sought to explain throughout this book, a lack of clear and basic rules addressing the most essential aspects of the Canadian constitution, combined with a lack of effective constraints by either the rules of the House of Commons or political parties on the powers of the prime minister, have disrupted the capacity of the House to fulfill its fundamental role. This undermines the principles and integrity of the people's Parliament as a democratic institution.

The resulting concentration of those powers in a single individual, including the power to summon, prorogue, and dissolve Parliament, does not belong in a robust democracy. Nor does relying on the personal discretion of an unelected governor general to constrain a prime minister from abusing those powers. Beyond the high level of disagreement on our constitutional conventions for determining what the governor general should or should not decide and under what conditions, relying on the governor general's discretion is antithetical to democracy: it harkens back to a pre-responsible-government era.

To fully realize the underlying principle of responsible government demands that neither the prime minister nor the governor general should make those decisions: the House must decide. These issues take us to the very heart of our democracy: whether the House still matters and what its role should be.

The 2011 election of a majority Conservative government led by Prime Minister Stephen Harper has put the most contentious of these issues to bed for a while—whether or not it is legitimate to change governments between elections if a government loses confidence or whether a prime minister has the right to demand a dissolution even when he or she has lost confidence. But majority government has not made all of the issues related to a prime minister's power over Parliament disappear, including the ability to abuse the governor general's powers for partisan purposes. For example, via prorogation, Prime Minister Harper can still unilaterally shut down parliamentary scrutiny. Further, the loopholes still exist in Prime Minister Harper's fixed election date law, so he can still dissolve Parliament at a time of his choosing and call a snap election when it suits his interests. Ironically, he may well face a political context similar to that of Prime Minister Chrétien, whose use of snap elections Harper once objected to so strenuously, with opposition parties dividing votes among themselves, ill-prepared to fight an election, in this case due to the recently announced elimination of party subsidies.

At the same time, the return to majority government does present an opportunity. This is a much more suitable time to deal with these problems than if we were firmly in the middle of a political or constitutional crisis. The opportunity should be used to thoughtfully consider and advance a reform agenda.

In that spirit, we turn to outlining our proposals for reforming responsible government in order to democratize the Canadian constitution. We argue that the prime minister should not be able to dissolve or prorogue Parliament or to put off summoning Parliament at his or her discretion or to decide when the government has lost the support of the House of Commons. We thus propose four reforms that directly address the constitutional issues we have examined. We also propose a number of reforms that could be undertaken by Parliament to further reform parliamentary governance and constrain the executive powers of the prime minister to undermine the House; and reforms that could be undertaken by political parties to make themselves more democratic, as well as to reduce the degree to which the parties have failed to constrain party leaders, especially when the leader is prime minister. We consider these proposals in light of a simple four-part test that should be applied to all proposals for democratic reform.

The chapter starts by considering the dynamics of reform, then introduces our four-part test. Next, we put forward our four proposals for democratizing the Canadian constitution. The chapter then introduces our other proposals for reform, focusing on the three sets of powers at the heart of this book: the discretionary powers assigned to the governor general, other executive powers assigned to the prime minister, and the powers associated with being a party leader. In putting forward the proposals, we are careful to demonstrate how these reforms satisfy our own four-part test and how best these changes could be made. We also discuss an important potential limitation of the reforms before moving on to anticipating and addressing some potential criticisms of what we are proposing. The chapter ends by affirming a simple maxim that has underpinned our analysis and our reforms: parliamentary democracy must prevail.

The Dynamics of Democratic Reform

While the dust was still settling after the 2011 election, in which the Conservatives had secured a majority government, pundits immediately began to discuss what the Conservatives should do with their majority. The *National Post* editorial board had the most interesting list of "conservative priorities" because, in addition to nine that were largely consistent with promises already made by the Conservatives, it added a tenth:

> Reinstate a culture of openness, transparency, and accountability on Parliament Hill. Now that the Conservatives have a majority, there is no excuse (not that there ever was) for the paranoia, secrecy, rule-bending, shirking of due process and committee bullying that rightly has become the subject of opposition ire in recent years. (*National Post* 2011)

This call for reform is significant because it comes from a staunch supporter of the Harper Conservative government. It is partly a frank and candid rebuke of the behaviour of the Harper government since 2006, partly an acknowledgment that the 2006 reforms promised by the Harper Conservatives before they took office have not materialized, and partly a recognition that what the Harper Conservatives had identified as needing reform in 2006 were real problems that still need to be addressed.

Reforms aimed at reducing the power of the prime minister have been part of an almost continuous process of democratization that has ebbed and flowed since 1867. They have focused on removing discretion from the prime minister over decisions that merely advance the governing party's partisan interests, not the public interest. Examples, as previously noted, include the creation of the Civil Service Commission in 1908, with legislation following a decade later, and in 1920 the creation of an independent chief electoral officer (CEO).

None of this is to suggest that partisanship is inherently evil, unseemly, or counter to good governance. Under responsible government, partisanship and partisan agendas are both expected and appropriate (Smith 1999). The system is adversarial by design and it is assumed that the public interest prescribes that there be a governing party able to exercise discretion over matters such as organizing and managing the Cabinet, directing government departments on most matters of administration, and generally promoting its agenda. A partisan agenda always underpins a government's policy platform and, in a parliamentary democracy, this makes perfect sense. In general elections, we choose between individuals whose public affiliations with political parties enable us to know what they stand for, and, in that connection, provide an agenda to vote for. When a political party is elected, has formed the government, and then acts to fulfill its "partisan" policy objectives, that is an entirely legitimate exercise; the party has a democratic mandate to pursue its agenda. For instance, if a fiscally conservative party campaigns on a plan to lower taxes and wins, then there is a reason to expect that taxes will be lowered, in keeping with its promise to the voters that reflects its ideological position, *if* the details of the party's proposals can garner the support of the House. There is nothing problematic about this. However, there is a problem when a party's quest for political power leads it to abuse its constitutional or other executive powers for partisan advantage in matters where the public has nothing to gain. In other words, there are times when the party's interest, if unchecked, can overshadow the public interest.

For instance, Prime Minister Stephen Harper's requests for prorogation in both 2008 and 2009 were designed to achieve partisan goals and had nothing to do with serving the public interest, just like previous prorogation abuses by Chrétien in 2003 and Macdonald in 1873. In each of these cases, Canadians had an interest in allowing Parliament to do its work, uninterrupted by the government's partisan tactics to shut down the House.

Abuse of power was also seen in 2008 when Harper called a snap election for partisan advantage. As noted in Chapter 2, he was not the first prime minister to do so. Diefenbaker in 1958, Pearson in 1965, Trudeau in 1968, and Chrétien in 1997 and 2000 had done the same.

These were among the dramatic instances of abuse of power in recent years. But, as we have described throughout the preceding chapters, the litany is getting longer and also encompasses other far less dramatic examples of the capacity of the prime minister and government party to run roughshod over the House of Commons, and especially its committees. The prime minister can do all of this because there are insufficient constraints on a prime minister who is willing to put the partisan interests of controlling the House and its committees ahead of the public interest in effective parliamentary democracy. Rarely, if ever, has public opinion constrained a prime minister who is willing to act in bad faith. Moreover, the state of parliamentary democracy has never been considered a decisive issue in an election.

Public opinion cannot be ignored, however. It is usually a prerequisite for reform, in that reform requires that the public appreciate the problem that a proposed reform addresses and that the reform is viewed as an appropriate response. Reforms to address the problem of unconstrained prime ministerial power over Parliament are likely to be undermined if experts and pundits are divided on whether certain actions constitute an abuse or not. If the actions of the prime ministers we have noted are not regarded by at least a substantial majority of experts, pundits, and politicians as abuses of power, however legal their actions may have been, there is unlikely to be a broad perception that there is a problem that requires democratic reform. Reforms are also likely to be undermined by the degree to which the media portray abuses of power as merely part and parcel of the "game" of partisan politics. If politics is regarded as a "no-holds-barred" sport, nothing can truly be abusive.

For their part, prime ministers are able to manipulate the disagreement and the cynicism surrounding the practices of summoning, proroguing, and dissolving Parliament, as well as confidence measures, in the pursuit of their partisan goals. How can prime ministers be held accountable for abusive behaviour and for acting in bad faith when there is no clear and common understanding of what is right and wrong and no firm rules about unwritten constitutional conventions? To be effective, unwritten conventions and standards of good faith require broad community understanding and acceptance. If there is no understanding and acceptance, there is little incentive for politicians to feel bound by them.

At the same time, reforms that create firm rules and clear standards of good faith do not emerge just because there is a problem. Two other conditions must be met. First, the proposals for reform must meet certain requirements in order to be effective. We outline these in the next section in relation to the democracy problem facing Canada. Second, a reform "movement" must emerge, a consensus that goes beyond one political party, even if one party is the primary mover of the proposals. Political reform does not just happen because there are proposals that meet certain practical requirements. Where reform is required but nothing happens, it is not generally because reform ideas are absent, but because a sufficient movement for reform has not materialized or has been undermined by the forces in favour of the status quo. We address some of these forces in the final section of this chapter.

Reform: Four Essential Questions

The story of Canada's parliamentary democracy is one of evolution and continual development, including numerous instances and periods of reform. These have often led to significant improvements in Canadian governance. But there have also been periods of relative stagnancy, stemming either from a failure of leadership to confront pressing problems and build popular support for reforms, or from a failure to implement well thought out reforms, even when they had broad public support.

The 2011 election campaign was hardly inspiring when it came to democratic reform. After defeating Prime Minister Stephen Harper's Conservative government over an unprecedented finding of contempt of Parliament, and highlighting what they considered to be Harper's elevating abuses of parliamentary government in the lead-up to, and during, the election campaign, the opposition parties' proposals for democratic reform proved at best disappointing, and likely induced greater cynicism. No easy feat.

With limited exceptions, even when they addressed substantive causes for concern, such as the prime minister's power to abuse prorogation, the proposals on offer were often vacuous. For example, both the NDP and the Liberals promised to put forward measures to restrict the ability of a prime minister to abuse prorogation to avoid Parliament, but neither provided any details as to how. One can only assume that they intended to implement their earlier flawed plans to restrict prorogation (as discussed in Chapter 2). Beyond the lack of details, other platform proposals reverted to general remarks about improving civility in the functioning of Parliament, like the NDP's (2011, 23) promise of "setting a new tone in parliament" or proposals that verged on gimmicks, such as the Liberals' (2011) call for a "People's Question Period." Given the heightened rhetoric that opposition parties used to describe Harper's abuses, one could hardly blame voters for being deeply cynical about their motives and for believing Harper's suggestion that opposition criticisms were little more than "partisan bickering" or "simply a case of the other three [opposition] parties outvoting us" (Delacourt and Whittington 2011).

The failure of Canada's political parties to advance a concrete, comprehensive reform agenda is nothing less than astonishing. For one thing, there is widespread agreement, transcending party lines, that the centralization and abuse of these powers are not recent phenomena, but, rather, long-standing problems. For another, we have experienced an even greater concentration of these powers in Canada and thus, not surprisingly, a greater abuse of these powers for partisan purposes compared with other Westminster systems such as New Zealand or Great Britain, both of which have taken concrete steps to address the situation.

Of course, the proposals we put forward in this chapter are far from the only reforms available for bolstering Canadian democracy. Many commentators and other individuals and groups have their own preferred reform measures, such as electoral reform, and the merits of each of these can—and should—be debated in terms of how parliamentary democracy is to be improved by its implementation.

At the very least, any reforms put forward, regardless of the source, should be able to demonstrate that they (a) are not likely to cause further damage to Parliament and our sagging institutions, as well as their proceedings; and (b) are distinctly and realistically likely to engender positive changes to the status quo. No proposal should be taken seriously if there is no coherent argument as to how it would meet these requirements. But, while important, even these minimum criteria are insufficient to judge the merits of any proposal for reform.

We propose a fourfold test that ought to be applied to any reforms, whether proposed individually or as part of a more comprehensive plan for democratic reform, consisting of four core questions:

1. Is there a clear, unambiguous stated objective attached to each specific reform that would enhance robust democracy under the parliamentary system while fully accepting the partisan basis of parliamentary democracy?
2. Do the specific reforms avoid relying on prime ministers acting in good faith or on public opinion as a deterrent? In other words, is the measure adequately fortified against loopholes?
3. Is there a clear mechanism by which the House of Commons can enforce the reform?
4. Do the proposed reforms entrench the power of the House in both minority and majority settings?

While these questions are all self-explanatory, it is important to underscore their importance. As much as possible, any reforms that ought to be considered should be effective in guarding against abuses of executive power in both majority and minority circumstances, enabling Parliament—and especially the House of Commons—to ensure that the reforms are adhered to, in keeping with their clear intention. As we have discussed throughout the book, it is simply not good enough to depend on measures that rely exclusively on public opinion and good faith to be effective. Doing so only reduces the constraints on a prime minister's power over Parliament to voluntary measures. This, as exemplified with Harper's fixed election date law, is inadequate in a contemporary democratic system. The demand for a clear, explicitly stated purpose is also in keeping with tests for the development of constitutional conventions (see Chapter 3). We should be skeptical of reforms that fall short on any or all of these questions.

Our Proposals for Democratic Reform

Stephen Harper was on the right track when he signalled his intention to end the prime minister's unconstrained power to call elections whenever most advantageous to the governing party. Ultimately, however, the fixed election date legislation passed by Parliament was deficient. It left a major loophole that could be exploited by a prime minister acting in bad faith, doing nothing to constrain this power. Nonetheless, the reform's objective was to secure better democracy by eliminating the capacity of the prime minister to abuse constitutional powers. This was a good starting point, but the absence of good faith on the part of the prime minister in calling the early 2008 election demonstrated the need for clear, binding rules to effectively constrain this and other powers.

Better parliamentary democracy in Canada requires that the House of Commons be *in session* to perform its fundamental democratic responsibilities as required. This prerequisite does not require that the House be continuously in session, with no breaks or elections. Rather, it means that the government should not be able to decide unilaterally when the House should be in session or not. Prime ministerial discretion over these matters, with no constraints other than public opinion, invariably leads to the abuse of power purely for partisan advantage, with no redeeming democratic purpose.

Some constraints can be adopted by adding new, firm rules that are reasonably straightforward, as outlined below. But changes should not be made arbitrarily; the rules should build on the basic principles and logic of responsible government as the democratic framework of Canadian parliamentary democracy. These principles require that:

- the prime minister and government must have the confidence of a majority in the House of Commons to govern; and
- when the prime minister and government lose the confidence of the House, they either resign so that a new government that has the confidence of the House can be formed, or the House is dissolved and an election is held.

The logic of responsible government holds that the people's elected representatives in the House, rather than the governor general or the prime minister, determine:

- who should form the government after a general election;
- when the government has lost the confidence of the House; and
- whether there should be a change of government without an election after the government has lost confidence or whether an election should be held.

The logic of responsible government has been both ignored and twisted over time. Our conventions never address constraints on the power to summon Parliament, and the Canadian constitution requires only that the House meet once a year. And even then it is up to the prime minister to advise the governor general to summon it. It is perhaps not surprising, then, that when Prime Minister Joe Clark delayed summoning Parliament for several months in 1979, governing even though his minority government had not yet met the House to test its confidence, there was no major public criticism. The fact that there might be a problem with the prime minister using this power to suppress the House was ignored.

The carelessness with which Canadian governments and parliaments have approached the exercise of power when a government does not have the confidence of the House is further illustrated by the absence of publicly known conventions to regulate what the prime minister and government may and may not do from the time they have lost confidence in the House until a continuing or new government has had confidence confirmed following a general election, including the period after the government has been defeated in the House and the prime minister has not yet resigned or a dissolution has not yet been granted. Elsewhere, as discussed in Chapter 2, these are referred to as "caretaker government" protocols or conventions. In Australia, Great Britain, and New Zealand, they are publicly available documents, meant to regulate the government and to guide both the governor general and the public service when the prime minister and government cannot satisfy the basic democratic condition of responsible government, that they no longer possess the confidence of the House. They can also be quite comprehensive documents. For example, New Zealand has established detailed protocols to guide confidence votes, government formation, and transition, and the roles of a range of actors in various circumstances, in addition to circumscribing the behaviour and decision-making power of prime ministers and governments who do not clearly have the confidence of the House. Such a document exists in Canada but it has not been made public. This vastly decreases its usefulness by making it impossible for observers or the public to determine whether its rules have been breached.

Before 2004, most Canadian constitutional experts, pundits, and politicians would have scoffed at the need for caretaker government conventions along the lines put in place in Australia or New Zealand. The typical responses would have been: too many rules, too elaborate, inflexible, and too fixated on procedures when judgment is required. A great deal of the support for the status quo came crashing down with the 2008 prorogation debacle, when the complete absence of agreement on our unwritten conventions was fully exposed. It became even more embarrassing, and potentially dangerous, when total confusion reigned about what the governor general could and/or should do if Harper was to lose confidence and demand another election, while a coalition with majority support waited in the wings. Many observers in our Westminster counterparts thought we looked second-rate.

The fact that Harper was able to abuse the power of prorogation and get away with it politically without plunging the country into a full constitutional crisis is not evidence that "the system worked" as some, perhaps even most, experts, pundits, and politicians astonishingly claim (see, for example, a number of contributions to Russell and Sossin 2009). On the contrary, it is evidence that our conventions, as practised, are not capable of constraining power that solely serves the partisan interests of the government. It also illustrates either a deficient understanding of the democratic logic of responsible government on the part of our leading political classes or a willingness to depart from it without making any effort to reform the system, including the establishment of other constraints on power consistent with a modern democracy. By allowing the prime minister to abuse constitutional powers, the practices of parliamentary government have become dominated and controlled by the prime minister in a way that would make even pre-1848 governors general (or the monarch) blush!

Developments since have only further muddied the waters, serving to strengthen the powers of the prime minister over both the government and Parliament and to further diminish the fundamental logic of responsible government. Stephen Harper's extension of this, with his assertion that only the electorate can select and dismiss a prime minister, should come as no surprise. His assertion is entirely consistent with the destructive trajectory of power in the Canadian system, even if it does elevate it to new heights. The fact that Harper's assertion cannot fit within the principles and logic of responsible government has not led the prime minister or his defenders to withdraw the assertion or to attempt a revised design of responsible government that might go some way to accommodating his claim.[1] His claim now constitutes yet another point of disagreement and confusion over the conventions of the Canadian constitution.

As we have argued, the reasons that Canadian prime ministers are subject to so little constraint have much to do with their capacity to act independently of the government ministers and the party's backbench MPs and to keep them in line through the various rewards and sanctions at their disposal. These include rewards like Cabinet positions and potential future ambassadorships, or sanctions such as withdrawing Cabinet

---

1. It might be noted that, as discussed earlier in this book, the same murkiness characterizes the government's proposals for Senate reform, with so much of the critical detail of a reformed Senate not addressed in any way and potentially left to be arbitrated by the provinces and territories on a one-off basis.

positions, dismissal from caucus, or possibly refusing to accept a member's future candidacy on behalf of the party. Another contributing factor is the prime minister's control of other mechanisms of executive power, including the political staff in the Prime Minister's Office (PMO) and the public service staff in the Privy Council Office. With precious few exceptions, the influence of the PMO has become the most important in the exercise of power. The ability of the PMO to speak for the prime minister has taken the blurring of the governmental and the partisan political spheres to new levels.

The influence of the PMO is not confined to the administration of government, however. The PMO extends its influence into the governing party itself, as it advises the prime minister on how to exercise his or her extensive powers of appointment to exert control over ministers, government backbench MPs, candidates/potential candidates, as well as the management of the party's national and local fundraising and campaign organizations. Needless to say, the concentration of key powers over the governing party has meant that the prime minister can easily dictate and manipulate the behaviour of government MPs and ministers as they undertake their responsibilities in Parliament, especially in Commons committees.

We want to be careful to repeat here that this does not mean that the prime minister necessarily gets everything he or she wants, or can control everything. There are a number of "counterweights" or "countervailing forces of power" that do limit a prime minister's power (see Bakvis 2001, for example). But generally they do not constrain the prime minister's use of executive powers or powers over the operations of the House of Commons or the Senate. The prime minister's ability to act independently of government ministers and the party's backbench MPs, and the relative powerlessness of either group to address what they consider to be abuses of executive power, go a long way to undermining an effective system of responsible government.

What needs to be done to correct this imbalance of power between the prime minister and the House—to democratize the constitution and reform responsible government? There must be a series of interconnected reforms that address three distinct but complementary sets of powers related to parliamentary governance:

- the discretionary powers assigned to the governor general but regularly exercised virtually unilaterally by the prime minister;
- other executive powers assigned to prime ministers; and
- the powers associated with being a party leader.

We address each of these areas in turn.

1. Four-Part Constitutional Reform

First, we propose that the power to summon Parliament after an election be fixed in law so that there is a maximum time frame within which a new government must face the House. A maximum limit is required to protect the House of Commons from a prime minister delaying meeting the House after an election. Although the House is terminated at dissolution, and MPs are no longer MPs, the prime minister is, in fact, still the prime minister and remains so for the duration of the election campaign. No matter what the results of the election are, constitutionally he or she has the "first right" to meet the House of Commons to see whether his or her government can hold its confidence. When no party wins a majority of the seats, it is often not entirely clear what will happen when the House reconvenes, since any of the parties would need support from another in order to govern.

As described in earlier chapters, most commonly in Canadian practice the party with a plurality forms government and is assumed to be able to gain the confidence of the House. There are a wide variety of scenarios where a prime minister might find it useful, from a political standpoint, to delay the sitting of the House. For example, he or she might seek to begin to govern without meeting the House if it is not clear that he or she has the support of the House. Or the prime minister might want to stir up public skepticism about a possible alternative government, including possible coalition governments, in order to dissuade opposition parties from joining forces and teaming up against the prime minister's party when it has won a plurality, but not a majority, of seats. Therefore, we propose that after a general election, the House of Commons must be summoned within 30 days, as is required by the Australian constitution.[2]

Turning to our four-point test from page 211, we outline here how this proposal meets the four criteria that we propose to apply to all suggestions for reform. First, the democratic objective of establishing a deadline for summoning the House is clear: to protect the House, the people's representatives who are elected to hold the government to account, against being prevented from expressing a lack of confidence in a new government, or from being able to scrutinize a government that intends to govern without meeting the House for a prolonged period. This would ensure that the House could meet and conduct its business, independent of any political concerns on the part of the prime minister. The measure does not rely on the good faith of the prime minister to uphold its integrity, because there is no discretion involved on the prime minister's part: the summoning of the House would happen automatically, 30 days after the election, if it had not occurred before. Because it would happen automatically, no further enforcement mechanism is required. If an expected government failed to show up, the House would be able to press on without it, including voting confidence in another government. The measure would have the same effect and function whether any party won a majority of seats in the House or not.

Second, we propose a more robust requirement for fixed election dates. Harper's reform, as we have stated, started on the right track. Proper fixed election dates have the potential to remove the discretion

---

2. Germany and Ireland also require that Parliament meet within 30 days of an election, whereas Denmark, Norway, and Sweden require Parliament meet within two to three weeks (see Boston 1998).

FOUR-PART CONSTITUTIONAL REFORM

Summary of Proposals

- establish a deadline requiring the House of Commons to be summoned within 30 days after a general election
- establish fixed election dates every four years on a specific date, binding both the prime minister and the governor general, unless a majority of two-thirds of MPs approve a motion to dissolve Parliament for an early election
- adopt the "constructive non-confidence" procedure
- require the consent of a two-thirds majority of the House of Commons in order to prorogue Parliament

---

of the prime minister to abuse the power of dissolution when the prime minister has a majority, as Chrétien did in 1997 and 2000, or even a minority, as Harper himself did in 2008. But they also have the potential to make it clear that the prime minister does not have a virtual right to dissolution particularly when he or she has lost the confidence of the House, as was simply assumed when Harper announced the dissolution that triggered the May 2011 election, after the House had passed a Liberal motion of non-confidence in his government.

A fixed election date regime that relies on the prime minister acting in good faith cannot be effective, as we saw in 2008 when Harper ignored his own law and dissolved the House. The governor general, as discussed in previous chapters, did not hesitate to accept his advice and the Federal Court made clear its view that the constitution gave the governor general complete discretion to dissolve Parliament. An effective fixed election date law must thus be binding on both the prime minister and the governor general, with no discretion for either to address special circumstances.

We do recognize the possibility that in some unusual circumstances it might be necessary to dissolve Parliament before the four-year fixed election date occurs, as a safety-valve mechanism of sorts.[3] But, again, the problem of majority government presents itself; we must ensure that a majority government prime minister cannot get an early dissolution simply because of party discipline. To address this need, we couple the fixed election date with a recommendation that the House can only be dissolved before the four-year scheduled election date with the support of a supermajority of two-thirds of MPs.

The democratic objective of this reform is clear: to ensure that any decision to dissolve Parliament—dismissing it entirely and undoing the work of its committees—would have to come from the House, not the prime minister alone. It would terminate the ability of a prime minister to call a snap election to force voters to choose at a moment designed to capitalize on their ignorance, because parliamentary scrutiny would be disrupted, or to seize on a perceived moment of opposition weakness. Snap elections carry no benefit for the public and have been far too common in Canadian history. It would also mean that any early election, in whatever unusual circumstances it might be necessary, is fully sanctioned by the House. Like the deadline for summoning Parliament, this measure does not rely on the good faith of the prime minister, because the virtual right of a prime minister to dissolution and a new election would simply be eliminated. Implemented properly, neither the prime minister nor the governor general would retain discretion to ask for or grant an early dissolution. In normal circumstances, dissolutions would occur automatically, just before pre-scheduled elections; in exceptional cases, early dissolution would only be triggered when the House approved

---

3. Eugene Forsey (1953, 228) asserted that early dissolution would be legitimate when a Parliament "is nearing the end of its maximum term, or when some great new issue appears, or when a redistribution act or a new franchise act or a new electoral system has been adopted, or when all possible alternative governments have been tried and have failed." We suggest that a change in the leader of the party that forms the government could also be a valid reason for an early dissolution.

it by a two-thirds vote. It would effectively remove future governors general from decisions related to dissolution.

This supermajority threshold would ensure that there was multiparty agreement on the need and decision to dissolve; even a majority government could not, in most circumstances, meet this threshold on its own. In most instances of majority government in Canadian history, the two-thirds threshold would have been sufficient to require at least some support from the opposition parties, with few exceptions: in 1958, John Diefenbaker's Progressive Conservatives elected 208 MPs in a House of 265 (78.5 percent); and in 1984, Brian Mulroney's Progressive Conservatives elected members to 211 of the House's 282 seats (74.8 percent). So, as long as the government caucus does not comprise more than 66 percent of the House, this reform would eliminate the opportunity for prime ministers to silence the House when it suits them. The only loophole that the proposed measure does not address is that it does not guard the House against the preferences of a majority government that exceeds 66 percent of the House of Commons. In the last two decades, the likelihood of any one party electing more than 66 percent of the seats has been strongly diminished as more parties have won seats in the House. Should the number of parties contesting seats in future elections change dramatically, adjusting the percentage requirement might be necessary.

Third, to address the near constant use of brinkmanship by both the government and opposition, we propose the adoption of the *constructive non-confidence* system. As discussed in Chapter 5, in a minority government situation the prime minister is tempted to play brinkmanship whenever it appears possible to get the opposition majority to back down from opposing the government's agenda, if the agenda has popular appeal and/or the government's standing in public opinion polls suggests that an election would be to the government's advantage. The prime minister can simply declare a vote a matter of confidence and more or less dare the opposition to defeat the government. However, the opposition parties are also tempted to play brinkmanship, to persuade the government to amend its agenda to accommodate their demands. They do this by threatening the government with withdrawal of confidence and thus, in the Canadian practice, triggering an election, when public opinion is less favourable to the government and the opposition parties' electoral fortunes appear to be on the rise. This brinkmanship has also been an opportunity for party leaders to exert excessive party discipline over caucus, especially the prime minister, who can stake the party's fortunes on nearly every vote.

Under the *constructive non-confidence* system, as enacted in a number of other parliamentary democracies, including Germany, Spain, and Belgium, confidence in the government can only be withdrawn with an explicit non-confidence motion. This would require a simple statement that confidence has been lost, as long as the motion also clearly states which opposition party leader would be willing and able to form an alternative government with the support of a simple majority of MPs. There would be no doubt about what constitutes a vote of confidence because, upon declaring no confidence in the government, the House would have to identify the member of Parliament who would become the new prime minister. No other government legislation, motions, or financial votes, including the Speech from the Throne or the budget, would be considered confidence matters or could be so declared by the government. The adoption of this system would eliminate the need for the three-line whip or any like-minded reform that seeks to reduce party discipline. Once a constructive non-confidence motion has passed, and the majority of MPs who would support the alternative government have been identified through a vote in the House, the prime minister would be required to resign and the governor general would be required to appoint the new prime minister and government. This would be a binding rule. It would entail no discretion on the part of the governor general, and especially no second-guessing on the viability or stability of the new government, whether it is a single-party minority or a coalition minority or majority. The new government's viability would be assessed only through the fundamental logic and requirement of the democratic system of responsible government: that the government must be able to command the confidence of the House.

Again, the democratic objective of this reform is very clear: it would impede both the government and the opposition from using the brinkmanship of confidence as a substitute for taking their role in our democratic governance seriously. The government would no longer be able to bully the opposition into supporting measures it genuinely believes are not in the best interests of the country for fear of triggering an election. In situations of minority government, a government that wanted to implement its agenda would have to take the concerns of the House seriously, unlike the current system. Opposition parties would not be able to simply blackmail the government into accepting an opposition agenda instead of undertaking serious scrutiny of government performance and decisions. This rule would allow opposition parties to defeat a government only if they were prepared to support another government from the same House. In turn, the act of withdrawing confidence in government as the most serious mechanism of accountability would carry a suitable weight with a very significant consequence for the government: loss of power. It would also eliminate confusion about what counts as a confidence vote and in what circumstance, and allow the prime minister to rule over those determinations with no room for "alternative interpretations."

Neither the opposition nor the government would be able to game this reform. It is explicit about what is required of the opposition (an explicit non-confidence motion that also indicates who would lead a new government), the government (resignation and no role in the transfer of power or any possibility to request dissolution), and the governor general (whose role is simply to appoint the new prime minister); the only discretion would reside with the House. In this way, the good faith of the prime minister is not required. If a prime minister were to refuse to resign, it would amount to an actual constitutional crisis: a prime minister attempting to usurp power with no legitimate claim to do so. The governor general would have to make it clear that he or she had dismissed the prime minister and call on the new government in the face of the outgoing prime minister's objections. The key, though, is that the governor general would not be acting with discretion in doing so. These acts would all occur in accordance with explicit and binding protocols for the transfer of power in the event of the passing of a constructive non-confidence motion, similar to the New Zealand protocols for transferring power. It should be noted that, because, as discussed in Chapter 4, the usual standards of party discipline mean that majority governments are not vulnerable to losing confidence (and for the same reason do not rely on brinkmanship as a mode of governing), this kind of motion is not likely to occur in majority situations, though it would still be applicable. In the rare case in which a majority government lost confidence, the reform would function in the same manner and to the same effect.

Fourth, as we have mentioned in previous chapters, several prime ministers, in both minority and majority government situations, have taken advantage of the prerogative power to prorogue the House of Commons in order to escape its scrutiny. To address this problem, we propose that prorogations of the House of Commons happen only with the consent of the House of Commons and, specifically, with the support of a supermajority of two-thirds of members. The supermajority is necessary to protect the ability of the House to effectively scrutinize majority government even when it might be embarrassing or damaging to the government, because a simple majority threshold that would be effective during a minority government could be met with support from the governing party caucus alone.

When prorogation is being used for its standard purpose—to briefly pause the operations of the House as a way to structure government business, usually when a government has fully implemented its existing agenda and is initiating a new session kicked off by a new Speech from the Throne announcing its new objectives—there should be no problem securing the two-thirds support. In cases where a government is merely attempting to serve its own partisan interests, particularly in trying to disrupt the House to prevent it from holding the government to account or from withdrawing confidence, it will likely be unable to escape, even temporarily, through prorogation.

The democratic objective of this reform is to enhance parliamentary democracy in Canada by protecting the House of Commons from being silenced by a prime minister for purely partisan purposes. This proposal does not rely on good faith on the part of the prime minister because it transfers the authority for prorogation to the House, and eliminates any and all discretion on the part of governors general for the decision whether to grant a prime minister's request. Our proposal recognizes the House of Commons, our assembly of elected representatives, as the constraint on prime ministerial power, rather than the governor general. As with the safety valve for early dissolution, the only loophole that the proposed measure does not address is that it does not guard the House against the preferences of a majority government that exceeds 66 percent of the House of Commons.

OPENING THE CONSTITUTION

There are a variety of ways to enact the changes that we have proposed. The most effective means would be through formal, written constitutional amendments to remove the governor general's powers for proroguing and dissolving Parliament and to establish the new processes that we have proposed in their place, as well as to fix election dates, establish a maximum time limit for summoning Parliament after an election, and to entrench the constructive non-confidence system.

The failed fixed election date law reveals the inadequacy of legislative amendments to reform constitutional conventions when the powers of the governor general are not restrained or removed. Some would counter that a less flawed law would have proven more effective. While this is likely accurate, it is not entirely clear to what extent a law could be flawed but still be effective. For example, while the clarity of the Harper fixed election date law could unquestionably be improved upon, whatever wording a new law uses to attempt to constrain the role of the prime minister and governor general within the current distribution of power, the intended meaning of the wording would always be open to debate and even misrepresentation. Further, given the disputes over the development of constitutional conventions outlined in Chapter 3, it is not clear exactly which tests and, hence, which requirements must be fulfilled to be sufficient for the development of an effective law as a means of establishing a convention, especially given that the tests themselves, as discussed, are not entirely clear.

Of course, there is little appetite for "opening the constitution." There is a tangible fear, expressed by politicians, voters, scholars, and journalists alike, of opening the Pandora's box that is the constitution. Previous efforts at constitutional change, specifically the Meech Lake and Charlottetown accords, are infamous for their contributions to political instability and national discord. No one wants more of that, so suggestions for changes to the rules of the game are often rejected before they are considered on their merits. This collective fear of entering into constitutional negotiations and, hence, constitutional changes has become a major impediment to positive and necessary democratic reform and changes in Canadian politics. It renders us incapable of fixing real problems. It also reeks of immaturity as a country.

One way to mitigate both the fear attached to opening the constitution and any potential political instability would be to limit any constitutional amendment to our proposed package of four reforms, separate from any other measures—especially electoral system reform and Senate reform—that bring important and controversial issues of federalism into play. While the changes we propose require the consent of the provinces, they do not affect the legislative powers or rights of the provinces in any way. Provinces would have no sound reason to object to these reforms, and any effort to tie other, more politically controversial issues to such a package should be condemned as crass, obstructionist opportunism.

An alternative would be to articulate the processes in a formal government document, as was done in New Zealand's *Cabinet Manual* and is now being attempted in Great Britain. The guide itself would be an important first step for generating clarity and to ensure a broad understanding of the "rules." If this approach is taken, the opportunity should also be taken to make Canada's caretaker conventions public, which, as discussed in Chapter 2, have been kept secret. But the writing of any kind of touchstone handbook itself should not be accepted as sufficient. Explicit agreement of the relevant political actors should also be sought so that the provisions are respected as convention (and potentially recognized as such). If this approach were taken, it must be made clear that these procedures would not be mere "guiding principles," but would carry expectations as binding processes by, and on, all political participants—especially prime ministers. Although this would not remove the governor general's powers, the document would enunciate what is deemed to be convention for the use of the governor general in responding to requests (or demands) from a prime minister seeking to override the articulated processes.

2. Reforming Executive Power

While constraining the prime minister's power to arbitrarily and unilaterally exercise the discretionary powers assigned to the governor general will go a long way to empowering and protecting the House of Commons, we argue that further change is required to enhance our democracy. To this end, we suggest a series of reforms, which complement those proposed in the previous section and those that follow, with regard to party leadership. As in those areas, these reforms about the way the House operates would constrain the executive power held by the prime minister or create countervailing forces of power, again with the idea of reinforcing the principles and logic of responsible government. In order to empower and protect the House of Commons, we suggest the following reforms to the way the House operates: limiting the size of the Cabinet; allowing parliamentary committees to choose their own chairs for fixed terms through secret preferential ballots; setting opposition days on a firm schedule that cannot be unilaterally altered by the government; and reducing the number of political staff serving the government. We discuss each of these in turn here, explaining how each measure would advance the interconnected goals of constraining the power of the prime minister and bolstering the House of Commons.

As we discussed in Chapter 4, the Canadian prime minister has a number of instruments that can be used to maintain the loyalty of his or her caucus and to ensure responsiveness to his or her agenda; perhaps the most effective of these is the dispersal of rewards and sanctions. The worst form of punishment for an MP is to get thrown out of caucus; the most coveted reward is a Cabinet position, followed by the lower-profile positions of minister of state, parliamentary secretary, and committee chair. In Canada, there are no statutes or regulations that limit the number of people who can serve in Cabinet and parliamentary secretary positions, which means that if a prime minister is not averse to a large ministry (which includes Cabinet ministers and ministers of state or junior ministers), he or she can have many "carrots" at his or her disposal to dole out to government MPs. In exchange, those MPs are willing to defer to the prime minister's agenda and unlikely to constrain a prime minister's power or object to abuses of power. Ministers and parliamentary secretaries are the most "disciplined" people in caucus—in other words, the ones least able to speak independently on matters of policy and governance. Prime ministers expect, and, with only rare exceptions, get, effective Cabinet solidarity. Therefore, the larger the ministry, the more control the prime minister has within caucus and, by extension, within the House. Parliamentary secretaries are not part of the ministry, but they are expected to be every bit as disciplined as ministers. Further, by shuffling the Cabinet periodically, the prime minister keeps hope alive for backbench MPs that they might some day be promoted. And, of course, as mentioned in Chapter 4, there are a range of other appointments that can follow a career in the House that are also cherished rewards for loyal MPs.

First, we argue that the Canadian House of Commons adopt legislation to limit the size of ministries to a maximum of 25 individuals and to limit the number of parliamentary secretaries to eight. Ministries have gotten bulkier over the past century. Capping the size of the ministry to less than 10 percent of the membership of the House would put a limit on the number of rewards a prime minister can distribute. Reducing the power to create incentives may smooth the way for ministers to speak out against abuses of power and for government party backbench MPs to take their role of scrutinizing and holding the government to account more seriously.

Ministerial responsiveness is not the only issue here; the sheer number of ministers also poses a practical problem. Although it might seem counterintuitive, a smaller ministry would actually be more powerful, because it would be more capable of deliberating and providing sound policy advice. The larger the Cabinet, the less capable it is of conducting effective dialogue and deliberation. Large Cabinets, like the one that Prime Minister Harper appointed after the 2011 election consisting of 39 ministers, are too large to function as effective decision-making bodies. This has led some to conclude that Cabinet has ended up serving as a focus group while the prime minister relies on other political appointees for advice, a development that only isolates the House of Commons from the true locus of power (Savoie 1999).

While some might charge that a cap of 25 is too restrictive, this reform would actually make Canada more consistent with international standards. Britain, Australia, France, Germany, Italy, Japan, the Netherlands, and the United States (among others) all manage with 20 ministers or less (see, for example, Coyne 2011). Nor would Canada stand alone in formally restricting the size of the ministry. In Britain, two pieces of legislation limit the size of the ministry: the *House of Commons Disqualification 1975*, which limits the number of ministers who can sit and vote in the House, and the *Ministerial and Other Salaries Act 1975*, which limits the amount of money that can be paid out in ministerial salaries (United Kingdom 2010). The latter has been circumvented by the practice of having some ministers serve in an unpaid capacity, but the idea of statutory limits on the size of ministries is a good one.

This reform proposal meets the criteria established earlier in the four-point test for reforms. Its democratic purpose is to reduce the number of appointments at the prime minister's disposal as loyalty incentives, which undermine the operation of responsible government. Having fewer appointments to dole out reduces the size of the dedicated group of MPs in the ministry who are unlikely to constrain the power of the prime minister. It should also increase the likelihood that backbench MPs will act as something other than trained seals clamouring to benefit from the prime minister's power of appointment, and will perhaps even take seriously their role in scrutinizing and holding the government to account. It will also make the ministry a more useful actor in the policy process, mitigating the prime minister's reliance on political appointees in the PMO and the Privy Council Office. This limitation should be placed in statute so that the prime minister would be forced to accept the rule and so that the House of Commons could expect that he or she would accept it, without having to rely on the prime minister's good faith. Additional legislative measures could be considered to preclude any potential unpaid members of the ministry. The House as a whole would benefit from a more effective ministry, because it would re-establish clear lines of individual ministerial responsibility and accountability as well as collective ministerial responsibility according to the edicts of the system of *responsible government.* The effect of the change would be the same whether a prime minister commanded a minority or majority government.

Second, we propose that committee members, using secret preferential ballots,[4] select House of Commons' committee chairs and that committee chairs should retain their positions for the duration of the parliamentary

---

4. Preferential ballots invite voters to rank-order the candidates according to their preferences. Initially, votes are counted by first preferences. If no candidate wins a majority, the candidate with the lowest amount of "number 1" votes is taken off and those ballots are redistributed to other candidates according to second preferences. This process continues until someone wins a majority.

REFORMING PARLIAMENTARY GOVERNANCE

Summary of Proposals

- adopt legislation limiting the size of ministries to a maximum of 25 individuals and the number of parliamentary secretaries to 8 at any given time
- use secret preferential ballots by committee members to select House of Commons' committee chairs for the duration of the parliamentary session
- adopt a set schedule for opposition days in the House of Commons that cannot be altered by the government unilaterally
- reduce, by 50 percent, the partisan political staff complement on Parliament Hill

---

session. As we discussed in Chapter 4, the position of committee chair is one of considerable responsibility and prestige in the parliamentary context. Almost all of the committees in the House of Commons are chaired by a government MP during a majority government and it is the prime minister who chooses who gets to fill these positions. This is yet another "carrot" that the prime minister can dangle in front of caucus members to reward their cooperation and loyalty.

In addition to being one more perk dangled in front of backbenchers, because the prime minister appoints committee chairs, their first loyalty is to the prime minister instead of to their committee members. This can have a significant effect on the attitudes and behaviour of chairs. Specifically, a chair who feels beholden to the prime minister might also feel inclined to protect the government and, as chair, has the authority to structure committee proceedings in such a way as to shield the government from the criticism and scrutiny of opposition members and witnesses who appear before the committee. We have seen this happen already. As discussed in Chapter 4, in 2007 the media learned of a "handbook" that the Prime Minister's Office had distributed to committee chairs, instructing them how to steer committee proceedings in the government's favour (Martin 2007). At times, this kind of behaviour makes it impossible for committees to perform their necessary scrutiny function. It strikes at the heart of the legislature's ability to hold the government to account.

Again, this reform easily fits with our test for reforms. The democratic purposes of this proposal are to restrain the power of the prime minister to undermine the work of parliamentary committees and to protect and enhance committees' ability to scrutinize the government effectively and to hold it to account. Parliamentary committees are an essential part of a modern parliament's capacity to hold the government and its individual ministers to account. If chairs were to retain their positions for the entire session, they would have enough time to become comfortable in their roles and to gain a more complete understanding of their assignments. The fixed terms for chairs would prevent a prime minister from replacing one chair with another who is more loyal to his agenda. While no one expects government committee chairs or other government MPs on a committee not to play some defensive role on behalf of a government under duress—even if it is under duress for good reason—committees cannot perform their functions if chairs are acting solely as agents of the government, undermining parliamentary process without any regard for impartially presiding over proceedings. The capacity of committees should be further bolstered by providing them with more resources and staff; clear rules that allow opposition members to have a greater say in witness selection, including under majority government; and rules that provide greater flexibility for more uninterrupted time to question witnesses, allowing more effective probing of issues.

There is, of course, no way of prohibiting a prime minister from instructing caucus as to who he or she would like to see chairing committees. But, along with the other reforms proposed here, establishing this rule as part of the Standing Orders of the House of Commons, which would allow the House, through the Speaker, to enforce it, might diminish the effect of those instructions. The election of committee chairs by committee members would empower the House of Commons by giving MPs the ability to choose their own committee chairs and by empowering the committees in their capacity to hold government to account. In majority governments, government MPs would outnumber opposition MPs on committees, and, given the excessive party discipline that is ever-present in Canadian politics, would likely elect a government MP chair of the prime minister's choosing. The confidential preferential ballot would then allow (though not force) committee members to reach across party lines by providing an opportunity for them to support candidates from other parties as well as from their own. That means that there would be an incentive to be responsive to the committee rather than to follow the orders and carry out the will of the prime minister. In times of minority government, opposition members would have the numerical advantage over government MPs and the result of the vote would be harder to predict, because any candidate would need votes from at least two party caucuses in order to be successful.

Third, we recommend that opposition days in the House of Commons occur according to a set schedule that cannot be unilaterally altered by the government, as is the case now. Opposition days, as mentioned in Chapter 3, are days on which the opposition parties (rather than the government) control the agenda in the legislature. Opposition days provide opportunities for opposition MPs to introduce private members' bills and motions of their own. Most important, it is an opportunity for opposition parties to put forward a non-confidence motion in the government. The government's ability to schedule opposition days is, therefore, an especially useful tool for prime ministers in minority government situations. Both Paul Martin and Stephen Harper were able to escape losing confidence by shifting opposition days.

Delaying opposition days is a way of silencing the House of Commons and preventing it from holding the government to account. No public purpose is served by a prime minister's ability to keep a government alive when the House has lost confidence in it, because the doctrine of responsible government dictates that governments must maintain the confidence of the legislature in order to have the legitimacy to govern. Even with the modest limits on how long opposition days can be put off by the government, prime ministers can still delay opposition days in order to avoid votes of no confidence that they know are forthcoming, as we discussed in Chapter 3. (Not to mention that they can still prorogue Parliament when their ability to shuffle opposition days is insufficient.)

The democratic purpose of this proposal is obvious: to protect the House of Commons' ability to express its lack of confidence in the government as it sees fit without the possibility of the prime minister preventing it from doing so, regardless of the consequences for the government. This rule should also be made part of the Standing Orders of the House of Commons, which would make it enforceable via the Speaker. The power would simply be taken away from the prime minister, who would have no choice but to comply. The House would be empowered by this measure, because opposition members, as elected representatives, would have regular opportunities to introduce bills and motions, including non-confidence motions, without interference from the government.

Fourth, we propose that the political staff on Parliament Hill be cut by 50 percent. It is especially important that this change be implemented in a manner that ensures that the most severe cuts affect the Prime Minister's Office. The PMO is the prime minister's political machine. It includes a chief of staff, speechwriters, communications experts, planners, and other staffers, all of whom advise the prime minister on appointments, policy, public relations, and virtually everything else. There is no reason to demonize political staff generally. They play a number of vital roles for ministers, including contesting public service advice, providing their own political and policy advice, monitoring policy implementation, and political communications. Having political staff also helps to keep the public service out of partisan politics.

But the increasing size and clout of the political staff is a problem. Prime Minister Trudeau is well known as the first prime minister to establish a robust PMO; subsequent prime ministers, including Prime Minister Harper, have not departed from this model, and have even intensified it. As we have argued earlier, political staff in the PMO have become an important part of the conduct of the prime minister's power over government MPs, including ministers, with staffers often tasked with essentially "whipping" government MPs' behaviour outside of the House beyond votes, ensuring that they are toeing the government's official party line through the distribution of talking points, tightly controlling all media interaction, and the like. As stated earlier, the PMO also directs the political staffs of the ministers on all matters of priority to the prime minister. Political staffers from the PMO also do not shy away from giving politically motivated advice to ministers and public servants, decreasing the likelihood that ministers will ever receive impartial, independent, objective advice that is free from partisan considerations. PMO staff have effectively come to play a central role in the broad operations of government.

Our recommendation to cut the size of the political staff meets the test we've set out. Cutting the political staff of government, and especially the PMO, serves the democratic purpose of reducing the prime minister's power as exerted through political staffers. It would also, from the perspective of good governance, reduce politicization over processes that are meant to remain non-partisan and impartial. It is an essential part of good governance that political staffers not be involved in those matters of implementation and administration of government operations and public service delivery where impartiality is meant to prevail, or in the management of public service policy or public service staffing. We recommend that the proposed limitations on staffing complement and budget be set in statute, similar to the limits on the size of the ministry and number of parliamentary secretaries, above, so that the prime minister is forced to cooperate and so that the House of Commons is tasked with enforcing his or her compliance. Also, like the limits on the numbers of the ministry and parliamentary secretaries, the limits on political staff would have the same effect in both minority and majority circumstances. The budget savings from cuts to political staff could even be used to offset any increased costs in better staffing and resourcing House committees.

3. Reforming Political Parties

First, we propose restoring the power of caucus to dismiss the party leader, including a sitting prime minister, and to appoint a new leader. As was described in Chapter 2, all Canadian parties select party leaders via a national leadership convention that allows the party membership to participate in the selection of the leader (even if the particularities of that selection process vary by party). This replaced the previous practice of allowing party MPs to select the leader from their own ranks. The change was embraced as enhancing the democratic legitimacy of the selection process by broadening the range of actors who have a say in choosing the leader. But an unintended consequence of this change has been that it granted the party leader an incredible amount of security in the role, by eliminating the caucus's ability to remove a sitting party leader, including one who is prime minister.

While some might suggest that restoring the power of caucus to remove a party leader and appoint a new one is a step backward for democratizing party leadership contests, it should be noted that this need not completely undermine the capacity for a broader group of party members to select leaders. Parties could stipulate that in any case where a party leader was deposed by caucus a new leader could only be appointed on an interim basis by caucus. Parties could also require that a new national leadership convention be held within a specified period to allow membership to select a new leader (including potentially returning a leader who had been dismissed) in line with the party constitution.

The democratic purpose of this reform is to correct the relative powerlessness of party caucus members to address what they consider to be abuses of executive power, as well as to empower a party caucus to take action against a leader who is not acting in the party's interest or

---

REFORMING POLITICAL PARTIES

Summary of Proposals

- restore the power of party caucuses to dismiss the party leader, including a sitting prime minister, and to appoint a new interim leader
- remove the party leader's power to approve or reject party candidates for election in each riding

---

who has unduly sidelined the wishes of caucus. In addition to being an important countervailing force against a prime minister willing to abuse power, which is rarely in a party's interests, it should also diminish the excessive party discipline that has come to be a blight on partisan politics in Canada. Parties in other Westminster systems, such as those in Australia and Britain, have retained, and applied, this power (see Chapter 4). A prime minister would be forced to think twice about how restrictive he or she is willing to be in silencing even, and most importantly, backbench government MPs, or demand that caucus "speak with one voice."

Implementing this reform would require changes to party constitutions and would in no way rely on a prime minister's good faith, as he or she would have no role in the actual exercise of the power. If implemented, it would be left to the party caucuses to make use of the power as they see fit. The effectiveness of this reform in diminishing excessive party leadership should be heightened to the extent that it is implemented alongside the other reforms that we have proposed, such as limiting the number of Cabinet appointments and limiting the power of party leaders to interfere in local riding contests (see below). It should be noted that while cliques within a party caucus could abuse this power, they run the risk of angering party membership and the ability to secure their individual candidacy.

Second, we propose that the *Canada Elections Act* be amended to remove the party leader's power to approve or reject the official party candidates for election in each riding. Instead, we propose that local riding associations (now that they are legally recognized and registered by Elections Canada) should legally be invested with the power to declare candidates in line with the general requirements of a party's constitution.

The democratic purpose of this reform is twofold. First, it would remove the power of the prime minister to sanction "disloyal" MPs who wish to seek re-election. Second, it would make the selection of local candidates more democratic by keeping it at the local level, thereby preserving the process of candidate selection as a vital role for party members to play in the electoral process. This would help to strengthen the representative role of political parties. Leaders should not have the power to veto or interfere in local candidate contests. The arbitrary and ad hoc manner in which party leaders have come to interfere in local nominations, creating disparate local processes across the country even within a single party (see Samara 2011, 2010) lacks transparency, can be easily abused, and serves no democratic purpose. Indeed, the only purpose, as Conservative MP Michael Chong has pointed out, is an implicit sanction for MPs who are thinking about not toeing the party line, which is especially powerful for prime ministers who want to escape scrutiny or stifle dissent. This undermines the functioning of responsible government because it diminishes the likelihood that government backbench MPs would do anything more than seek to protect the government. While some may caution that the capacity of the leader to approve party candidates has served valuable purposes (for example, to screen out deplorable potential candidates or to select candidates from underrepresented groups, including women), these issues could be addressed by other means. And, in cases where party leadership simply has a preferred candidate, those individuals would still be free to attempt to secure candidacy in line within the prescribed process.

This reform does not rely on a prime minister acting in good faith since it would legally remove specific powers now held by party leaders and assign them to local riding associations. Enforcement would fall to the riding association and party executive to defend the appropriate process for candidate selection against a party leader who still wanted to attempt to overrun the decision of a riding association. We do recognize that parties must retain safeguards against potential abuse by the riding associations. National campaign bodies are already empowered to be a check on riding associations. Overruling the riding association because of allegations of corruption or impropriety should require the approval of multiple individuals, including the head of the national campaign, other party officers, and the head of the party executive (the party president or equivalent position), to minimize the risk that a prime minister or other party leader might single-handedly and inappropriately interfere. While there is no way to completely eliminate the informal influence of party leaders, this would eliminate their unilateral interference. Also, if our proposal to restore the power of caucus to depose a party leader were adopted, any party leader contemplating defying these constraints on his or her power would be open to dismissal by caucus colleagues.

Other Possible Reforms

It should be noted that while some of these reform proposals are new, not all are. A number of them have been put forward elsewhere. For example, Peter Russell (2008) has also supported the adoption of the constructive non-confidence system. Russell (2008) and Jonathan Boston (1998) both embrace a 30-day deadline for recalling the House. Coyne (2011) has also suggested the need to cut Cabinet. And Aucoin and Turnbull (2004) have signalled the problems with the prime minister's *virtual right* to a dissolution and the need to remove it.

The proposals we put forward are far from the only reforms available for bolstering our democracy. Many commentators and other individuals and groups have their own preferred reform measures aimed at addressing a range of different particular issues through different means. Other potential reforms include the following:

- Introduce measures that are likely to improve decorum and scrutiny in the House, such as making changes to the Standing Orders and conventions that govern Question Period to allow longer, more thoughtful questions and responses; and even remodel the physical layout of the House of Commons to reduce the worst of the schoolyard-level taunts and behaviour regularly on display.
- Establish new avenues for public participation that embrace social media and technological advances in an effort to modernize politics and parliamentary government. Proposals in this area often tie in the efforts of *open government* movements that seek to make much more government information and data freely and easily available, especially in light of Canada's diminished access to information regime.
- Propose measures for decreasing the politicization of public administration and services and limiting the capacity of prime ministers to centralize government decision making, such as removing the power of the prime minister to staff the senior public service—including Order in Council appointments, deputy ministers, associate deputy ministers—and to assign power and responsibility to the Public Service Commission to create an independent staffing process and reduce the prime minister's control over the public service.
- Introduce measures to enhance the democratic legitimacy of different elements of our parliamentary system, such as the adoption of some kind of proportional representation for electing members to the House of Commons, and Senate reform that includes electing senators.

Some will be perplexed as to why we have chosen not to put forward proposals in these areas, but our objective was not to cast a broad reform agenda here. We have taken care to restrict our proposals to those reforms likely to be most effective in addressing the specific problems that we have targeted with this book: that is, the ability of Canadian prime ministers, through their abuse of power, to undermine the democratic principles of *responsible government* and Canadian democracy. Indeed, in some cases, these other reforms could even exacerbate current problems or make them more common.

For example, it is clear, as described in Chapters 4 and 5, that the limits of the first-past-the-post system have a significant distorting effect in translating votes cast into seats in the House of Commons. Whether one supports electoral reform or not, there can be little doubt that this system erodes the democratic legitimacy of government. But we feel strongly that if some form of proportional representation were enacted in the absence of the reforms we are proposing, it would simply intensify a number of the problems that we are hoping to correct, including the ability of the prime minister to use prorogation to shut down parliamentary scrutiny and the use of executive power to interfere with and obfuscate the ability of an opposition party to vote non-confidence in a government. It would also likely ensure the continuation of brinkmanship by both the government and the opposition. Depending on what system of proportional representation was chosen, these problems could be further exacerbated, potentially allowing the prime minister to establish a rank-ordering of candidates and adding a further "carrot" to a prime minister's repertoire for demanding greater loyalty and compliance. This is clearly not desirable.

That is not to say that any of these reforms, including electoral reform, should not be enacted, but that the merits of each of these can—and should—be debated in terms of how they would improve parliamentary democracy. We argue that the most effective way to assess the potential benefits is to consider any proposals that satisfy a basic standard of not likely causing further harm, in light of the four-part test we introduced in this chapter.

We briefly turn our attention in the next three sections of the chapter to address, first, what some might see as a potential hazard of our proposed reforms, and some potential criticisms of our reform agenda.

Is a Stalemate Possible?

We want to clearly recognize that one potential hazard of adopting this four-part reform is a parliamentary stalemate. Because the adoption of the constructive non-confidence system demands that only explicitly worded non-confidence motions that also identify a new prime minister (who has the support of the majority of the House) are matters of confidence, it becomes possible under this system to defeat all government legislation and even the budget without causing the government to fall. It should be carefully noted that a stalemate could have consequences of varying degrees of significance. In other words, not all potential stalemates would have grave or significant consequences.

Of gravest concern are situations under which a minority government would not be able to gain sufficient support to pass its budget and obtain supply[5] to finance the operations of government. In addition, some will also be concerned with the potential inability of a minority government to pass legislation, pointing to the recent American experience during the Obama presidency, though most will consider this as less disconcerting.

A true budgetary or legislative stalemate could occur only when three conditions are met: (1) a minority government is not able to gain majority support to pass its budget, or any legislation, and is unwilling to put forward further alternatives; (2) two-thirds majority support for an early dissolution in the House is not possible; and (3) no opposition party is able and willing to gain majority support for an alternative government under the constructive non-confidence system. Only when all three conditions are met has a full stalemate been arrived at. However, the combination of either the first and second or the first and third conditions can also produce a temporary budgetary or legislative stalemate.

---

5. The process by which a government submits its projected annual expenditures and, upon approval, receives appropriation of revenue and authorization to spend the money accordingly.

Unlike the current system, the prime minister would not have the right to dissolution tucked up his or her sleeve to escape the situation with a snap election. The prime minister would also not be able to use confidence to frame a threat of "forcing an unwanted election" to harangue the opposition into supporting the government's budget. Likewise, the opposition's existing leverage to extort concessions from a government by threatening a vote of non-confidence would also be eliminated.

A number of points should be considered in deliberating the likelihood of a stalemate. First, the possibility that a sitting minority government might not find majority support for its budgetary measures or legislative agenda is inherent in the Westminster system. A government has no right to implement its agenda as it sees fit without sufficient support from the House. Indeed, withholding support is among the greatest powers held by the House. Second, given the relatively tight ideological spectrum in Canadian federal politics, any deadlock would likely be the result of political egotism or tactical calculations, rather than serious disagreements on policy or priorities. Even then, there is no incentive to create any kind of stalemate. What makes these scenarios highly unlikely, then, is that the parties must keep in mind that the electorate could, and likely would, react in one of three ways: (1) it would be apt to punish any government unwilling to compromise; (2) it would punish the opposition party or parties stridently opposed to letting the government have supply; and/or (3) it would support an alternative government or early dissolution.

The most likely possibility where potential electoral sanctions might not be effective would be a regional or separatist party. But given the realities of seat distribution in the House, no one province has the one-third seats necessary to single-handedly force a stalemate as a strategy to render the government ungovernable. For example, even if the Bloc Québécois were to capture all 75 seats in the province of Quebec, it would not have enough seats to single-handedly prevent the House from approving a budget, or passing legislation, or an early dissolution with two-thirds support.

Third, to the degree that a prolonged stalemate is likely to be the cause of political egotism or tactics on the part of a party leader or his or her advisers, our proposal that parties reinstate the capacity of caucus to replace a leader, even a sitting prime minister, would constrain leaders who are unwilling to compromise. Given that such stridency and efforts to engender distrust and dysfunction are highly unlikely to be in a party's best interests, we should expect that a caucus with the power to terminate that behaviour would not tolerate it.

Finally, if this package of reforms were to be adopted, one would expect that, as a precaution to avoid possible stalemates, minority governments would be keen to secure support through informal or formal arrangements with one or more other parties. These formal arrangements could be coalitions or other agreements of support for minority governments, often referred to as confidence and supply arrangements, as are common in New Zealand, where a single party has not won a majority of seats since the adoption of electoral reform.

On this basis, we think that the very limited risk of a stalemate is tolerable when considered against the benefits of the constructive non-confidence vote reform and our proposed limits on early dissolution. As suggested earlier in this chapter, the constructive non-confidence system should reduce the effect of excessive party discipline and should severely reduce the brinkmanship, blackmailing, and bribery that have come to epitomize the recent Canadian experience of minority government.

Against Reform. Period.

We must also dismiss the idea that reform is inherently bad or ineffective, or that it necessarily has perverse consequences that would be worse than anything that we have become accustomed to. If this attitude had prevailed in the 1840s, responsible government itself would have been rejected.

Three general anti-reform attitudes seem to permeate the discussion of how we should address the flaws in our current system. Some observers have simply denounced reform under the suspicion that any change would bring negative consequences that we cannot anticipate in advance, and embraced the status quo. But fear of the unknown, if indulged, prevents any and all change without properly and thoroughly considering the strengths and drawbacks of actual reform proposals. Others fear that "cherry-picked" piecemeal reform measures would upset the careful balance in parliamentary systems by introducing elements that do not fit with the overarching structure. The assumption here is that the component parts of parliamentary systems—such as unwritten conventions, prerogative powers, and confidence votes—join together to make an organic whole and that changes to component parts can have negative consequences for the entire system. Finally, some seem to think that we have now achieved a Pareto optimality of democratic reform of sorts where, regardless of the faults of the current system, no further improvements are possible without causing greater overall damage to democracy. This view is far too pessimistic. It is of course the case that the outcomes of reform are never fully certain in advance, including how different reforms will interact and reverberate throughout the system. It is quite possible that further reforms might one day be required to achieve a desired outcome. But we must take a balanced approach in assessing the potential advantages and disadvantages of possible reforms and how they will fit with the current system, all the while being mindful of the strengths *and* the weaknesses of the status quo.

Those who are dogmatic in their resistance to change invariably end up misrepresenting reality and/or denying the problems that exist with the status quo. The danger in staking out one's support for the status quo, even if it is done in the guise of embracing the least bad alternative, is that it clings to public opinion as a sufficient deterrent for the abuse of power. For instance, Pepall (2010, 13) dismisses the idea of fixed election dates for Canada's House of Commons as a measure "to solve a problem that doesn't exist." He says that "[i]f fixed election dates are such a no brainer, at worst harmless, how is it that we did without them for so long and so many parliamentary democracies still do?" (ibid., 11). To support his point, he goes on to say (ibid., 14):

> It is impossible that a government could decide on an election date on the basis of partisan political calculations without the opposition and the press being aware of them and free to make them an issue. The sanction that prevents governments from abusing the power to pick election dates is the judgment of the people on the appointed day.

The logic here is appealing, but flawed. Elections are blunt instruments by which to express political preferences. The decision about where to place the "X" could be affected by a whole host of short-term factors specific to the election (including the candidates, the party leaders, and the major issues) and long-term factors specific to the voter (age, religion, and level of education). It is impossible to determine whether, and to what extent, any individual factor affects the voter's ultimate choice. We simply cannot draw the conclusion, for example, that if a government is returned to office after a strategic election call, then voters had no problem with the early call.

A good example of this is Pepall himself. In addition to being *against reform*, Pepall was also quite outspoken in his criticism of Harper's first prorogation. Writing at the time, Pepall (2008) was unflinching in his criticism of Governor General Michaëlle Jean's decision to grant Prime Minister Harper's request, plainly concluding, "She did the wrong thing." And Pepall's criticism was not limited to Jean. He also castigated Harper: "Jean and Harper have carried us back over three hundred years to the time before men had figured out how to make responsible government work." Yet, despite his unequivocal defence of the legitimacy of the coalition taking power between elections, as well as his castigation of the prime minister for requesting the prorogation and the governor general for granting it, Pepall (2008) offers a *mea culpa* of sorts: "The reader should know that I am a Tory and abominate the Coalition and all its elements. Despite my condemnation of Harper, I shall, as always, vote Tory in the next election, whenever it is. If the prorogation derails the

Coalition and even gets Harper his majority, I shall be so far pleased." Even as an ardent critic of Harper's abuse of prorogation, Pepall is willing to vote for Harper's Conservatives in the face of this breach.

In pledging his vote allegiance to the Conservatives, Pepall himself demonstrates how inadequate it is to rely exclusively on "the judgment of the people on the appointed day" as a "sanction that prevents governments from abusing their power." Public opinion cannot be used as a barometer to test the system's functionality or integrity. What is "right" becomes what the government can get away with, and rules and principles don't mean a thing. We must resist this path to democratic decay by being clear about what our constitution means and about what restraints it places on the conduct of power.

To the degree that individuals might object to the principles and logic of responsible government, more sweeping reform is possible. But substantive changes, that include formal foundational elements of our parliamentary institutions, would be necessary to ensure that proper constraints on power are established.

Flexibility and Evolution or Firm Rules?

Even among those who are not dogmatically opposed to reform, not everyone will agree with our position that there is a need for reform. And, even among those who do agree that change is required, not all will agree with the measures we propose. Although we cannot address all criticisms, especially those not yet rendered, we do want to address two points here. Some contend that enacting firm, clear, and binding rules to govern the powers of summoning, proroguing, and dissolving Parliament, as well as the process required to withdraw confidence from a sitting government, precludes both the flexibility said to be a virtue of the Westminster constitutional system and further evolution in the Canadian version of this system.

For example, this issue emerged in the wake of a workshop led by Peter Russell in January 2011 (mentioned in Chapter 1), to address the problem presented by "the lack of clarity and agreement around important unwritten conventions of our parliamentary system of government" (Russell and Milne 2011, 1). The event "brought together constitutional scholars, experienced officials in government and Parliament, and individuals well connected to the leaders of all of the parliamentary parties at the federal level" in an effort to attempt to build consensus in the advance of any future constitutional crisis as nearly developed at the time of the 2008 prorogation (Russell and Milne 2011, 2).

The workshop's report notes that "participants discussed at length the pros and cons of producing some kind of authoritative statement of important constitutional conventions. They considered carefully the experience of other Westminster parliamentary democracies reported above. Concerns were expressed about the danger of making inflexible those elements of the constitutional system that should be left free to develop through political evolution" (Russell and Milne 2011, 5). For example, when it came to the issue of the legitimacy of changing governments between elections when a government of the day loses the confidence of the House, the workshop was unable to come to any consensus about whether it was ever legitimate for such a change in government or under what conditions such a change would be legitimate. The discussion of this issue in the report concludes that, "This is a matter that will likely be determined by evolving political practice rather than a settled constitutional convention" (Russell and Milne 2011, 6).

This reasoning seems to suggest that firm rules preclude flexibility or evolution in the system and is an implicit endorsement of the status quo. We have allowed our constitutional conventions to be "defined" through "evolving political practice" over a period of decades and we have arrived at a point in our political and constitutional evolution where our constitutional conventions are meaningless. As discussed in Chapter 3, our constitution has come to be "whatever happens."

We firmly disagree that the adoption of a few clear, firm rules precludes any flexibility or evolution. Having clear rules in place to protect against unconstrained power has not inhibited other jurisdictions from undertaking significant reforms that have led to major evolutions within their systems, nor has it undermined the flexibility that has allowed considerable variation in the operation of their systems. For example, as discussed in Chapter 5, New Zealand has undertaken electoral reform, adopting a form of proportional representation before the 1996 election, and has experienced far more flexibility and innovation in terms of government formation than we have, even though it has adopted rules that more clearly circumscribe power and shape the most fundamental aspects of the Westminster constitution, such as the processes for the formation of government. The key distinction is that in New Zealand power is clearly entrenched in Parliament. The democratic principle is that neither the prime minister nor the governor general should decide: the House must, and does, decide.

Democracy Must Prevail

In this chapter, we have outlined our proposals for reform and explained how these changes would place clear boundaries on the powers of the prime minister. Our intent is not to make the Canadian parliamentary system rigid, inflexible, or incapable of change, but rather to address problems that compromise the integrity of Canadian parliamentary democracy. Fixing the current situation, we have argued, requires both a reaffirmation of the *principles* and *logic* of responsible government as the basis of the Canadian system of parliamentary government *and* a radical shift of particular powers away from the prime minister to the House of Commons, the eminent parliamentary body of our democracy, to reflect this logic and these principles.

The point here is not to remake the House into a quasi-executive body that it was not intended to be. Instead, the point is to demand a constitution that ensures that the House has the capacity to effectively fulfill its traditional core role: to review and then approve or reject the government's legislative proposals; to scrutinize the government's administration of public affairs; to hold the prime minister and other ministers to account for their performance (collectively and individually); and to withdraw its confidence in the prime minister and government, as deemed necessary.

While there is no silver bullet, the changes we are proposing help to correct some of the greatest deficiencies of our democracy, as well as to help improve the day-to-day fractiousness that had come to characterize the period of minority government between 2004 and 2011 in Canada. In this environment, brinkmanship outpaced statesmanship as the primary mode of governance and Parliament itself came to be seen, often with good reason, as an irrelevant and ineffective waste of time, energy, and money. Our proposals ought to address some of the worst excesses of the system, both in majority and minority contexts, to ensure that parliamentary proceedings matter in a way that they scarcely have for some time. Power would actually be entrenched in the House rather than in the hands of the prime minister.

Democratizing our constitution and parliamentary system of governance demands change. The concentration of powers that we have focused on in this book cannot be permitted to remain in the hands of a single individual who is able to undermine democratic governance at his or her will. Further, relying on an unelected official, the governor general, as the sole safeguard against the abuse of that power, even if we had a widely agreed upon understanding of how our system is to work—which we don't—does not belong in a robust contemporary democracy. Our proposal to prescribe, in writing, protocols for the operation of some of the most fundamental aspects of parliamentary democracy, including summoning, proroguing, and dissolving Parliament, and forming and dismissing governments, would correct a major deficiency of Canadian democracy. As we have demonstrated in this chapter, realigning power through these proposals with the House, as well as other integral aspects of the system, including Cabinet, riding associations, and party caucuses, would effectively entrench power with the people's democratically elected representatives: the members of the House of Commons. Further, it would do so whether the context was a minority or a majority government and would not rely primarily on either public opinion or the prime minister acting in good faith to be effective. Both have proven ineffective in the Canadian experience.

Again, it should be stressed here that there is no silver bullet to building a better Canadian democracy. Our approach has been to focus on how power is, should be, and can be organized and deployed in ways that secure and enhance the public good, loosely defined, rather than partisan interests. Achieving reform will not be an easy mountain to climb. The weight of the carelessness with which we have allowed our democracy to erode for many decades itself creates a heavy momentum. For instance, we've had 85 years to sort out the confusion over the King–Byng affair but we've failed to do so. Further, this does not even begin to layer in the considerable interests who relish the status quo, including, most importantly, all-powerful prime ministers and would-be prime ministers who aspire to that level of power. It's also not clear who would be the driving force behind change. Serious questions have come from different directions about the capacity of the press, so-called constitutional experts, opposition parties who have squandered opportunities to demand change, and a largely apathetic citizenry, to be the driving force.

However, one thing is clear: the status quo is intolerable. Now, with a new majority government and some of the most contentious issues placed firmly on the backburner, we have an important opportunity. This might be the most suitable time to attempt to address these problems. Failure to do so, as we have failed to do in the past, whether because of fear of the unknown, fear of the difficulty of addressing these problems, or out of self-interest, would be an egregious collapse on all our parts. Our failing democracy depends on whether we can *and will* use this opportunity to thoughtfully consider and advance reform.

References

Aucoin, Peter, and Lori Turnbull. 2004. Removing the virtual right of prime ministers to demand dissolution. *Canadian Parliamentary Review* 27 (2): 16–19.

Bakvis, Herman. 2001. Prime minister and Cabinet in Canada: An autocracy in need of reform? *Journal of Canadian Studies* 35 (4): 60–79.

Boston, Jonathan. 1998. *Governing under proportional representation: Lessons from Europe*. Victoria, NZ: Institute of Policy Studies, Victoria University.

Coyne, Andrew. 2011. Cut it in half and no one would notice. *Macleans.ca*, May 16. http://www2.macleans.ca/category/blog-central/canada-blog/andrew-coynes-blog/.

Delacourt, Susan, and Les Whittington. 2011. Debate: Harper and Ignatieff's six-minute showdown. *The Toronto Star*. http://mobile.thestar.com/mobile/NEWS/article/973852.

Forsey, Eugene. 1953. Professor Angus on the British Columbia election: A comment. *Canadian Journal of Economics and Political Science* 19: 226–230.

Liberal Party of Canada. 2011. *Your family. Your future. Your Canada.* http://www.liberal.ca/files/2011/04/liberal_platform.pdf.

Martin, Don. 2007. Harper government whips Tories into line with secret handbook. *The Calgary Herald*, May 18. http://www.canada.com/calgaryherald/columnists/story.html?id=b8122d51-95e8-4b29-b99b-34217406425d.

National Post. 2011. A Tory majority checklist. May 4. http://www.nationalpost.com/todays-paper/Tory+majority+checklist/4722137/story.html.

New Democratic Party. 2011. *Giving your family a break: Practical first steps.* http://xfer.ndp.ca/2011/2011-Platform/NDP-2011-Platform-En.pdf.

Pepall, John. 2008. Harper's game and the Queen's government. December 7. http://www.pepall.ca/archive_article.asp?YEAR=&VRT=355.

Pepall, John. 2010. *Against reform*. Toronto: University of Toronto Press.

Russell, Peter H. 2008. *Two cheers for minority government: The evolution of Canadian parliamentary democracy*. Toronto: Emond Montgomery.

Russell, Peter H., and Cheryl Milne. 2011. *Adjusting to a new era of parliamentary government: Report of a workshop on constitutional conventions*. Toronto: David Asper Centre for Constitutional Rights.

Russell, Peter H., and Lorne Sossin, eds. 2009. *Parliamentary democracy in crisis*. Toronto: University of Toronto Press.

Samara. 2010. *The accidental citizen?* http://www.samaracanada.com/downloads/Samara_Report_The_Accidental_Citizen.pdf.

Samara. 2011. *"It's my party"*: *Parliamentary dysfunction reconsidered.* http://www.samaracanada.com/downloads/ItsMyParty.pdf.

Savoie, Donald. 1999. *Governing from the centre: The concentration of power in Canadian politics.* Toronto: University of Toronto Press.

Smith, Jennifer. 1999. Democracy and the Canadian House of Commons at the millennium. *Canadian Public Administration* 42 (4): 398–421.

United Kingdom. 2010. *Too many ministers?* House of Commons Public Administration Select Committee, Ninth Report of Session, HC 457, 2009–10. London: The Stationery Office Limited. http://www.publications.parliament.uk/pa/cm200910/cmselect/cmpubadm/457/457.pdf.

Index